Business Ethics

Sunday Ethic – Monday World

Business Ethics

Sunday Ethic — Monday World

Second Edition

Ted Batson and Blake J. Neff

TRIANGLE PUBLISHING

Business Ethics: Sunday Ethic — Monday World, Second Edition
by Ted Batson and Blake J. Neff

Direct correspondence and permission requests to one of the following:

Triangle Publishing
Indiana Wesleyan University
1900 West 50th Street
Marion, Indiana 46953

Web site: www.trianglepublishing.com
E-mail: info@trianglepublishing.com

Batson, Ted and Neff, Blake J.

ISBN: 978-1-931283-45-8

Cover and Graphic design: Lyn Rayn

Printed in the United States of America

Contents

Preface

One by-product of the Industrial Revolution has been the compartmentalization of knowledge. Compartmentalization—the separation of ideas or processes into isolated categories[1]—has proven efficient in the manufacturing world, but it often leads to the acceptance of false ideas in the academic world. For example, universities have long attempted to train students to be ethical decision makers. Under a compartmentalized system of thought, students are taught ethical philosophies and theories, managerial strategies, and accountability procedures as if they were independent and somewhat unrelated elements in the business process. But anyone working in the "real world" knows that these elements of decision making are inseparable. A decision in one area will affect all the other areas in some way.

In an effort to overcome the artificial barriers of compartmentalization, this book teaches ethical principles intertwined with the five basic managerial functions. Based on integrated instruction in basic ethics and managerial knowledge, it uses a case study approach to stimulate students' analytical skills. Most of the case examples are drawn from real-life experiences, and all interviews are with owners and/or managers who have demonstrated managerial success and ethical decision making in the small-business world. Names and selected occupations have been changed to protect the participants' privacy.

Another unique feature of the text is that it integrates Christian faith with the practice of business ethics. We address questions similar to those posed by David Noonan, author of *Aesop and the CEO*: "Why mix business and morals? An overwhelming majority of us believe in God. Can we separate our spiritual beliefs from our conduct in work? Can we suspend our moral code of behavior once the Sabbath is over? We are obliged to live good lives. We can't live one set of morals for home and a different set for work."[2] *Business Ethics: Sunday Ethic—Monday World* seeks to integrate godly principles with the business environment.

In these pages students are invited to examine their own belief systems, challenged to investigate the strengths and weaknesses of secular ethical philosophies and theories, encouraged to explore biblical principles and teachings in the context of their personal lives and the business setting, and assisted in the development of a personal framework for guiding their ethical decision making.

To keep up with current events in the business world, it is recommended that the students apply their ethical growth to ethical dilemmas found in recent business journals, newspapers, and media sources. We recommend that students and professors use Google® or other search engines to identify current websites containing ethical cases from career areas of their choice.

Endnotes

1. See *Merriam-Webster's Collegiate Dictionary,* 11th ed., s.v. compartmentalize.
2. David Noonan, *Aesop and the CEO* (Nashville: Thomas Nelson, 2005), xv.

1

Why Learn about Ethics?

Unless the LORD builds the house, those who build it labor in vain.

— Psalm 127:1

Chapter Challenges

A careful review of Chapter 1 should enable the reader to:

- Develop a deeper understanding of the relationship between differing views of moral standards and ethics.

- Have a better grasp of human characteristics that tend to either facilitate or impede ethical decision making.

A father wanted to teach his adolescent son a lesson on managing the family business. Does the son understand how the family partnership conducts business?

"Suppose a customer is shortchanged by ten dollars. You know the customer has been slighted, but no one else is aware of the problem. What do you do?" the father asked.

Seeking clarification, the son responded, "You mean, do we tell the customer?"

"Well . . ." his father said somewhat tentatively. "What I am really asking is do we tell our partner?"

What was the father's lesson? Cheating is okay if no one knows about it? Such one-dimensional thinking reflects the norm in today's American business climate. David Noonan, noted business consultant, points out that "One needs only to pick up a newspaper or turn on the news to see how far many corporations have strayed from moral business practices and efficient management."[1]

Evidences include:

- Coca-Cola admitted to rigging taste tests on its new frozen drink.[2]
- Tokyo Electric Power, the company behind Japan's postearthquake nuclear crisis, has allegedly been involved in a long list of accidents and cover-ups over the years.[3]
- Mitsubishi admitted to covering up defects to postpone a recall.[4]
- The BP oil spill in the Gulf of Mexico emerged as unquestionably the environmental catastrophe of the century, but some argue that it also demonstrates an ethical crisis.[5]
- Bank One was fined by National Association of Security Dealers (NASD) for allowing late trading of its mutual funds.[6]
- Weatherford International LTD, an oilfield services company, disclosed errors in its tax accounting leading to adjustments of more than $100 million in its financial statements from 2007 to 2010. The necessary adjustments involve errors in determining tax liabilities.[7]
- Raj Rjaratnam, described by US attorney Preet Bharara as "one of the most educated, successful, and privileged professionals in the country," became the thirty-fifth person to plead or be found guilty of insider trading during a federal crackdown extending from 2009 to 2011.[8]

As a result of these and countless other irregularities, the need for sound teaching in ethical management sparks little debate. In Washington, D.C., the more specific debate focuses on how to legislate morality. Should there be tougher penalties for white-collar crime? Would additional administrative regulations help? How about requiring the chief executive officers of major corporations to sign their companies' financial statements, thus personally vouching for their accuracy?

On university campuses, the question becomes one of appropriate emphasis. Should ethics be taught? What department or division should offer the course? Should business majors be required to study ethics? Is there enough emphasis on ethics in business schools?[9]

Ethics Defined

Manuel Velasquez, a leading writer in the field of business ethics, defines business ethics as "a study of moral standards and how these apply to the systems and organizations through which modern societies produce and distribute goods and services and to the people who work within these organizations."[10] Batson and Neff define business ethics as the application of moral standards to the structures, policies, systems, and decision-making processes that facilitate the production and distribution of goods and services and affect the treatment of people within the organization and the greater society. Both aspects of this definition raise two important questions: (1) Whose moral standards are to be used? (2) What is the best way to apply moral standards or principles in our business, societal, and personal lives?

Source of Moral Standards

If ethics is the study and/or application of moral standards, what is the most reliable source of moral standards? Whose moral standards are to be used? The following summary gives highlights of Western ethical thought in the Christian era:

God Implanted Moral Principles in the Human Mind

The French philosopher René Descartes (1596–1650) believed that God implanted moral standards in the inner man; they revealed themselves as innate ideas.[11]

Fulfillment of Our Need for a Peaceful Society

English philosopher Thomas Hobbes (1588–1679) believed that moral standards are the visible manifestation of humanity's mutual need to live in a peaceful society. "In the state of nature men were more or less equally powerful and, therefore had equal rights; being fundamentally egoistic, they were in a continual state of war and this made their lives 'nasty, brutish and short.' To remedy this men agreed to give up their rights to a sovereign who should maintain peace and order."[12] The state therefore ultimately determined what was right conduct.

Inner Moral Law

The eighteenth-century German philosopher Immanuel Kant (1724–1804) believed that through the rigorous use of reason he had discovered the source of basic principles of moral standards within the human being. He wrote, "Two things fill the mind with ever new and increasing admiration and awe, the oftener and more steadily they are reflected on: the starry heavens above me and the moral law within me." Kant's emphasis was on human reasoning and not God as the source of moral law.[13]

A Moral Sense

An eighteenth-century Scottish philosopher, David Hume (1711–1776), proposed that morality cannot be arrived at through reason and therefore is something felt by humans: a moral sense. What is morally right gives humans a sense of pleasure, and what is evil gives a sense of pain.[14]

God

The earliest monotheistic believers maintained that God was the source of moral standards and that these standards were revealed in two primary ways. (1) Scripture passages such as Ephesians 1:9–10, Romans 1:18–20, and Romans 2:14–15 demonstrate general revelation of standards such as those found in nature, held in common by human beings, or demonstrated in history. (2) Passages such as 2 Peter 3:1–2 and 2 Kings 22:11–13 demonstrate the reliance of God's people on the authority of Scripture for God's special or inspired revelations. VandenBerg refers to the two revelations as "two books" and acknowledges that "because God is the author of both 'books'—the physical world and the Bible—so the argument goes, there can be no disagreement between the two books."[15]

To accept God as the source of morality one must believe (1) that God exists; (2) that God is a just and moral being; and (3) that God's creations—the universe and its inhabitants—are created to reflect God's moral character. If one accepts these premises, the secular philosophical arguments citing human reason or human characteristics as the independent sources of moral standards give way to the deeper, divine source of moral standards. The previously mentioned philosophers as well as more recent philosophers, ethicists, and practitioners who hold these "secular" perspectives have unknowingly discovered God's morality and not some "new morality" that is independent from God.

Best Way to Apply Moral Standards

Let's look at basic question number 2: what is the best way to apply moral standards in our business, societal, and personal lives? The answer is through the use of critical-thinking skills. In the secular world, this statement seems to be accepted without question. In the Judeo-Christian world, critical thinking has sometimes been seen as an act against faith. The following four assertions show how and why critical thinking is indeed a part of a mature Judeo-Christian ethical decision-making process.

- Critical thinking is from God. God is the creative, intelligent creator of the universe and all that is in it, including humanity and the human's ability to think. Note Genesis 1:26: "And God said, 'Let us make man in our image, after our likeness.'"
- The Christian use of critical-thinking processes does not analyze God, but rather human statements about God. This use of critical thinking is one God-ordained way for us to arrive at God's truth.[16]
- Reasonable Christians seek to use critical-thinking skills to learn how to test their own understanding of and application of God's moral truth. This is different from the secular rationalist who seeks to define moral truth through the use of reason.[17]
- God is not subject to human limitations, but God is subject to the system of logic. Because he is the holy God, there are things that violate his holy character that he cannot logically do. In Hebrews 6:18 we see that it is impossible for God to lie, and in James 1:13 we find that it is impossible for God to be tempted. In the realm of logic, he cannot make a three-sided circle or a round square.

This book subscribes to the propositions that God is the true source of morality and that God created within humans the ability to use critical-thought processes in the application of his standards of morality in business, societal, and personal situations.

Ethical Decision Making: A Cord with Five Threads

This book is based upon the belief that the learning of applied business ethics is best addressed by a systems approach that visualizes the study and application of ethics for the workplace as a cord with five threads. Like a cord with five threads, five major continua influence the quality of an ethical decision. The stronger the component threads, the stronger the cord. Conversely, weaker component threads produce a weaker cord. Weak or missing threads increase the likelihood of poor and possibly unethical decisions.

Thread 1: Managerial Knowledge

Managerial Knowledge Continuum

Lack of Knowledge				Much Knowledge
-10	-5	0	5	10

Knowledge of managerial functions—planning, staffing, controlling, organizing, and directing—is a critically important thread in the ethical decision-making cord. Of course, a high level of managerial knowledge will not ensure a high level of personal or business ethics. But not knowing managerial expectations and standard procedures provides fertile ground for the germination of unethical practices and unethical decisions.

For example, in Chapter 7, the failure of management to develop a long-term business plan at "Hur Ministries" leads to an ethical dilemma. Similarly, at "White's Garage" in Chapter 10, management clearly does not understand the staffing function, which also produces an ethical dilemma.

Good managerial skills not only can safeguard against circumstances that contribute to unethical decisions, but also can reduce a manager's sense of inadequacy. Helping the student understand the interconnectedness between managerial knowledge and the other four threads of ethical decision making is a key aspect of every chapter in *Business Ethics*.

Thread 2: Managerial Skill

Managerial Skill Continuum

Low Skill				High Skill
-10	-5	0	5	10

How well one can implement the five managerial functions reveals a manager's skill level. The potential for higher skill development is directly proportional to a manager's knowledge. For example, one cannot become skilled in planning with only limited knowledge of the planning process. The same holds true for the other managerial functions. Like lack of knowledge, lack of skill in any managerial function opens the door to situations that increase the likelihood of unethical decisions or actions. Conversely, the higher one's skill level, the lower the probability of inadvertently making unethical decisions or acting unethically.

In the "West Park Apartment" scenario of Chapter 12, a manager understands the importance of providing quality leadership. But she lacks an adequate skill level when it comes to implementing authority as a leader. This managerial deficiency leads to an ethical problem.

In the "Pit Stop" case in Chapter 16, management recognizes the need for team development. The skill to lead team-building efforts, however, has yet to be developed. An ethical question surfaces as a result.

Thread 3: Personal Ethical Position

Figure 1.3. Personal Ethic Continuum

Personal Ethic Continuum

Vague				Well Defined
-10	-5	0	5	10

A manager's personal sense of right and wrong may range from vague to well defined. In a biblically based belief system as a manager's understanding of Scripture and natural law and their applications matured, one's ethical position would move toward the well-defined end of the continuum, resulting in a potentially higher incidence of ethical decisions and actions.

At "Oak Dale Bed and Breakfast" in Chapter 8, young Joanna has yet to develop her personal ethic in a structured way. As a result, she fails an ethical test precipitated by her attempt to adopt her superior's ethical system.

More mature managers in the "Decker and Associates" scenario of Chapter 19 have a similar problem. In this case, an ethically and legally problematic situation develops because managers fail to act on a well-structured ethic.

Again, one continuum does not "work" independent of others. One manager may have a fairly well defined ethical system but constantly become embroiled in unethical situations and actions because of inadequate managerial skills.

While we would like to believe that adopting a Judeo-Christian belief system would eliminate unethical practices in the business world, evidence speaks otherwise. A look at the comparative statistics between leaders in ministry and the general population reveals a striking similarity in areas such as adultery, divorce, abuse of power, and financial misconduct. It appears that a "head knowledge" of biblical standards by itself is not a solution to unethical behavior in the personal and business arenas.

However, without a well-defined ethical system, there is little chance for success in consistently making ethical decisions as a manager. Throughout *Business Ethics*, therefore, the reader is encouraged to develop a personal statement of ethical position. We unashamedly believe the Judeo-Christian worldview provides the best possible foundation for ethical standards and action. Hence, we encourage students to develop, adopt, and internalize the Christian worldview. This will assist them as they attempt to solve the ethical dilemmas of the case studies found in this textbook, as well as in future managerial positions.

Thread 4: Personal Motivation

Figure 1.4. Personal Motivation Continuum

Personal Motivation Continuum

Self-centered				God-centered
-10	-5	0	5	10

The personal motivation continuum separates self-centered on one extreme from God-centered on the other. Moving toward the God-centered pole of the continuum moves one closer to acting with godly rather than selfish interests. One premise behind *Business Ethics* is that, in the final analysis, motivation will trigger the use of knowledge, skills, and a sense of right and wrong to bring about either ethical or unethical decisions and/or actions.

"What would Jesus do?" While inadequate as a decision-making rule, this popular question does encourage a process that involves establishing a motivational system based on God's will rather than human self-will. In Chapter 17, "The Workman's Benefit Insurance" case describes a manager who has adequate knowledge, skills, and beliefs. His motivations, however, are not God-centered. The result is an ethical dilemma. Similarly, at "Dupont Men's Wear" in Chapter 18, a business couple must consider their personal motivations after having worked out their personal ethic.

Self-centered motivation provides the intangible element that often overrides knowledge, skills, and beliefs. While secular philosophies and theories tend either to encourage self-interest or set up rules by which to govern self-interest, *Business Ethics* attempts to guide readers in understanding what truly has value in directing actions—a God-centered eternal existence.

Thread 5: Critical-Thinking Skills

Figure 1.5. Critical-Thinking Skill Continuum

		Critical-Thinking Skill Continuum		
Opinion-centered				Logic-centered
-10	-5	0	5	10

This continuum illustrates the extremes of foundations for decision making: nonfacts supporting opinions accepted without question on one extreme and substantiated facts used in a systematic application of analytical skills on the other extreme. The authors believe that it is safe to say that most adults in positions of responsibility wish to make quality decisions to advance the company's and their own interests and futures. But why do so many fail to employ critical-thinking skills even though they may have been trained to do so? Neil Browne and Stuart Keeley offer some insights into this puzzling situation with their assertion that inappropriate mental habits impede the use of critical-thinking skills.

Browne and Keeley suggest that the following human mental habits cloud critical thinking and muddle the decision-making process:[18]

The Seductive Quality of Personal Experience

One's own personal experiences are just that—personal and therefore more emotionally intense than the experiences of others heard secondhand. This means we tend to value our own experiences more than those of others. When managers make decisions based solely on their personal experiences, they limit the size of the sample of observers to only one. Though the use of personal experience as the primary or total basis for decision making saves time and energy, making generalizations on such a small data base is considered unreliable and ill advised in all professional fields.

Belief in a Just World

Browne and Keeley propose that human beings have a built-in need for a comfortable and fair world. This psychologically driven need for the security of a just world can unknowingly cause managers to ignore obvious data that might disturb their level of comfort even though the data raise questions concerning the ethicality of a course of action.

Stereotyping

Stereotyping, based in a positive or negative bias, is characterized by a preset notion about the qualities of members of a certain group; it often inhibits approaching a situation with openness to gather and consider all data needed to make an ethical decision. In the high-pressure management world, stereotypes are tempting because they save time and effort in the decision-making process.

Urge toward Simplification

Managers are constantly pressured to greater efficiency. However, along with efficiency comes an urge to oversimplification. The fewer the data gathered, alternatives considered, or processes employed, the less time, mental energy, and processes it takes to arrive at a decision. However, as in reliance on personal experience, when the number of alternatives is limited, the "best decision" options are reduced.

Belief Perseverance

Critical thinking is hindered in an environment that fosters firmly held assumptions that the manager's or team's beliefs are not biased, but the beliefs of persons who disagree with those prized assumptions are perceived to be biased. This belief perseverance is founded in a manager's psychological need for certainty. A manager's or team's beliefs are often reinforced by an exaggerated sense of competence. This is a characteristic of "group think," and it limits the possibilities for reaching the better and/or more ethical decisions.

Availability of Information

When making decisions, there is a human tendency to rely on our memories and other handy sources of information; it is less time consuming and expensive than carefully researching data. In this scenario, the easier the information is to retrieve, the more valuable we perceive it to be. But what if the needed information is not the easiest to retrieve? The quality of analytical thinking is jeopardized because of ego and laziness, opening the door to unethical situations.

Myth of "the Right Answer"

There is a psychological need on the part of many managers to find the *right* answer before moving forward. But the complexity of human interactions is so great that there almost always are a variety of possible, good decisions about the ways to resolve interpersonal dilemmas. As Dr. Larry Lindsay of Indiana Wesleyan University would say, "Don't get trapped in paralysis of analysis." Skilled critical thinkers focus their analysis on making an appropriate selection from the identified data-based options rather than expending unnecessary energy chasing the illusive right answer. This false application of critical thinking—paralysis—creates an uncertainty within the organization, and inaction in some situations may be as unethical as a premeditated unethical action.

What Is an Effective Way to Learn Ethical Decision-Making Processes?

We believe that active learning leads to the deepest levels of skill and understanding. Unless the reader becomes an active learner, this book's content is nothing more than another collection of philosophies, theories, experiences, and opinions. However, when the reader is an active participant in learning, *Business Ethics* becomes a guide to self-knowledge and self-directed growth. As the reader embarks on the study of this book, the authors encourage the use of personal analysis and reflection in conjunction with the analysis of selected biblical, philosophical, theoretical, and experiential elements presented herein.

Questions Discussion

As a manager seeking to expand your knowledge and skill in ethical decision making, respond to the questions below:

1. As a manager involved in day-to-day decision making, which of the two definitions of business ethics presented in this chapter is more useful to you? Explain why.

2. From your vantage point as a member of the business community, rank the five threads of the decision-making cord in their order of importance, giving your reasons for placing each cord at its particular ranking.

3. Of the mental habits that can cloud the critical-thinking process, which two have you witnessed most often in your workplace or social setting? Give an example of each and explain the impact on the decision-making process.

Endnotes

1. David Noonan. *Aesop and the CEO* (Nashville: Thomas Nelson, 2005), xv–xvi.
2. Margaret Webb Pressler, "Coca-Cola, Burger King End Dispute," *Washington Post*, August 13, 2003.
3. "Scandal-ridden Energy Company behind Japan's Nuke Crisis," *CBS News World*, March 17, 2011.
4. Guy Dresser, "Mitsubishi 'Sorry' for Cover-up," *London Evening Standard*, June 29, 2004.
5. Valerie Elverton Dixon, "The BP Oil Spill and Religious Environmental Ethics," *The Washington Post*, June 2, 2010.
6. "In Brief: Bank One Unit Fined $400K, Late Trading," *American Banker*, January 13, 2005.
7. "Wetherford Shares Plunge as Tax Accounting Errors Disclosed," *Wall Street Journal*, March 2, 2011.
8. Joseph Slife, "Insider Out: Hedge Fund Billionaire Found Guilty of Fraud," *World*, June 4, 2011.
9. Julian Friedland, "Where Business Meets Philosophy: The Matter of Ethics," *Chronicle of Higher Education*, November 13, 2009, A26–27.
10. Manuel G. Velasquez, *Business Ethics: Concepts and Cases,* 5th ed. (Upper Saddle River, NJ: Prentice-Hall, 2002), 14.
11. Bruce N. Waller, *Consider Ethics: Theory, Readings, and Contemporary Issues* (New York: Pearson Longman, 2005), 7.
12. G. J. Dalcourt, "History of Ethics," in *New Catholic Encyclopedia*, 2nd ed. (New York: Gale, 2003) 5:395, s.v. "Ethics, history of."
13. Immanuel Kant, *The Critique of Practical Reason and Other Writings in Moral Philosophy,* trans. L. W. Beck (1788; repr. Chicago: University of Chicago Press, 1949), 259.
14. David Hume, *A Treatise of Human Nature*, 2nd ed., with text revised by and variant readings by P. H. Nidditch (Oxford: Clarendon Press, 1978), 470–74.
15. Mary L. Vandenberg, "What General Revelation Does (and Does Not) Tell Us," *Perspectives on Science and Christian Faith* 62, no 1 (March 2010):16–24.
16. Norman L. Geisler and Ronald M. Brooks, *Come Let Us Reason: An Introduction to Logical Thinking* (Grand Rapids: Baker Books, 1990), 17–18.
17. Geisler and Brooks, *Come Let Us Reason,* 18.
18. M. Neil Browne and Stuart M. Keeley, *Asking the Right Questions: A Guide to Critical Thinking,* 9th ed. (Upper Saddle River, NJ: Prentice-Hall, 1990), 168–73.

Notes

2

An Ethical Framework

Be a good worker, one who does not need to be ashamed.

— 2 Timothy 2:15 (NLT)

Chapter Challenges

A careful examination of Chapter 2 should enable the reader to:

- Identify the role of a Judeo-Christian worldview in building a system of ethics.
- Define the term *ethics*.
- Explain the role of stakeholders in making ethical decisions.
- Recognize informal systems of ethical decision making.

Increasingly business failure is being viewed as ethical failure. For example, Rushworth M. Kidder, president of the Institute for Global Ethics, argues that what started as an economic recession in the fall of 2008 actually was an ethics recession. He believes that attitudes of managers at every level, coupled with a culture-wide tolerance for lack of integrity, led to the financial collapse.[1]

Perhaps the ethical problems of modern American business stem from the fact that managers are bombarded with pressures from all sides as they strive to balance the management equation in their everyday decision making:

Efficiency + Effectiveness = Profits

This simplistic approach to business has a negative impact on the public. John Ward, chairman and CEO of Russell Corporation, notes, "Recent research studies have indicated that the public believes that many CEO's are not ethical and that they leave their values at the door of the office in pursuit of the almighty dollar. Yet, we know of the 15,000 public companies, only a handful is creating this highly negative perception. However, the abuse that we have seen by those few companies goes beyond anything that I thought would or could occur, and is creating a major mistrust of business."[2]

In spite of negative results, this equation represents the totality of management for many business leaders, even as they regularly confront foreign competitors, new technologies, workforce demands, and myriad other challenges. How are managers to carry out their short- and long-term fiduciary responsibilities to owners and customers, as well as their human responsibilities to employees, themselves, and their families?

> *Fiduciary responsibilities*: the responsibilities of a person who has the power and obligation to act for another under circumstances which require total trust, good faith and honesty.[3]

The Three-E Equation

Many Christian business managers have added a variable to the manager's decision-making equation. For them, the equation might be called the Three-E Equation:

Efficiency + Effectiveness + Ethics = Profits + Long-Term Stability

Some Christian managers, however, continue to accept the belief that the stakeholders' hunger for stronger and stronger bottom lines is incompatible with the addition of ethics as illustrated in the Three-E Equation. As a result, Christians in business are often left with cognitive dissonance; that is, they hold two opposing views simultaneously. Their Christian beliefs maintain that certain principles are absolutes and contribute to the well-being of individuals and society. However, the business setting often uses an action system that honors higher profits above the well-being of individuals or moral values. In some cases, the well-being of an entire society is subordinated to profit. Managers at Enron and their accountants at Arthur Andersen are accused of using just such an action system.[4]

Since many Christian business managers live in constant cognitive dissonance—believing the teachings of Jesus but practicing business in ways that are completely opposed to those teachings—they experience a high level of stress and frustration. One has to wonder what impact this level of discord has on a manager's self-image and resulting relationships with employees, family, and the community. Ironically, it is possible that this level of frustration may foster an environment that leads to managerial ineffectiveness and reduced profits.

Therefore, it is imperative for Christian managers especially—and all managers generally—to have a well-established framework and a belief system to guide the decision-making process. Without such a system, managers often will make decisions erratically, decisions that are dictated by the "squeaky wheel" or a blind desire to maximize profits at any cost. To gain the managerial knowledge, skill, and motivation to develop and refine an ethics-based decision-making framework and to operate it from a Judeo-Christian worldview, it is necessary to "*study to show thyself approved*" (2 Timothy 2:15 KJV). Such study must focus on the secular world of ethical theory and business management practices as well as on biblical principles, attitudes, and decision-making skills. With these skills properly integrated, the manager can formulate and begin to internalize a personal ethical position.

> *Judeo-Christian worldview*: those principles, attitudes, and values that influence every area of life and that grow out of an acceptance of God's standards as revealed in his creation and holy Scriptures.

Informal Systems of Ethics

Ethics is a part of the fabric of American business. Imagine running a business where no one could be trusted. In such a world, the suppliers all would be liars, the bank would be out to steal businesses, and all employees would be loafing when the boss was not watching. Fortunately, most people do have a sense of right and wrong and follow some kind of moral code, possibly learned in their youth from significant role models. They have at least an informal method of making decisions that could include elements of self-protection and goodwill toward a high moral ground.

The Self-Protection Approach

The self-protection approach to ethical decision making has long been used by business managers as well as others. The approach consists of asking a series of questions designed to protect the manager's public image and self-esteem. They include but are not restricted to:

- How will my image or reputation with my employer be affected if I make this decision?
- Would I want my children to know what I am doing?
- Would I want this decision or course of action to be published with my name on the front page of the local newspaper?

The Common Moral Beliefs Approach

The common moral beliefs approach uses commonly accepted moral principles that a child would be taught by ethical caregivers. The person using this application of the informal system of ethics might ask questions such as:

- Is it the right thing to do?
- Is this the fair thing to do?
- Am I following the Golden Rule?

Problems with the Socratic Model

The questions in these two variations of the informal system of ethics represent a *Socratic model* of decision making. Named after the Athenian philosopher Socrates, this model uses a series of questions that lead to a logical conclusion. When answered objectively, these generally lead business managers to ethical decisions. However, they also present some real problems for managers:

- They do not encourage a causal analysis of the decision.
- They do not examine the decision's extended consequences.
- They do not identify the persons affected or the issues involved.
- The self-protection approach is motivated by fear or self-interest.

Ethics Defined

If the informal system of ethics is too shallow, then how does one make sound ethical business decisions? The answer lies in understanding the nature of ethics. *Ethics* is a system of moral values that is applied in a consistent way to one's personal, social, and business life.[5] To apply those moral values effectively, one must understand the structural levels at which ethical dilemmas occur, what parties are involved in the dilemmas, and how a particular decision will affect them. In addition, one must know how to formulate and consider various courses of action. Failing in any of these four areas may lead to an ineffective decision, resulting in unintended consequences.

> *Ethics*: A system of moral values that is applied in a consistent way to one's personal, social, and business life.

The Ethical Dilemma

In business, as in other areas of life, an ethical dilemma occurs when a moral conduct issue is at stake or when the economic needs or desires of a business conflict with its responsibility toward people, the environment, or social institutions.[6] Formulating the proper decision to resolve the ethical dilemma calls for an understanding of many variables. One of the most compelling variables involves determining whose needs are driving the demand for a decision. This requires careful analysis since people have a variety of needs, some of which are not expressed or obvious.

At the Personal Level

The first source of needs is at the *personal level*. Dilemmas at the personal level directly confront the decision makers and require them to make individual decisions. A key question in this situation is, what do I do to meet my needs?

For example, suppose Byron has been passed over for a promotion. The promotion is given to an employee with fewer years of experience in the industry and in the company. Should Byron file a complaint with a regulatory agency? The answer relates primarily to Byron's needs.

Or suppose the husband of Tina's best friend has made sexual advances toward Tina. Should Tina tell her friend and risk ending their friendship or her friend's marriage? This is a personal issue that Tina herself must resolve.

At the Organizational Level

Organizations establish policies, systems, and structures to ensure that operations run smoothly and organizational goals are attained. At the second or *organizational level*, the manager makes decisions on behalf of the company or the organization with the purpose of meeting the needs of the organization. When faced with a dilemma, a manager operating at this level should ask, "Did this situation occur as the result of meeting a perceived organizational need as the organization formulated or applied a policy, procedure, system, structure, or goal?" That is, has the company created this moral dilemma while striving to meet other organizational needs? The manager's decision must balance the needs of the organization, as presented in the form of established policies, systems, structures, and goals, while attending to the company's responsibilities to others.

In Tina's case, the unwanted sexual advances could constitute sexual harassment if they occurred at work. In that case, the situation directly relates to the company's policy-making and legal responsibilities. The company managers want to resolve the situation not only to protect a fellow employee, but also to protect the company's assets and future. This is especially important because the design of the company's planning, controlling, and reward and punishment systems inadvertently may set the stage for unethical decision making.

At the Societal Level

A third level of needs occurs at the *societal level*. Societies protect and advance their needs by adopting economic, legal, social, and political systems that determine how a business should operate within the culture. A key question to ask is are market forces, governmental regulations, laws, or political processes and ideologies that are outside my direct control dictating boundaries for my decision? Here the issues that directly affect the success or even the survival of the company originate from systems outside the company. Conventional wisdom calls for managers to absolve themselves of personal responsibility at the societal level, because the systems are outside their control. But is it ethical to allow these systems to limit decisions, or is it ethical for these managers simply to comply with society's requirements? Do managers who are Christians have a biblically based standard that overrides society's standard?

The Christian manager should ask this important question: is it possible in the short run to do the ethical thing—based on an ethical belief system grounded in both a Christian worldview and an understanding of ethical philosophy—while in the long run working for positive change in the economic, legal, social, and political systems? Such an approach could amount to being salt and light to the world (Matthew 5:13–14).

At the Legal Level

One societal system affecting a business is the law and its regulatory role. A major guiding principle for many business leaders is the belief that if it is legal, it is ethical. This is based on the belief that in a democratic society the law represents the will of the people and, therefore, represents what is morally just in the society. Conscientious managers should analyze this belief by asking themselves a series of short questions: "Does the law really represent the will of the majority of the people in every situation or even the majority of situations? . . . Do laws truly represent the changing moral values of society or the constant moral values of God? . . . Are the forces and conditions that caused laws to be enacted the same or even similar years later? . . . Is there consistency in the application of the law to all segments of society?"[7]

Workplace law can provide examples of the pitfalls of using the law as the sole criteria of ethical behavior. The responsibility of employers to their employees is, by law, determined in some areas by the size of the company. For example, in the United States, while the employees of large companies receive company-subsidized health-care plans and the benefits of family leave when a child is born, small businesses are legally exempt from offering the same advantages to their employees.[8] If laws truly represent the will of the people, then the majority of Americans believe that only employees of large companies and their families deserve affordable health care and related benefits. Some observers conclude that since this scenario is legal, it is also morally right. When the law is seen as the primary measure of right and wrong, morality is determined by a majority of people or a few individuals in the judiciary. All managers have the responsibility to obey the law of the land. They also have the responsibility to ask a deeper question: do society's laws represent the final standard for my ethical decision making, or are they the beginning point?[9]

At the Political Level

The political system in which the company exists is a second societal system that influences decision making and introduces ethical dilemmas. Yet sometimes political systems send mixed signals. Let's examine a hypothetical example. A farmer in the Carolinas is considering the most effective use of his property. Should he plant tobacco or vegetables? Economic pressure tells him that to produce a strong bottom line, he should plant tobacco. What's more, the political system seems to support this decision by subsidizing tobacco farmers, providing low-cost loans and other financial aid for natural disasters, and artificially supporting the price of tobacco on the domestic trading market. At the same time, other sectors of the US political system are banning the advertisement of tobacco products to certain markets, placing age requirements on the purchase of tobacco goods, and sponsoring health-related lawsuits against tobacco companies. The farmer very well may say that he has no control over the political system and its flaws and that he is free to plant tobacco. After all, a portion of both the political system and the legal system seem to agree and even encourage the planting.[10]

Stakeholders and Ethical Decision Making

Another key question for consideration in ethical decision making is, who are the *stakeholders* in a given decision? Typically, stakeholders in a company decision are employees, suppliers, customers, stockholders, and the community at large.[11] For example, in deciding whether to raise tobacco or vegetables, the hypothetical farmer may consider his employees' need for jobs, his family's need for security, or his community's need for economic stability. But other stakeholders should also be considered in the farmer's decision, for example, the consumers who may contract cancer or the taxpayers who support the health-care and welfare systems for cancer patients. When these secondary stakeholders are added to the equation, the decision to grow tobacco or vegetables becomes a more significant ethical dilemma.

> *Stakeholders*: individuals, groups, or environments that have a stake in a particular decision.

We've considered whose needs might be driving the need for a decision. A business manager must also consider who will be affected by a decision and weigh options in this light. For instance, the manager must anticipate the needs of all stakeholders affected by the decision, policy statement, or new structure. Sometimes the aggregate effects on larger, more remote groups of stakeholders—such those living in the community where a company is located—hold more potential for good or harm than the effects on stakeholders within the organization.

Stakeholder consideration is especially important to those who believe that people are made in God's image. However, the consideration of people alone does not provide the moral standard for a decision. It is also important to think through how God's creation will be affected. For the Christian manager, the appropriate standard comes from God's moral system.

Ethical Decisions Don't Ensure a Perfect World

Ethical decisions often harm some stakeholders while helping others. One manager switched suppliers to obtain cheaper raw materials. She made this decision for the purpose of keeping her business viable and to protect the owners, employees, and community in which the business was located. As a result, however, the supplier's business failed, harming its owners and employees—in the same community.

Some decisions have extended results that are difficult to anticipate. A manager may resolve a dilemma in the short run and set in motion an unexpected extended consequence. That was the case for the New Orleans chef who created a blackened redfish entrée. He had no idea that his business innovation and nutritional dish would become so popular worldwide that it would endanger the world's redfish population.

While not all unexpected results of ethical decisions are as far reaching, they can be just as undesirable. On his first day on the job, one middle manager sent a morning memo to all lower level managers and staff. He believed he was doing the right thing by providing employees with up-to-date information for optimum job performance. However, before 10 a.m., he received a call from the corporation's main office. The chief executive officer (CEO) demanded to know how, on his first day on the job, the new manager had made his staff so angry that they were threatening a walkout. What the manager did not know was that his predecessor also had a daily morning memo, which he had used to discipline and embarrass subordinate managers and employees. People feared that their new boss was using the same approach. The middle manager's motives were ethical and his openness in sharing information eventually led to positive long-term outcomes, but the short-term results were nearly catastrophic.

This example also illustrates another facet of ethical decision making. Decisions always involve personal implications. Decisions may trigger the company's reward or punishment systems, strengthen a manager's relationship with God, or otherwise affect the manager's personal life. However, the results of *not* making the ethical decisions usually are much more costly.

When applying a sound ethical decision-making process to a dilemma, managers will find many solid solutions with varying degrees of acceptability. A simple yes or no answer will seldom suffice. In the short run, weighing the pros and cons of various acceptable solutions involves additional energy and time. In the long run, however, managers generally save costly time and energy in damage control and corrective actions by using a sound process for ethical decision making.

Questions Discussion

1. Describe a situation in which you or an acquaintance, acting in a managerial role, used the Three-E Equation to resolve an operational or manufacturing problem at work. What were the results of this approach? How would the results have differed if only effectiveness and efficiency had been considered? What if only efficiency had been considered?

2. Describe an ethical dilemma that occurred at the organizational level and the managerial decision to resolve it. Who were the relevant stakeholders? Which stakeholders benefited from the actions taken to resolve the dilemma? How did they benefit? Which stakeholders did not benefit from or seemed to be harmed by the action taken? How? Did the dilemma directly relate to the enforcement of a company policy or procedure? Which policies or procedures? If possible, describe an alternative action to resolve the dilemma that would have produced fewer and/or less severe negative outcomes for stakeholders.

Endnotes

1. Rushworth M. Kidder, *The Ethics Recession: Reflections on the Moral Underpinnings of the Current Economic Crisis* (Rockland, ME: Institute for Global Ethics, 2009).

2. John F. Ward, "Restoring Corporate Trust: The New Imperative for Ethics, Integrity and Diversity," in *Leaders on Ethics: Real World Perspectives on Today's Business Challenges*, ed. John C. Knapp (Westport, CT: Praeger, 2007), 19–25.

3. Law Dictionary law.com Law Dictionary, accessed September 9, 2010.

4. Wendy Zellner, Stephanie Anderson Forest, et al. "The Fall of Enron," *Business Week*, December 17, 2001.

5. *Webster's Ninth New Colligate Dictionary* (Springfield, MA: Merriam-Webster, 1989), 426.

6. LaRue Tone Hosmer, *The Ethics of Management*, 3rd ed. (Chicago: Irwin, 1996), 136.

7. Hosmer, *The Ethics of Management*, 59–65.

8. Anjel Vahratian and Timothy R. B. Johnson, "Maternity Leave Benefits in the United States: Today's Economic Climate Underlines Deficiencies," *Birth: Issues in Perinatal Care* 36, no 3 (September 2009): 177–79.

9. Hosmer, *The Ethics of Management*, 75.

10. Duff Wilson, "Congress Passes Measure on Tobacco Regulation," *New York Times*, June 13, 2009.

11. Robert Phillips, *Stakeholder Theory and Organizational Ethics* (San Francisco: Berrett-Koehler, 2003).

3

Three Ethical Systems

The sum of your word is truth, and every one of your righteous rules endures forever.
— Psalm 119:160

Chapter Challenges

A careful examination of Chapter 3 should enable the reader to:

- Identify the primary components of three major secular ethical systems.
- Recognize the strengths of each of the three major secular ethical systems.
- Understand the weaknesses of each of the three major secular ethical systems.

The search for what is right, just, and proper has fueled civilized societies since ancient times. Often these efforts have been based on a society's drive to understand and apply God's written Word and/or God's natural revelation. This search also has focused on finding a system that does not depend on God at all. The guiding forces in these latter attempts have ranged from one extreme of serious application of logic (reason) and philosophy to the opposing extreme of personal fulfillment of an individual's basest desires. This chapter will introduce and explain three prominent ethical systems.

Utilitarianism

An ancient ethical system is *utilitarianism*, in which the end result is important, not the motivation or the means by which the end is achieved. As a philosophy, utilitarianism became more refined in England in the nineteenth century, but this system has roots in the earlier Greek system, *telos,* which emphasized the end results of an action or the consequences of the action; utilitarianism is sometimes referred to as a consequentialist theory. In utilitarianism, managers try to identify the positive and negative end results of an action. If the positives outweigh the negatives, the decision is considered to be ethical.[1]

For example, when a colleague took over the presidency of a failing college, an in-depth study revealed that overstaffing some academic departments was seriously draining the institution's limited resources. The decision was made to reduce the workforce substantially in those areas. The tenets of utilitarianism qualify this as an ethical decision. The rationale, according to utilitarianism, is that it is better for some of the staff to lose jobs than for the college to be forced to close. Closing the college would have a negative impact on all employees and students, as well as on the college's creditors and the surrounding community.

Utilitarianism and the Stakeholder

To apply utilitarianism effectively, managers must consider the impact of their decisions on all stakeholders involved. We generally think of people when we refer to stakeholders, but stakeholders can include the earth and its ecosystems, as we saw in the Chapter 2 example of the New Orleans chef. In the case of the college president, the obvious stakeholders were the college's faculty, staff, students, and creditors, as well as the community into which the college contributed culturally and economically. Less obvious but no less important stakeholders included the families of the faculty and staff, the institution's alumni and donor base, the state's academic community as a whole, and future generations of students hoping to attend a college with the same kind of ethos as the one that might have been closed. When a decision has to be made, a skilled decision maker is able to identify key stakeholders, whether or not they appear at the top of an early list.

What Price Harm?

Utilitarianism is not concerned only with the number of stakeholders potentially benefited or harmed by a decision, but also with the degree or amount of benefit versus the amount of harm. In general, if the amount of harm to the few is severe and the amount of benefit to the many is slight, then the right, just, and proper thing to do according to utilitarianism is to make the decision that protects the few from severe harm.

For example, when viewed through utilitarianism's ethical lens, one would have to question whether a state lottery is ethical. The vast majority of people who play the lottery lose, which is why the lottery makes so much money. The overwhelming majority of these lottery losers are low-income people. The money they lose in the lottery translates into food, clothing, and other necessities and services that they or their families will not receive. Most citizens benefit from the lottery's payments to the state through reductions in their taxes. But the reduced taxes are a very small percentage of the average citizen's total income. The loss of lottery-generated tax breaks would, in most cases, not reduce the level of basic needs available to those individuals and their families. In this case, utilitarianism would determine the state lottery to be unethical because the negative effects on the poor and their children are significantly greater than the tax reduction benefits to the general public.

The Negative Harm Principle

A specialized and unique application of utilitarianism, the *negative harm principle*, generally is applied to questions about the rights related to safety and health. Its key element refers to whether a manager's decision has caused or avoided physical harm to stakeholders. Harm to the health of the stakeholders overrides other nonhealth benefits of a manager's decision.[2]

> *Negative harm principle*: specialized application of utilitarianism in cases that could impact stakeholders' health and safety.

For many years the federal government, through its school lunch subsidy program, offered peanut butter to the nation's school children. This provided hundreds of millions of children with a good source of protein and zero cholesterol fat, two positive characteristics. However, a small percentage of children are born with an allergy to peanut products. This allergy can be so severe that a teaspoon of peanut butter may cause death. Many school lunchrooms have stopped offering peanut butter despite its known benefits (to the many) because of its devastatingly harmful potential (to a few). This is an example of the negative harm principle at work. The same principle also can apply in business to issues related to worker safety, product safety, environmental safety, or to any issue involving physical harm to people.

Utilitarianism's strength is in its impartiality. The stakeholders are considered both as subgroups and as a whole. An individual's self-interests, such as those of the manager, an employee, or a customer, are not an overriding consideration. Decisions based only on friendship, family relations, or political allegiances do not stand the utilitarian ethical test. Many aspects of the American legislative and judicial systems reflect this ethical philosophy.[3]

The Flaws of Utilitarianism

Utilitarianism also has several weaknesses. The first is operational; it is often difficult to identify the relevant stakeholders.[4] This is caused in part by a manager's inability to completely set aside personal emotions and look for all relevant stakeholders. It is especially true when the manager or business entity must make decisions while under attack by one or more stakeholder groups or when relevant stakeholders enter the picture late.

For example, the US Food and Drug Administration has approved and then later withdrawn medicines or food products from the marketplace because the products later were discovered to cause birth defects. Unborn babies became relevant stakeholders after the original approvals were made.

The second weakness also is an operational one; it is almost impossible to accurately weigh the results of decisions on the various stakeholder groups.[5] The results may be more than just economic. They also may be psychological, social, or political.

Perhaps the most profound weakness of utilitarianism is its indifference to the needs of individuals or smaller stakeholder groups when weighed against the needs of a larger set of stakeholders.[6] In the example of the financially struggling college, the individual needs of those being released were set aside in favor of the needs of the larger stakeholder groups.

Other examples of utilitarianism are more insidious. Voting laws in eastern states disenfranchised first-generation American citizens who had immigrated from Ireland and Middle and Eastern Europe. This was done to keep in power the political systems that represented the established majority. Like many other nations, America's past includes the terrible institution of slavery. Slavery oppressed the powerless for the benefit of the powerful. At its worst, utilitarianism demonstrates that the benefit to the majority can become evil totalitarianism to the minority.

Ethical Egoism

One dictionary defines egoism as "the tendency to be self-centered, or to consider only oneself and one's own interests."[7] When applied to ethical behavior, egoism states that the ethicality of a decision is determined by the decision maker's self-interest. Thus the person who works hard and sets aside short-term gratifications in order to attend college and then graduate school because of perceived future psychological, social, and economic benefits operates from the position of *ethical egoism*. The department manager who makes decisions designed to improve the department's efficiency so that it (and in turn she) appears to be more effective in the eyes of upper management also is applying ethical egoism.

Strengths and Weaknesses

Ethical egoism's primary strength is that it can be an effective motivational tool. Sales representatives or production managers who consistently make decisions to improve their departments' performance to gain large bonuses, to protect their jobs, or to be known as the best, fit this model.

However, the ethical egoism model for decision making also can reflect ethical, operational, and organizational weaknesses. For instance, it tends to put emphasis on the short term at the expense of the long term. One acquaintance, known as a highly successful insurance salesman, offers an example of ethical egoism's weaknesses. In his desire to maintain his position as the division's top salesperson, along with the accompanying financial rewards, he made the decision to write policies with larger and larger benefits without weighing the policyholder's ability to pay or the long-term effects on the company's financial health. In the short run, this practice gained him larger commissions and salesperson-of-the-month bonuses. In the long run, these oversold policyholders were unable to continue to pay. This caused them to lose their coverage, the company to lose money, and ultimately the agent to lose both his job and his lavish lifestyle.

A second weakness is that this approach to decision making leads to the dissolution of organizational vision. When decisions are based solely on the best interest of an individual or a department, the company's mission, goals, other departments, and systems take a backseat.

Consider, for example, a university basketball team with a starting lineup of five high-scoring individual stars. They become the highest scoring team in the league and possibly in the college's history. Yet they barely have a winning season. That is because each person's desire to pad his personal scoring average takes precedence over the team goal of winning games. Five highly motivated individuals do not automatically make a team. A team requires putting aside personal interests for the good of the group.

A third weakness of ethical egoism involves the lack of an effective mechanism to settle disputes between and among various self-interests. Every manager acts in his or her own best interest. This position says that self-interest, even at the expense of others, is the right thing to do. The inevitable result of ethical egoism is anarchy, which is characterized by undercutting, backbiting, and other negative effects on the company's general health.[8]

Kantian Ethics

Immanuel Kant established a set of ethical decision-making principles called *imperatives* that form the basis of Kantian ethics. Examples of imperatives include always telling the truth and never stealing. In his quest to develop a usable ethical system, Kant developed what is called the *categorical imperative*. This is an important standard meant to guide behavior, a standard that should never be broken. The categorical imperative is composed of two formulations. The first states, "Act only on that maxim through which you can at the same time will that it should become a universal law."[9] Kant's second formulation of the categorical imperative states, "Act in such a way that you always treat humanity, whether in your own person or the person of any other, never simply as a means, but always at the same time as an end."[10]

> *Categorical imperative*: two standards or formulations must be met to satisfy Kantian ethics: (1) the universal-law standard, act only on a maxim that you would be willing to become universal law, and (2) the treatment-of-others standard, treat others as an end not a means to an end.

You should be able immediately to see how this model differs from the first two ethical decision-making positions. Unlike ethical egoism, Kant's system emphasizes impartiality to individuals and groups. It is built around obligations and duties. When one person has duties, Kantian ethics automatically implies that others have rights. If these duties are obligatory, personal desires alone no longer control decision making. Unlike utilitarianism and ethical egoism, the end result and personal desire do not determine ethical behavior. Instead, the fulfillment of moral obligations or absolutes in the form of the categorical imperative defines the ethics of managerial actions.

Two Sides of the Kantian Coin

Let's look again at the two formulations of Kant's categorical imperative. Formulation 1 states, "Act only on that maxim through which you can at the same time will that it should become a universal law." This formulation is built on several primary principles, including the use of reason in ethical decision making, obligation to duty, and what Kant termed the principles of universalizability and reversibility. In effect, before enacting a decision, a manager must ask, "Would I want all other managers in a similar situation to make the same decision (universalizability)?" A second question is, if I were the person being affected by this decision, would I want my manager to make the same decision that I am considering (reversibility)?[11] In a sense, a manager has the obligation to help define the high moral ground for an entire industry through ethical decision making. It is a matter of duty.

Formulation 2 states, "Act in such a way that you always treat humanity, whether in your own person or in the person of any other, never simply as a means, but always at the same time as an end."[12] This axiom recognizes the rights of others and the manager's duty toward them as well as to oneself. This prohibits the manager from manipulating or using people only as a means to gain a goal. Duties-based ethical systems do recognize that all members of an organization contribute value toward meeting the organizational goals. Kantian ethics also asserts that each person is an individual with needs, talents, and goals, all of which must be respected. Creating a workplace culture that balances the means-and-ends equation is a foundation stone of many modern models for effective business.

Kantian Strengths

Kantian ethics as a whole passes the test of logical consistency. The categorical imperative teaches that some things are right in every situation. It acts as an anchor to keep managers from being swayed by either changeable emotions or foreseen outcomes of decisions.

The United States Supreme Court adhered to the Kantian emphasis on consistency by applying his principle of universalizability in denying the requested vote recounts in a small portion of the state of Florida in the 2000 presidential election. If they had allowed a recount in that county, should the votes in every other county in Florida, or in the nation, be recounted as all possibly had some errors? The justices received scathing denouncements by individuals caught up in the emotions of the time, exacerbated by their lack of knowledge of the electoral process and the United States Constitution. Kant would say that the justices had to apply the universilizability principle because not doing so would undermine the electoral process.

A second strength of Kantian ethics is its ability to bring about the recognition of right and wrong. This involves duties based on unchanging principles called imperatives, which are universal rules. Additionally, right and wrong responses are based on the rules, not on an individual's personal wishes, emotions, or circumstances. Kantian ethics counteracts the human tendency to rationalize that a certain behavior—because of some personal reason—is wrong for one person, but right for another.

A third strength of Kantian ethics involves rationality. There are as many definitions of what is rational as there are principal stakeholders in a given ethical dilemma. However, a decision that can be rationally supported is still better than one that cannot be rationally supported.

Kantian Weaknesses

Kant's concept of imperatives includes weaknesses. First, duties may conflict. Some duties may be more important than others, leading to internal conflict. The rule never to lie may conflict with the rule to protect the lives of individuals. Corrie ten Boom was a Christian who lived in German-occupied Holland during World War II. When Nazi officers repeatedly questioned her about whether or not her family was harboring Jews, she faced a terrible dilemma: either tell the truth and send people to their deaths or lie to save the Jews.

Conflicting duties may have been the issue in June 2007 when Billy Donovan, the highly successful head basketball coach of the Florida Gators flip-flopped on whether he would remain at the University of Florida or join the NBA as head coach of the Orlando Magic. Donovan reportedly signed a multimillion dollar, five-year contract with the Magic. Only six days later, he returned to the University of Florida, having apparently experienced some difficulty in sorting out his contractual obligations from his obligation to loyalty to university-team recruits.[13]

A second weakness in Kantian ethics is that circumstances cannot always be ignored if we have real concern for people. Ten Boom looked at the implications of telling the truth. In this situation, rational logic was broken down by human need. Knowing which circumstances cannot be ignored and which are less pressing is a key leadership skill—one that effective leaders continue to hone on a daily basis.

Ethical Systems Comparison Chart

As a means of synthesizing the key concepts of the three ethical systems, fill in the cells in the Ethical Systems Comparison Chart below.

Ethical Philosophy or Theory	Main Characteristics	Strengths	Weaknesses
Utilitarianism			
Egoism			
Kant's Imperative Formulation 1			
Kant's Imperative Formulation 2			

Questions ❓ Discussion

Using your comparison chart as a guide, respond to the following questions:

1. With which of the elements in the ethical systems comparison chart do you feel most comfortable? Explain your answer, giving specific reasons that reflect your beliefs and the key elements of the ethical position.

2. Which ethical philosophy or theory is most prevalent in your workplace? Provide examples.

3. Is any one of the ethical philosophies or theories described in this chapter sufficient by itself to guide a manager in making ethical decisions? Explain your answer and give examples.

Endnotes

1. Bruce N. Waller, *Consider Ethics: Theory, Readings, and Contemporary Issues* (New York: Pearson Education, 2005), 49.
2. John R. Boatright, *Ethics and the Conduct of Business*, 2nd ed. (Upper Saddle River, NJ: Prentice-Hall, 1997), 383.
3. Joseph W. Weiss, *Business Ethics: A Managerial, Stakeholder Approach* (Belmont, CA: Wadsworth, 1994), 66.
4. Manuel G. Velasquez, *Business Ethics: Concepts and Cases*, 4th ed. (Upper Saddle River, NJ: Prentice-Hall, 1998), 76.
5. Velasquez, *Business Ethics*, 76.
6. Weiss, *Business Ethics*, 67.
7. *Webster's New Universal Unabridged Dictionary*, 2nd ed., s.v. egoism.
8. Scott B. Rae, *Moral Choices: An Introduction to Ethics*, 2nd ed. (Grand Rapids: Zondervan, 2000), 29.
9. Kant, *Groundwork of the Metaphysics of Morals*, trans. H. J. Paton (New York: Harper & Row, 1964), 61.
10. Kant, *Groundwork of the Metaphysics of Morals*, 96.
11. Velasquez, *Business Ethics*, 95.
12. Immanuel Kant, *Groundwork of the Metaphysics of Morals*, 61.
13. Associated Press, "Very Apologetic Donovan Returns to Florida," NBCSports.com, June 7, 2007.

Notes

4

Christianity and Ethics

Make me to know your ways, O Lord; teach me your paths. Lead me in your truth.

— Psalm 25:4–5

Chapter Challenges

A careful examination of Chapter 4 should enable the reader to:

- Define the term *natural law*.
- Explain the principles of Old Testament ethics.
- Understand the basics of New Testament ethics.

"There's no such thing as business ethics," declares leadership expert John C. Maxwell in his provocative little book of the same title.[1] Maxwell contends that all ethics are personal and suggests that ethics boil down to one simple maxim, the Golden Rule. "Whatever you wish that others would do to you, do also to them" (Matthew 7:12). That, according to Maxwell, is the sum and substance of business ethics and of ethics in general.

Someone may argue that the Golden Rule is a Christian principle and therefore has no appeal or applicability to those of other religious faiths. Maxwell demonstrates, however, that some version of the Golden Rule exists in nearly every culture and in every major religion of the world. His research uncovered passages strikingly similar to the Christian Golden Rule in the holy writ of several faiths, including Islam, Judaism, Buddhism, Hinduism, Zoroastrianism, Confucianism, and Bahai.[2]

We do not wish to undermine the importance of the Golden Rule, but it can become a cliché that covers every situation without thought. Therefore, we take a more comprehensive view of ethics and expand the concepts of God's natural law and God's revealed law in Scripture. This chapter will provide the reader with specific examples.

Natural Law

Without using the term, Maxwell has declared the Golden Rule to be a part of *natural law*. Natural law is sometimes referred to as eternal law or even human nature. Robert Van Wyk notes: "Natural law is regarded by its supporters as transcending custom and the laws of particular societies because some aspects of human nature are the same for all human beings."[3] Natural law suggests that right and wrong are written on the hearts of human beings by nature itself. It is the belief in a moral standard independent of a particular society's customs or rules of law.

The great thirteenth-century theologian and philosopher Thomas Aquinas is credited with developing the concept of natural law. This approach was also foundational to the thinking of English philosopher John Locke. In America, Thomas Jefferson expressed natural law's strong influence on him when he penned these words in the Declaration of Independence: "We hold these truths to be self-evident, that all men are created equal, that they are endowed by their Creator with certain unalienable Rights . . ."[4]

Two Emphases

Today the term *natural law* is used primarily in two ways. Scott B. Rae explains the first context of natural law, writing of the universal principles that are found in our society as well as in most societies around the world. Universal values include justice, fairness, respect for an individual's dignity, the obligation not to harm others, truthfulness, and prohibitions against killing.[5]

While many moral standards are culturally derived, those that exist across cultural boundaries, according to this understanding, are derived from natural law. Proponents of this view maintain that certain values exist in enough different cultures to warrant the belief that these truths are written naturally on the hearts of individuals. These adherents argue that where differences exist in mores between cultures, these differences result from something other than natural law.

Second, the term *natural law* sometimes refers to what occurs naturally in creation. Environmentalists adopt natural-law thinking when they declare pristine wilderness to be superior in any and every case to development. The Roman Catholic Church has used a natural-law argument in its traditional opposition to birth control. Contraception, the Catholic Church suggests, interrupts the natural created order and, thus, is morally wrong.

Nearly Derailed

According to Rae's analysis, natural law also played a significant role in the Clarence Thomas confirmation hearings in October 1991. Rae believes Thomas's belief in natural law nearly derailed his confirmation as a justice of the United States Supreme Court. He suggests that the mood of the hearings and the attitude of many members of the Senate Judiciary Committee shifted when Thomas vocalized belief in natural laws.[6]

Rae theorizes that the media and other liberal observers found Thomas's belief in natural law frightening for two important reasons. First, natural law has been used too frequently to oppress minorities and women. Ultraconservatives, for example, have argued that superior male leadership qualities exist in nature and have offered that as a basis for keeping women out of decision-making roles. Others have suggested that whites are superior to blacks in the natural state. These historic misuses of natural law may have prompted some members of those groups to find Thomas's advocacy of natural law unacceptable.

Some may have found Thomas's belief in natural law unacceptable for a deeper reason: natural law represents a God-centered ethic. The existence of a universal right and wrong presupposes the existence of a higher authority—a higher authority that has declared that standard. In its rush to secularism, modern America has become much more comfortable with man-centered rather than God-centered ethics.

Most Christians would agree with Judge Thomas's opponents on the first point. If Thomas intended to use natural law to suppress women and members of his own race, few would find his ethic acceptable. On the second point, however, orthodox Christians would generally find themselves in agreement with Thomas and natural law. (By orthodox, we refer to the biblical Christian church worldwide, not specifically to the Eastern and/or Russian Orthodox Churches.) Most Christians agree that right and wrong are correctly understood in God-centered rather than human-centered ethics. Further, Christians believe that while God has written right and wrong on the hearts of human beings, as understood by natural law, God also has revealed his ethic in another way. Believers look to God's special revelation of moral right and wrong in the Old and New Testaments.

Old Testament Ethics and Holiness

The ethics articulated in the Old Testament and foundational to Judaism and Christianity are based upon the principle that human beings are created in the image of God. "God created man in his own image, in the image of God he created him; male and female he created them" (Genesis 1:27). That we are created in the image of God explains why life preservation is so central to Judaism and orthodox Christianity. One does not destroy that which has been created in God's image.

Being created in the image of God also emphasizes a godly lifestyle. To be ethical, according to the Old Testament writers, is to be godly. And since *holiness* is an attribute unique to God as revealed in Old Testament literature, it follows that to be more like God is to be more holy. God's command to the people of Israel in Leviticus 11:44 (NRSV) sums up Old Testament ethics: "For I am the LORD your God; sanctify yourselves therefore, and be holy, for I am holy." The emphasis is on the responsibility of the Hebrew people to keep the covenant between them and God by being like God.

Theologian Allan Coppedge writes: "Never has the Christian Church needed to place a greater emphasis on holiness of character than in our day. But human holiness cannot be understood without reference to divine holiness."[7] Perhaps the insurgence of less ethical behavior in today's culture can be linked to its inability or unwillingness to understand God's holiness and his requirement to be like him.

While the Old Testament outlines many characteristics of the holy life, three emerge as foundational to the study of ethics as applied to business and management: justice, equality, and integrity.

Justice: God's Measuring Line

The Old Testament declares that the holiness of God issues in *justice*. Accordingly, God's true (ethical) followers are people of justice. We probably think first of its punitive aspects when we think of the word *justice*. But justice involves a standard for both punishment and reward. Isaiah 28:17 (NKJV) refers to justice as God's "measuring line," a way to correct imbalances. The concept of justice as applied to business and management today can best be understood when broken down into four component aspects.

Biblical Contractual Justice Principle

Contractual justice occurs when an exchange of promises creates a special relationship or contract. The Old Testament demonstrates contractual justice when God deals with the people of Israel in a special way in exchange for their agreement to follow him. God demonstrates contractual justice through a covenant with Israel: "Now therefore, if you will indeed obey my voice and keep my covenant, you shall be my treasured possession among all peoples, for all the earth is mine; and you shall be to me a kingdom of priests and a holy nation" (Exodus 19:5–6).

> *Contractual justice*: justice that occurs when an exchange of promises creates a special relationship called a contract.

Contractual justice still exists today. Ethical business people believe that the terms of a contract are binding. To violate a contract is to be unjust and thus unethical. On the other hand, the court dockets are filled with cases involving principals who have violated or severed their contractual relationships. Contracts are thus not eternal in spite of their moral and ethical dimensions.

Biblical Distributive Justice Principle

Questions of injustice surface when some people struggle to provide for their needs, while others enjoy an abundance of the world's goods. This is a matter of *distributive justice*. God implies distributive justice when he gives these commands in Leviticus 19:9–10 (NRSV): "When you reap the harvest of your land, you shall not reap to the very edges of your field, or gather the gleanings of your harvest. You shall not strip your vineyard bare, or gather the fallen grapes of your vineyard; you shall leave them for the poor and the alien: I am the LORD your God."

> *Distributive justice*: justice that emerges from questions regarding the distribution of wealth.

Biblical Compensatory Justice Principle

The rubric of justice also includes *compensatory justice*. God often negatively or positively compensates certain people or people groups for their behaviors. For example, the Egyptians received harsh treatment at God's hands for enslaving God's chosen people. "I will lay my hand upon Egypt and bring my people the Israelites, company by company, out of the land of Egypt by great acts of judgment" (Exodus 7:4 NRSV). God authorized compensatory judgment when he instructed the people of Israel to ask the Egyptians for gold and silver articles prior to their exodus from Egypt (see Exodus 12).

> *Compensatory justice*: long-term justice that emerges from compensation for injustices of the past.

In an interesting twist on the concept of compensatory justice, a modern-day Egyptian attorney, Nabil Hilmi, has planned to sue the world's Jews for that ancient plunder.[8] Apparently the suit would focus on whether compensation to modern Egyptians is due in light of ancient compensatory plunder by the Israelites. Such are the thorny questions of justice.

Closer to home, more recent, are arguments about affirmative action programs in America. These arguments essentially stem from a variety of views on compensatory judgment. Some argue that it is unethical to give preferential treatment on the basis of race when hiring or offering opportunities in higher education. Others contend that preferred treatment is ethical and necessary in order to compensate for the injustices of the past. The latter group sees social ethics as mandating compensatory justice. The former group sees unqualified equality as the most just and most ethical basis of behavior.

Biblical Interrelational Justice Principle

God is concerned for those who are vulnerable. As with God's commands for impartiality in other types of justice, Deuteronomy 24:14–15 reminds us that it applies *to interrelational justice* as well: "You shall not withhold the wages of poor and needy laborers, whether other Israelites or aliens who reside in your land in one of your towns. You shall pay them their wages daily before sunset, because they are poor and their livelihood depends on them" (NRSV). Just application or violation of interpersonal justice is determined by the *interrelational justice principle*, which states that interactions between human beings—God's creation—regardless of station in life must not unjustly damage the integrity, personal dignity, and sense of worth as well as public identity of an individual or groups of individuals. Violations of the interrelational principle may emanate from the misuse of power (positional, physical, wealth, or emotional). Abuses of this principle in the workplace can take the form of bullying, sexual harassment, and employment and advancement discrimination.

> *Biblical interrelational justice*: justice that emerges when power is not abused by one party to gain an unjust domination over another.

Equality: The Principle of Impartiality

A second characteristic of God's holiness and the holy life is *equality*. Throughout Scripture, God encourages his people to deal equally with one another. A classic Old Testament account poignantly reveals this truth. According to God's instruction, the prophet Samuel was to search for the next king of Israel among the sons of a man named Jesse (1 Samuel 16:1–23). Samuel nearly overlooked the youngest son, David. But indeed David was God's choice to succeed Saul. The principle of equality is summarized in God's explanation to Samuel: "Do not look on his appearance or on the height of his stature, because I have rejected him [Eliab, David's older brother]; for the LORD does not see as mortals see; they look on the outward appearance, but the LORD looks on the heart" (1 Samuel 16:7 NRSV). That is to say, God viewed all of the sons of Jesse equally. He did not treat the firstborn with more deference than the youngest, as was the custom of that time.

The Old Testament concept of equality is reinforced in the New Testament command to show impartiality in passages such as Romans 2:9–11, where God makes it clear that he does not show favoritism, even to his beloved children of Israel when he said, "There will be anguish and distress for everyone who does evil, the Jew first and also the Greek, but glory and honor and peace for everyone who does good, the Jew first and also the Greek. For God shows no partiality" (NRSV). The *principle of impartiality* holds that decisions regarding individuals, groups of individuals, or entities are to be based in their actual performance or other task-related qualifications and not in non-task-related characteristics such as group membership.

The principle of impartiality discredits practices such as stereotyping. Stereotyping in the workplace occurs when a trait such as low or high intelligence, inferior or superior manual skills, honesty or dishonesty, laziness or initiative are exaggeratedly applied to an individual or group. Stereotyping often involves stakeholders of a particular gender, color, regional origin, ethnicity, or other group membership. One of the authors earned his way through college working in the school's cafeteria. He was quickly promoted until he was the highest paid student worker on campus, the assistant director of the cafeteria. He was told by the director that the best assistant director she had ever hired had been from the author's high school; when given the opportunity, she always chose a graduate from that high school to be her assistant. The author has always wondered if he won the job on the merits of his ability to supervise students or because he was a graduate of a particular high school.

Integrity: The Principle of Veracity

A third attribute of God's holiness as demonstrated in Old Testament literature is *integrity*. God reveals himself throughout Scripture in terms of honesty and truth. Psalm 33:4 captures the essence of God's integrity. "For the word of the LORD is upright, and all his work is done in faithfulness."

As with godly attributes of justice and equality, truthfulness or veracity is expected of God's followers who aspire to ethical behavior. Hence, the psalmist prayed, "Make me to know your ways, O LORD; teach me your paths. Lead me in your truth and teach me" (Psalm 25:4–5).

Truthful Communication Corollary

The *truthful communication corollary* of the principle of veracity requires communication messages that are truthful in their content as well as in their intent. The manager does not present inaccurate information as truth or divert stakeholders from the truth through the use of techniques designed to mislead those for whom the communication is intended. Misleading techniques include:

Straw Person Fallacy: the distortion of the connection(s) of one or more stakeholders or of facts related to a managerial dilemma—meant to confuse the decision maker, causing decisions to be made on false premises rather than the real issue.[9]

Red Herring Strategy: the introduction of unrelated information with the intent of diverting the decision maker's focus from relevant facts so that the real dilemma will not be addressed or a decision more favorable to the deceiver will be made.[10]

Stalking-Horse Strategy: the disguising or concealment of intentions (plans or objectives) by one or more stakeholders by proposing a fictitious solution that is not likely to be adopted, thus masking true purposes.[11]

Appeal to Emotions Strategy: the use of emotionally charged language to influence stakeholders and distract the decision maker from relevant issues and data; generally this includes a strong statement about impending doom, failure, losses, etc., if a course of action is taken or is not taken.[12]

Accuracy of Information Corollary

Leviticus 19:35–36: "You shall do no wrong in judgment, in measures of length or weight or quantity. You shall have just balances, just weights, a just ephah, and a just hin: I am the LORD your God, who brought you out of the land of Egypt." The accuracy corollary of the principle of veracity has two major elements.

Credibility of Data Standard: The *credibility of data standard* deals with the credibility of sources of information used in communication and decision making as well as the methods of acquiring this data. Primary questions to be asked include: Were reliable, industry-accepted methods of data gathering employed? Were the data interpreted impartially according to their *prima face*, face value, rather than distorted for a particular purpose?

Transparency of Data Standard: The second element is the *transparency of data standard*, which deals with the availability of important, accurate, and complete data to all involved stakeholders—including the form in which the data is presented. A manager who fails to provide relevant information needed to understand why a decision is being made or how it is being implemented is violating the transparency of data standard. The manager who knowingly withholds relevant data or who purposely presents data in a form that will not be understood by the stakeholders or will mislead the stakeholders is also violating this standard. Common techniques used to violate this standard include:

- Equivocation strategy: a presenter of data purposefully uses a key word or phrase that has two or more common meanings. This is done for the purpose of confusing the stakeholders and influencing the outcome of the decision-making process.[13]
- Withholding important information strategy: pertinent information is purposefully omitted from the decision-making process to influence the decision in favor of or against one or more groups of stakeholders or to prevent a needed decision from being made.
- Unreliable data collection strategy: data is gathered through questionable techniques, with ineffective tools, or from dubious sources with the deliberate intent of obstructing the decision-making process or of manipulating the ultimate decision.

The truthful communication corollary speaks both of being truthful in communication, and also using only accurate and reliable data for judging assertions, people, and possible consequences of upcoming decisions. The desired result of such practices is the facilitation of harmony in the workplace, whether in operating procedures and practices or cooperation among co-workers and stakeholders toward stated goals.

Old Testament ethics, based on God's holiness, recognizes justice, equality, and integrity as the standards by which people should live, by which managers should manage.

New Testament Ethics and Holiness

A major difference between the ethical system presented in the Old Testament and in the New Testament is a shift in emphasis rather than overall approach. Jesus, the second person of the Trinity, maintains the holiness inherent in the Godhead and continues to demand holiness in his followers as the appropriate response of commitment to him. The New Testament ethic involves the imitation of Jesus Christ.[14]

To the principles of justice, equality, and integrity, Jesus and the early church add a strong emphasis on love as a standard of ethical behavior. Paul also insists that in light of Christ's coming, love is an important aspect of becoming more godly. "Therefore be imitators of God, as beloved children. And walk in love, as Christ loved us and gave himself up for us" (Ephesians 5:1–2). In his epistles, John concurs and spells out the necessity of loving other human beings as a response to God's character. He writes, "Beloved, if God so loved us, we also ought to love one another" (1 John 4:11).

The New Testament writers understood this new emphasis on love as a component of ethical, holy behavior in response to Jesus's specific commands. In what must have been considered shocking in Roman times, Jesus even went so far as to suggest that love must be extended to one's enemies. In his most famous sermon, Jesus taught, "You have heard that it was said, 'You shall love your neighbor and hate your enemy.' But I say to you, Love your enemies and pray for those who persecute you" (Matthew 5:43–44).

The Ethics of Love Principle: God's Concern for the Good of People

In Ephesians 2:4–5 God instructs us in the meaning of his love when he says, "But God, being rich in mercy, because of the great love with which he loved us, even when we were dead in our trespasses, made us alive together with Christ—by grace you have been saved." God's *ethics of love principle* is expressed in the Greek word *agápé*. This word is found only in religious writings and is generally used to describe God's love toward humanity and the expression of God's love through human beings toward others. Agape is a benevolent love. "Its benevolence, however, is not shown by doing what the person loved desires but what the one who loves deems as needed by the one loved."[15] This is an unselfish love that is reflected in the modern term *tough love*. In John 3:16 we read, "For God so loved the world, that he gave his only Son, that whoever believes in him should not perish but have eternal life." God's love toward humanity prompted an action initiating the way for forgiveness, even though humans did not ask for forgiveness or possibly understand their need for it.

In the application of the ethics of love, the manager factors this question into the decision-making process: how will my action concerning this person or group assist them in becoming better people as well as better employees? In short, this ethical principle requires management to be an instrument in the wholistic improvement of others as well as in their capacity of carrying out their responsibilities to the company. Keeping the right balance between these two factors is part of the manager's challenge.

Empowered by the Holy Spirit

Besides emphasizing love as a component of holiness, the New Testament introduces for the first time the presence and power of the Holy Spirit's indwelling the believer on a continuous basis. In the Old Testament, the Holy Spirit empowered one or more of God's people from time to time. In the New Testament, the Holy Spirit is a continual presence in every believer. While the specific moral decisions are the person's own responsibility, the Holy Spirit assists in the operation of conscience. This presence makes it possible for disciples to achieve holiness of heart and life.

Jesus had made a promise to his band of eager followers. "When the Spirit of truth comes, he will guide you into all the truth" (John 16:13). On the day of Pentecost, that promise was fulfilled. Immediately and boldly, the disciples began to demonstrate holy and ethical behavior. Acts 4:33–35 summarizes some of the characteristics of the early church:

With great power the apostles were giving their testimony to the resurrection of the Lord Jesus, and great grace was upon them all. There was not a needy person among them, for as many as were owners of lands or houses sold them and brought the proceeds of what was sold and laid it at the apostles' feet, and it was distributed to each as any had need.

In looking at this passage from an ethical point of view, we can say that the disciples:

- spoke *truth* about the Resurrection;
- ministered *justice* to those in need;
- attempted to facilitate *equality* among the brethren;
- acted with *love* toward others.

A central truth of the New Testament is that once followers of Jesus Christ are empowered by the Holy Spirit, they can become godly in their ethic. This happens because the Spirit enables them to live with holiness of heart and practice, as demonstrated in ethical justice, impartiality, integrity, and love.

Facing Moral Dilemmas

A Spirit-filled Christian relies on the Holy Spirit to live out godly, moral behavior. Yet evidence abounds that empowerment by the Holy Spirit is not the only factor in determining how a Christian will view or act in a particular situation. Two different Spirit-empowered believers can come to strikingly different solutions for identical moral dilemmas. Further, the same two Christian managers can seek to interpret the same biblical truths yet reach vastly different conclusions.

For example, one entry-level supervisor sought to act lovingly and justly toward an employee who was a single mother. He agreed to punch her time card, giving her the extra twenty minutes she needed to get her child to an important dentist appointment. Upper management saw the matter differently, interpreting the supervisor's act as disregard for integrity (disobeying the rules) as well as undercutting equality (showing favoritism). The supervisor was disciplined for unethical behavior.

A Christian manager also can experience inner conflict when faced with various scenarios. Should the manager emphasize love over justice in one situation and equality over truth in another? What if the decision in the first scenario ethically contradicts the decision in the second scenario? Managers who wait until they are faced with such choices have waited too long. They must develop in advance a clear ethical position designed to encompass as many situations as possible. How to develop such a personal position is the subject of Chapter 5.

Questions ❓ Discussion

1. Compare and contrast each of the four types of biblical justice found in this chapter with secular utilitarianism as discussed in the previous chapter.

2. Cite specific biblical ethical principles from this chapter which you believe would be problematic. Explain why each of the principles might not work in the business world.

3. Compare and contrast the ethics of love principle discussed in this chapter with the two formulations of Kant's categorical imperative (see chap. 3).

Endnotes

1. John C. Maxwell, *There's No Such Thing as "Business Ethics": There's Only One Rule for Making Decisions* (New York: Warner, 2003), Preface.
2. Maxwell, *There's No Such Thing,* 22.
3. Robert N. Van Wyk, *Introduction to Ethics* (New York: St. Martins, 1990), 57.
4. National Archives, The Charters of Freedom, Declaration of Independence, www.archives.gov/exhibits/charters/declaration_transcript.html.
5. Scott B. Rae, *Moral Choices: An Introduction to Ethics,* 2nd ed. (Grand Rapids: Zondervan, 2000), 35.
6. For a review of the facts surrounding the confirmation hearings, see Gloria Borger and Ted Gest, with Jeannye Thornton, "The Untold Story," *US News and World Report*, October 12, 1992, 28–32. See also Orrin Hatch, *Square Peg: Confessions of a Citizen Senator* (New York: Basic, 2002), 141–62.
7. Allan Coppedge, *Portraits of God: A Biblical Theology of Holiness* (Downers Grove, IL: InterVarsity, 2001), 16.
8. "What about 400 Years of Slavery?" *World,* September 27, 2003, 8.
9. M. Neil Browne and Stuart M. Keeley, *Asking the Right Questions: A Guide to Critical Thinking*, 9th ed. (Upper Saddle River, NJ: Prentice-Hall, 2010), 77.
10. Browne and Keeley, *Asking the Right Questions,* 82.
11. *Merriam-Webster's Collegiate Dictionary,* 11th ed., s.v. stalking horse.
12. Browne and Keeley, *Asking the Right Questions,* 74.
13. Browne and Keeley, *Asking the Right Questions,* 75.
14. Richard A. Burridge, *Imitating Jesus: An Inclusive Approach to New Testament Ethics* (Grand Rapids: Eerdmans, 2007).
15. *The Hebrew-Greek Key Study Bible* (Chattanooga, TN: AMG, 1990), 1796.

5

Developing a Personal Statement of Ethics

But be doers of the word, and not hearers only, deceiving yourselves.

— James 1:22

Chapter Challenges

A careful examination of Chapter 5 should enable the reader to:

- Differentiate between three views for interpreting Scripture.
- Draft a personal statement of ethics.

"To Become a Better Man"

In the spring of 2003, reports surfaced that political pundit Bill Bennett had lost as much as $8 million over several years in high-stakes gambling.[1] As the summer heated up, so did the ethical questions surrounding Bennett's lifestyle. There were mixed reactions from conservative loyalists. On the one hand, Bennett's followers expected the former drug czar and editor of the best-selling *The Book of Virtues* to live above reproach. They believed their self-appointed hero of morality should have avoided such arguably unethical behavior.

On the other hand, many concluded that Bennett's personal life was his business alone. No one doubted that Bennett's income could support a gambling habit. He was never accused of illegal behavior. Hence, many took the position that no one really had been hurt by this aspect of his lifestyle.

Bennett himself responded to the debate with a concise analysis. Referring to his Roman Catholic belief system, he said simply, "Gambling is not a sin in my church."[2]

Within a few weeks, however, Bennett vowed that he was "now done with gambling. Period."[3] Cynics argued that his change of heart was strictly a result of his eagerness to reenter public life free from the baggage of national scandal.

Bennett himself declared the change to be the result of deep introspection and the development of a personal ethic that apparently went beyond that of the church. "I stopped a lot of the usual action in my life and have done a kind of inventory of myself . . . and that's been good for me. The task is, and put this in capital letters, to become a better man."[4]

What Changed?

Let's consider factors surrounding Bennett's decision to give up gambling.

- The church's position had not changed.
- Scripture had not changed.
- The acceptability of gambling had not changed.
- The legality of gambling had not changed.
- Bill Bennett's family circumstances had not changed.
- Only Bill Bennett's personal ethic had changed.

Bill Bennett's announcement of his personal inventory resulting in an updated personal ethic gained unusual nationwide attention. However, an ethical review is not an unusual activity. Leaders consistently discover the need to develop and perform according to a personal ethic. They find it necessary from time to time to review and update their own ethical position. As John Maxwell wrote, "Ethics is never a business issue or a social issue or a political issue. It is always a personal issue."[5]

Randy Cohen, who answers ethical questions on a regular basis for the *New York Times Magazine*, agrees. He writes, "In considering an ethical question, whether concerning the right conduct of an individual or the society within which we function, I refer to a set of principles I cherish as profoundly moral." Cohen declares that for him personally, "this constellation of values includes honesty, kindness, compassion, generosity, fairness."[6]

Scripture Only

Such was the case for Ethan, a Christian who owned and operated a retail business. Ethan maintained that his personal ethic was based simply on "Scripture only." He declared, "Along with the rest of my independent church, I believe the Bible. That's all the ethic I need."

On many issues, Ethan's approach worked satisfactorily. However, ultimately he was faced with a dilemma for which his "Scripture only" position was inadequate. Ethan had hired Jason, a teen from a troubled family, to work as a clerk in his business. He believed that he would have an opportunity to exert a positive Christian influence on Jason. The problem arose because Jason arrived late for work at least four days a week. Although the tardiness amounted to ten minutes or less, it clearly was a pattern. Ethan had repeatedly warned Jason about the importance of punctuality. Obviously, he needed to follow up on his warnings. The matter no longer involved Jason alone. Other employees were forced to cover for him in his absence.

Ethan faced an ethical dilemma. On one hand, the scriptural position was one of mercy and grace. On the other hand, there definitely were godly standards about the use of time. Further, there was the issue of fairness to other employees. Ethan asked himself, "Should I fire Jason or forgive him, so that I can continue to work toward his rehabilitation?"

Ethan's "Scripture only" ethic left him without a clear moral choice in this matter. He was forced to develop a more comprehensive ethical system. Many Christian managers faced with ethical dilemmas have developed such a system by first creating a personal statement of ethics. One of the purposes of this text, as we explained in the introduction, is to help the reader develop a personal statement of ethical position.

Building the Foundation

Before exploring the components of a personal statement of ethics, we need to examine the keystone upon which all Christian ethical positions are based—Scripture. Here we need to make a distinction between a "Scripture only" ethic and a "scriptural ethic." A "Scripture only" ethic sees the Bible as the beginning and end of ethical thought. A "scriptural ethic" builds upon Scripture as its foundation, but may include reason, experience, and tradition to structure a solid ethical position. It is important to remember that even a completely developed scriptural ethic does not answer every question, because Scripture can be interpreted in many ways. In addition, scriptural passages can be adapted to real-world scenarios in a number of ways.

Three Views of Scripture

Allen Verhey suggests three possible ways to use a scriptural ethic for real-world choices.[7]

Fundamentalist View

A *fundamentalist view* teaches that the biblical ethic is normative for today's culture, except for those passages originally intended to be temporary. Of course, debate arises when determining just which passages were intended to be temporary. For example, some strict fundamentalists maintain that Paul's indication to the Corinthian church that women should be silent is normative for today's culture (see 1 Corinthians 14:34–35). Some even see this passage as a general prohibition against any and all female leadership.

Some see issues other than this prohibition as Paul's primary focus in the Corinthian church. They reason that the prohibition against women in leadership is applicable only to that situation. Even among those who hold to the fundamentalist view, there is diversity of opinion and a need for a personal ethic founded on, but broader than Scripture.

Liberal View

Verhey identifies a second or *liberal view*. According to this position, a teaching is applicable to today's moral choices only if it is the Word of God as opposed to the human writer's viewpoint. Paul clearly identifies his own opinion in at least one passage, 1 Corinthians 7:12. Determining how much of the writer's opinion colors God's Word, as well as its overall applicability to today's ethical choices, is a springboard for much discussion among those who hold to the liberal view.[8]

Interpretive View

Finally, Verhey identifies what might be called an *interpretive view*. In this view, the Christian who is applying scriptural truth to moral choices must first determine the original intent of the passage. The intent, as opposed to the literal words, is then applied to any contemporary ethical decision.[9] As with the fundamentalist and liberal views, debates rage over the original intent of any number of scriptural passages. For example, the command "You shall not murder" (Exodus 20:13) is interpreted by some to apply at the moment of conception. Others interpret this command as applicable from the moment of birth. Thus, it is still necessary for one who holds to the interpretive view to consider and construct a personal ethical viewpoint.

Developing a Personal Statement of Ethics

Regardless of one's view of Scripture, the Christian business leader or manager needs to develop a personal ethic—a personal statement of ethical intent. This statement is built on an individual's understanding of Scripture and purports to anticipate ethical dilemmas that may arise. Correctly structured, it contains an appropriate anticipatory response. Scripture and faith can and should be foundational to the Christian's personal ethic, but each person must build upon the foundation of Scripture and faith to determine the appropriate response in any given situation.

Evidence indicates that today's business managers eagerly accept the challenge to develop a personal statement of ethics. If there was a time when business and professional leaders managed their organizations according to the explicit dictates of a church's teachings and rules, that day is past. Today's business leaders "want fact and freedom simultaneously. They respect the teachings of their religious traditions, but they want to be active participants in interpreting, applying, and sometimes redefining the rules meant to guide them."[10]

Increasingly, business managers and students of business are discovering the advantages of writing out their statements of personal ethics in advance of any moral dilemma. That way, when issues arise, they have given prior thought to what they believe and how they intend to behave.

No On-the-Job Philosophizing

As a supervisor in a small manufacturing plant, Chris took his faith seriously. He also thought it necessary to think through his foundational ethical belief system. He learned from experience that the day-to-day rush of planning and supervising the work of his eighteen employees left little time for on-the-job philosophizing over ethics. He also discovered that as he revisited his personal statement of ethics from time to time, it required a bit of updating and fine-tuning in light of things he discovered in his work. In time, however, he was satisfied that the statement adequately reflected his personal beliefs. He also was confident that when implemented in the real world in which he operated, the statement made him a more ethical Christian manager. Chris's well-thought-out and fine-tuned statement appears in Figure 5.1.

Figure 5.1. A Personal Statement of Ethics

Chris Ault

As a disciple of Jesus Christ, I believe that everything I do reflects him and his kingdom. Therefore, I will endeavor to make decisions based on the key question, "What would Jesus do?"

Often I will find the answer to this question in the Scriptures, which is God's Word of truth. Therefore, I must be a regular student of the Bible in order to be an ethical manager.

Sometimes the answer is not spelled out in Scripture. Then I must ask myself a series of follow-up questions:

1. Which decision would do the most good for the most people?
2. How would I want to be treated if someone else were making the decision?
3. Have I already made statements or in any other way given an indication of my decision that others may be counting on?
4. Recognizing that I will stand before Christ someday to be judged, what decision should I make?

Even using these probing questions is no guarantee that I will always perform ethically. Therefore, I will revisit this statement at least every three months to ensure that it is still leading me to ethical decision making. I also will pray regularly for my employees, suppliers, customers, and co-workers that God will prevent me from making decisions that will harm them.

A Personal Top Ten

Scripture is a key ingredient in Chris's statement, yet his position does not reflect interpretations of any particular passage. By contrast, another Christian manager incorporates interpretations of particular scriptural passages into her personal statement of ethics. Alison's statement appears in Figure 5.2.

Figure 5.2. A Personal Statement of Ethics

Alison Stewart

These are my top ten ethical guidelines:

1. Make every decision remembering that Jesus is watching.
2. Remember that Christian people are to be holy, just, and truthful.
3. Submit to your employer unless to do so would violate God's law.
4. Obey the government unless to do so would violate God's law.
5. Treat others as you wish to be treated.
6. Realize that all people are created in the image of God.
7. Recognize that since the Fall all human beings are born in sin.
8. Be honest and above reproach in all things.
9. Treat the environment as a specially created gift from God.
10. God first, others second, self last.

Alison's personal statement of ethics has been refined over several years of management experience. Initially, however, it was the result of an in-depth scriptural study, as well as the study of several important topics related to ethics.

Writing a Personal Ethics Statement

Your assignment, at the end of this chapter, is to formulate your personal ethics statement by first identifying what ethical concepts are important to you and prayerfully considering various scriptural passages to glean insight and information. Many resources are available to help you with this topical study. These include the concordance in your Bible, a good Bible dictionary, many Christian websites, the opinion of secular as well as Christian ethicists, and your own personal experiences.

Give special attention to those areas of life in which you are often tested. For example, one manager frequently lost his temper. He knew that he needed to be more patient. He resolved to include patience as both a personal goal of self-development and a component of his personal statement of ethics. To incorporate patience into his statement, he first conducted a topical in-depth study of Scripture to find what God's Word said about patience. Then he wrote the specific truths he learned in his personal statement of ethics.

A Sample Topical Search

Effective managers will be committed to the idea that a personal statement of ethics must be practical as well as philosophically consistent. As a result, reviewing a series of scriptural passages relating more directly to employer-employee relationships will prove fruitful. Read the following Scriptures with an eye to how they could be instrumental in developing a personal statement of ethics. Beside each Scripture, write a summary statement that explains how that passage relates to business ethics.

Your summary statements might include a reference to *respect* for co-workers, employees, and employers. This is important, as 1 Timothy 6:1 points out, because when we are disrespectful, we slander God's name. Your search also might have found *sincerity* and *wholehearted service* to be important attributes in employee-employer relationships. To incorporate these findings into a personal ethics statement, you would focus on these qualities in your draft. A sample wording might include some of these thoughts:

> I will put my all into my job and give my employer a full day's work for a full day's pay. I will perform even the mundane tasks with sincerity and thoroughness, and I will be busy at all times—not just when my employer is looking in my direction. I will treat everyone I come into contact with respectfully, even when that person does not reciprocate.

Summary of Biblical Investigation in Ethical Behavior

Sample Scriptures	Key Ethical Insights
Leviticus 19:1	
Deuteronomy 24:14	

Sample Scriptures	Key Ethical Insights
Malachi 3:8	
Matthew 20:1–15	
Luke 10:7	
Ephesians 6:5–9	
Colossians 3:23	
Colossians 4:1	
1 Timothy 5:8	

Sample Scriptures	Key Ethical Insights
1 Timothy 6:1	
Titus 2:9	
James 5:4	
1 Peter 2:18–20	

Integrating Faith and Practice

Having studied relevant Scriptures and reviewed the ethical positions of important secular philosophies, such as those presented in Chapter 3, a manager is ready to write a personal statement of ethics. From time to time, many managers review their position in light of some ethical dilemma or moral choice they face in the workplace. Sometimes they simply perform a periodic review of the statement to assess how recent spiritual or emotional development has influenced their personal ethical position. Over time, the statement becomes a vital part of who an individual is as a manager.

Of most importance, a personal statement of ethics can significantly impact a manager's day-to-day faith. That alone causes those who make the effort stand out among many of their Christian colleagues. "Most business managers acknowledge that religion played an important role in their moral upbringing.

Yet few say that religion significantly affects their daily business decisions."[11] Managers who develop a personal statement of ethics effectively integrate faith and practice. They become "doers of the word, and not hearers only" (James 1:22).

Questions ❓ Discussion

1. What are the strongest points in Chris Ault's statement of business ethics? What are the weakest?

2. Reread Alison Stewart's personal statement of ethics. What are the key elements with which you agree? With what points do you disagree?

3. What is the role of secular philosophies and theories of ethics in the formation of a personal code of ethics?

4. How does one's view of the value of people affect the adoption of the secular principles of utilitarianism, ethical egoism, and Kant's second formulation in the development of a code of ethics? Give specific examples from each to support your assertions.

Endnotes

1. Jonathan Alter and Joshua Green, "Bennett: Virtue Is as Virtue Does?" *Newsweek*, May 12, 2003, 6.
2. Editors, "To Become a Better Man," *World*, August 9, 2003, 24–25.
3. "To Become a Better Man," 24–25.
4. "To Become a Better Man," 24–25.
5. John Maxwell, *There's No Such Thing as "Business Ethics"* (New York: Warner, 2003), 13.
6. Randy Cohen, *The Good, the Bad, and the Difference* (London: Atlantic Books, 2002), 10.
7. Allen Verhey, *The Great Reversal: Ethics and the New Testament* (Grand Rapids: Eerdmans, 1984), 170.
8. Verhey, *The Great Reversal,* 170.
9. Verhey, *The Great Reversal,* 170.
10. Alan Wolfe, *Moral Freedom: The Search for Virtue in a World of Choice* (New York: W. W. Norton, 2001).
11. Edward D. Zinbarg, *Faith, Morals, and Money: What the World's Religions Tell Us about Money in the Marketplace* (New York: Continuum, 2001).

Assignment: First Draft

Review the ethical systems of Chapters 3 and 4. What particular aspects of any of these philosophies can you apply to your personal statement of ethics? Then examine the Scriptures below and write a summary statement after each verse describing how that verse relates to business ethics. Be sure to include the Scriptures we highlighted in the sample topical search above. To assist you, we have chosen three concepts essential to a personal statement of ethics and listed relevant Scriptures.

Use the space at the end of this chapter to write the draft of your personal ethics statement. Be sure to include any important truths you have already discovered as a business manager or in your everyday interactions.

My personal statement of ethics will include the quality of justice:

- Exodus 23:1–8
- Ecclesiastes 5:8
- Ecclesiastes 7:7
- Isaiah 1:17
- Isaiah 56:1
- Lamentations 3:35–36
- Luke 10:7
- John 7:24
- Romans 14:17
- 1 Corinthians 6:12
- 1 Corinthians 13:6
- James 5:4

Are there any other Scriptures you wish to include on justice as it relates to ethics?

Review justice as it was presented in Chapter 4. What aspects are applicable to your personal ethics statement?

My personal statement of ethics will include the quality of impartiality:

- 1 Samuel 16:7
- Job 31:13–15
- Psalm 33:13–15
- Proverbs 22:2
- Matthew 20:25–27
- Matthew 23:8
- Acts 10:28
- Romans 2:9
- Galatians 3:28

Are there any other Scriptures that you wish to include on impartiality as it relates to ethics?

Review impartiality as it was presented in Chapter 4. What aspects are applicable to your personal statement of ethics?

My personal statement of ethics will include the quality of integrity:

- Exodus 20:16
- Exodus 23:1
- Deuteronomy 25:13
- Psalm 119:29
- Psalm 120:2
- Proverbs 3:3
- Proverbs 11:1
- Matthew 15:19
- 2 Corinthians 8:21
- 1 Thessalonians 4:12
- 1 Thessalonians 5:22

Are there any other Scriptures that you wish to include on integrity as it relates to ethics?

Review integrity as it was presented in Chapter 4. What aspects are applicable to your personal statement of ethics?

My personal statement of ethics will include the quality of love:

- Leviticus 19:18
- Deuteronomy 10:19
- Psalm 133:1
- Proverbs 10:12
- Proverbs 15:17
- Matthew 5:41–47
- Matthew 19:19
- John 15:12
- Romans 12:9
- Ephesians 5:2
- Philippians 2:2

Are there any other Scriptures that you wish to include on love as it relates to ethics?

Review love as it was presented in Chapter 4. What aspects are applicable to your personal statement of ethics?

Personal Statement of Ethics

Name _____   Date _____

6

The Christian Manager as Ethical Decision Maker

*If you call out for insight and raise your voice for understanding . . .
Then you will understand righteousness and justice and equity.*

— Proverbs 2:3, 9

Chapter Challenges

A careful examination of Chapter 6 should enable the reader to:

- Differentiate between issues of fact, value, and policy.
- Understand criteria for ethical decision making.

Case Study

Sunset Manor Retirement Center

Ever since earning her RN license more than fifteen years ago, Julie Fredericks has worked at Sunset Manor Retirement Center. In addition to providing traditional nursing home care, Sunset Manor serves the housing needs of retirees who select from among a variety of local independent living arrangements. Julie has always preferred working in the Alzheimer's unit, where she supervises a staff of five nursing assistants on the day shift. Together they care for fifteen patients.

The patient-to-caregiver ratio is high, because the needs of the residents are great. Sunset Manor has a fine reputation among both clients and competitors for providing above-average care. The commitment to quality is one reason Julie finds her work so rewarding. "The residents are so sweet, and there is just the right combination of nursing and administration. I love my job," Julie told a friend recently.

A Difficult Decision

Today, however, Julie is not so sure. She has just received word that she must release one of her five assistants. The memo from the front office indicates that after careful budget review and analysis, administrators have determined that employee costs are simply too high in the Alzheimer's unit. Asked to reduce the staff by one member, each shift supervisor has been instructed to submit the name of one employee to the Personnel Department.

Julie loathes the idea. "Those administration types simply don't understand the heavy demands of working with our special needs people," Julie complains to her second-shift counterpart. "Our responsibilities take more time and energy than those in other areas of Sunset Manor."

"I refuse to do it," her colleague responds. "I'm convinced it is morally wrong to understaff this area. I won't participate in the hatchet job. If they intend to lay off any of my people, they will do it without my help."

"Disobeying orders doesn't seem like the correct approach," Julie argues. "I don't think I have much choice, although I certainly wish for the residents' sake that we had some alternatives."

Later Julie sits with personnel files spread before her, trying to decide which of her five nursing assistants should be let go. She wants to be fair both to the employees and to the residents. The decision proves to be extremely difficult.

The Personalities Involved

Sally Chambers has been with Sunset Manor nearly as long as Julie and plans to retire in about three years. She demonstrates careful efficiency in her approach to the workload and seems to accomplish more than other staff members. But Sally sometimes becomes obsessed with the need to meet specific goals. Forging ahead with government-mandated paperwork, she can be abrupt, even rude, to residents and their families. Even so, Julie appreciates Sally's attention to detail, since Julie has never enjoyed these kinds of mundane tasks.

Janice Robinson is the complete opposite of Sally. She loves the people in the unit almost to the exclusion of administrative responsibilities. She could sit for hours and visit with residents or their families. Family members often comment positively on her caring attitude. "It is about people work, not paperwork," Janice loves to say. As a single mom with two elementary-age children, Janice depends on her salary at Sunset Manor to provide for the family.

Angie Franklin, the newest member of Julie's staff, joined the team as a replacement only a few months ago. Already Julie has come to depend heavily on Angie's knowledge and ability. She attends school at night and in less than a year will complete her nursing degree. Julie routinely gives her more responsibility than she does the other assistants. In fact, she encourages Angie to practice her nursing skills within the limits of propriety and the law.

Jake Minor, the only male member of the staff, has played a unique role during his five years at Sunset Manor. The others depend on Jake to lift patients or perform other strenuous tasks. Jake came to Sunset Manor after his conversion to Christianity and several subsequent months of drug rehabilitation. With no family and few outside interests, he came to Sunset Manor wanting to lead a more productive life. He pours his heart and soul into his work. More than once he has commented to Julie that few places would have offered him the second chance he needed. "I owe my life to Sunset Manor," he explains.

Regina Munson rounds out Julie's staff. Perhaps better than anyone else at Sunset Manor, Regina understands the residents' needs—and they love her. In addition to her work at Sunset Manor, she cares for her own aging mother at home. Some believe she has heavy financial responsibilities. Others call her a workaholic. For whatever reason, Regina has proved to be an extremely dependable employee. In fact, records indicate that she has not missed a single day of work in the nearly five years since she was hired.

What Is Right?

Complicating Julie's decision, Sunset Manor does not have a union. In addition, company history provides very little precedent for decision making in workforce reduction. Julie goes over the files repeatedly, trying to decide which staff member to release. The more she thinks about it, the more her second-shift counterpart's idea of refusing the task appeals to her. Julie even wonders if she should offer to quit, basing her decision on being asked to do something she finds unconscionable.

"I just don't know what is right," she declares. "I don't even know *how to decide* what is right."

On Background

Criteria for Ethical Decision Making

Julie acknowledges both that she must make a difficult decision and that she feels inadequate for the task. She joins a large segment of managers that finds constant decision making to be one of the most difficult aspects of their jobs.

Norman Augustine, former CEO of Lockheed Martin, reportedly said, "My most difficult business decision had to do with the closing of a number of plants. These downsizing decisions are, of course, intended to be in the best interest of the company and the shareholders, but can be quite devastating for the employees who are required to find employment elsewhere. . . . The human price is immense, but so too are the consequences of failing to face the problems one confronts."[1]

As Julie wrestles with the options available to her, she will certainly consider both the ethics of her dilemma and the ethics of decision making in general. To this end she may want to consider six aspects of ethical decision making.

Recognize That Not All Decisions Are the Same

Her current dilemma may prove to be one of the most agonizing in Julie's managerial career. Through a ripple effect, her decision stands to affect the lives of many others. To be an ethical decision maker, Julie needs to acknowledge the gravity of the situation and carefully weigh all options. This means she will have to devote more time and emotional energy to this decision than to less critical issues, such as choosing a supplier for a particular product or scheduling employee days off.

To better understand the differences in decisions, view them as involving three types of issues:

- fact
- value
- policy

Ethical decision makers readily recognize the differences in these three types of issues. Further, they recognize the need to deal differently with decisions involving issues of fact than with those involving value or policy.

Decisions Based on Fact

Because they consider the truth or falsity of an assertion, decisions surrounding *issues of fact* are generally the easiest to make. Most managers find it relatively simple to collect the data and then make a decision based on issues of fact. For example, a manager who reviews product safety data recognizes that a particular product may be harmful to the consumer. She follows preset guidelines that assess the potential for and severity of injury. The product in question will either meet the guidelines or it will not. An issue of fact determines the product safety manager's course of action.

Decisions Based on Value

Decisions surrounding *issues of value* consider the relative worth or rightness of a particular course of action. In such questions, one manager's ethical and honest conclusion may differ from another manager's ethical and honest conclusion. Julie's second-shift counterpart has decided that it is morally wrong to lay off an employee in her unit. She has made a decision of value not to participate. Julie instead has determined that it is morally wrong to violate the instructions of an employer. She is proceeding with the layoff, having come to a different conclusion on the question of value.

Decisions Based on Policy

Decisions of policy usually involve the word *should*. They focus on which course of action *should* be taken. This contrasts to decisions that *must* be taken (related to questions of fact) or decisions *determined* to be superior to an alternative course (related to questions of value). For example, a manager who buys a higher-priced, lower-quality item from one supplier may do so based on a policy decision. The manager may be willing to pay the higher price and accept the lower quality because of issues of loyalty, commitment, or customer service. In short, he concludes, "In this case I should pay more because . . ."

Analyze a Situation from Many Points of View

Since Julie's decision potentially will impact a host of people, she will want to examine the position of as many stakeholders as possible in the analysis phase of decision making. She must consider her own administrators at Sunset Manor, her five staff members, the staff members' families, and her counterpart on the other shift. Julie's decision even includes her counterpart's employees, who will see Julie taking managerial responsibility while their own supervisor fails to act. Certainly and perhaps most important, Julie will have to take into account the effect of her decision on the clients in the Alzheimer's unit. While it would be easier if she limited the analysis phase to her own needs and wants, such self-centered behavior must never be an option for the ethical Christian manager.

Be Action Oriented

The ethical decision maker must make decisions in a timely fashion. Julie would be acting irresponsibly if she made a snap decision or simply flipped a coin. However, because of the many perspectives she has to consider, Julie also is in danger of becoming so enmeshed in the analysis that she fails to make a timely decision. Managers are ultimately paid for decisions, not analysis. Ethical decision makers avoid the "paralysis of analysis." To drag the decision out beyond the point of reasonable analysis also challenges ethical standards. Delaying necessary decisions yields unethical results through the unproductive use of time.

- Every day that Julie does not announce her decision is another day that one employee cannot prepare for termination.
- Every hour that Julie spends in the decision process is an hour that she cannot give to her employer in other profitable endeavors.

Issue of fact: decisions that consider the truth or falsity of an assertion.

Issue of policy: decisions that consider what course of action should or should not be taken.

Issue of value: decisions that consider the relative worth or rightness of an issue.

Acknowledge Emotional Bias

A young man declared to his latest romantic infatuation, "I'll always love you. I know because I've never felt this way before about anyone." Decision making on the basis of feelings may prove adequate in "puppy love." However, it seldom provides a solid basis for sound managerial decisions.

In the decision-making process, Julie must do her best to distance herself from emotional involvement with her employees. Since Julie is human, some emotion is bound to be present, and the emotion must be accepted and acknowledged for Julie to make an ethical decision.

Emotional bias can creep into managerial decisions in various forms. One manager found it difficult to discipline employees in a certain age group, because they reminded him of his own parents. Another made poor decisions regarding employee time off because of her own unacknowledged guilt about the amount of time she spent away from home and family. Yet another manager found it difficult to be objective concerning a policy on tuition reimbursement. She had worked long hours and made significant sacrifices for her own education without the convenience of that benefit.

These managers will move toward more ethical decision making when they recognize their own emotional issues in these areas. They may find it useful to think of personal emotion as one of the many perspectives included in appropriate analysis. Having acknowledged their biases, they can then move on to more objective analysis through other points of view.

View Results Realistically

Few circumstances dictate either 100 percent negative or 100 percent positive outcomes. Yet some managers seem to insist on seeing the future as exclusively one or the other. Julie tends to view the problem at Sunset Manor as either (1) things stay the same or (2) quality is totally destroyed.

A fund-raising executive for a nonprofit corporation insisted on avoiding goal setting. "A goal only limits my thinking," he argued. "Without it we have the potential to raise unlimited resources." Such a rose-colored view denies reality. Another manager refused even to consider a product price increase, saying, "If we decide to raise prices, we'll never sell another unit." Such thinking undoubtedly overstates potentially negative outcomes.

Ethical decision makers routinely examine potentially positive and negative outcomes. They recognize that in actuality they probably will realize some combination of both.

Search for Causal Links

- A basketball coach declares, "The last time we played zone defense, we lost; therefore, we will never play zone again."
- An investor states, "Every time I sell on Friday, the market opens higher on Monday. I'll never sell again on Friday."
- A sales representative reasons, "Whenever I stay away from the home office for longer than one week, I lose sales. I'm not taking two-week trips anymore."

In each situation, these managers have made a fatal error in decision making. They have examined two independent pieces of information and assumed a causal link. The coach lost because of injury to his key scorer. The investor's small holdout had no real impact on the total market. The sales representative failed to consider his practice of usually not taking Friday afternoon phone orders when he is out of the office.

Failing to discover correct causal links leads to faulty decision making. The ethical decision maker researches and analyzes information carefully, searching for the correct links and, subsequently, the correct course of action.

Julie faces a complex situation and must make a very difficult decision. She may have developed her own approach to dilemmas, or she may seek the advice of other managers for input into her analysis and decision making. In either case, as she wrestles with her judgment, she should use the six criteria above to reach an ethical decision.

A Guide for Ethical Decision Making

It is important to keep in mind that *business ethics* is the application of moral standards to the structures, policies, systems, and decision-making processes that facilitate the production and distribution of goods and services. This application of moral standards affects the treatment of people both within the organization and society. Keeping this definition in mind, we define the *managerial ethical dilemma* as any situation when the economic needs and desires of the company come in conflict with its social responsibilities. On the interpersonal level, the same situation would occur when a person with some type of power uses that power to violate the person or dignity of another person or group of persons.

The following seven-step decision-making process will help you organize data and analyze options as you make an ethical decision.

Step 1: Identify the Stakeholders

Most business decisions begin with economic considerations and have human consequences. Identify the relevant stakeholders in the situation by asking yourself, "Who stands to benefit, and who will probably be harmed economically by the decision(s) made in this situation and why?" Should the decision(s) involve the exercise of power, in a moral or immoral way, by one person over an individual or group of individuals, who will receive benefit and whose person or dignity will be violated?

Step 2: Identify Noncompliance Issues

Since business operations are governed internally by company mission, policies, and standard operating procedures as well as externally by state and federal guidelines and laws, it is important to identify any lack of compliance. As a manager, you have a responsibility to the laws of the land and the policies of your company. A second question to pose is, have any laws or company standards been broken?

Step 3: Identify the Managerial Ethical Dilemma

Now that you have gathered information about stakeholders' economic and/or personal gains or losses and compliance with legal and company standards, you are ready to identify the ethical dilemma. Remember that a managerial ethical dilemma exists when the economic needs or desires of the company come in conflict with the company's responsibility to the stakeholders inside and/or outside the company. In one sentence, identify the ethical dilemma.

Step 4: Identify Dilemma Resolution Decision(s)

If you are expected to resolve a managerial ethical dilemma where a manager has already made a decision(s), what was that decision or series of decisions? If you are confronted with a managerial ethical dilemma, what decision(s) would you need to make to resolve it?

Step 5: Conduct a Biblical Analysis

Conduct a biblical ethical analysis by applying ethical standards found in Chapter 4. Ask yourself: "Is the decision(s) previously made or the one(s) I am considering supported or prohibited in God's written and/or revealed revelation?"

Step 6: Conduct an Analysis Based on Secular Ethical Systems

Conduct a secular ethical philosophy analysis. Ask yourself, "Is the decision(s) already made or that I am considering making supported or prohibited by the secular ethical philosophies found in Chapter 3?"

Step 7: Determine Degree of Ethical Appropriateness

Using the results from steps 2, 5, and 6, make your best determination about the ethicality or unethicality of the decision(s) analyzed.

Toward an Ethical Christian Worldview

Ephesians 6:5–9

Slaves, obey your earthly masters with deep respect and fear. Serve them sincerely as you would serve Christ. Work hard, but not just to please your masters when they are watching. As slaves of Christ, do the will of God with all your heart. Work with enthusiasm, as though you were working for the Lord rather than for people. Remember that the Lord will reward each one of us for the good we do, whether we are slaves or free.

And in the same way, you masters must treat your slaves right. Don't threaten them; remember, you both have the same Master in heaven, and he has no favorites (NLT).

It is estimated that when Paul penned these words to the church at Ephesus nearly 50 percent of the 120 million people living in the Roman Empire were slaves. The master-slave relationship was an obvious way for Paul to teach on the subject of obedience.

Although it never directly attacked the institution of slavery, Christianity effectively broke the fetters of the slave by lifting the servant to a higher plane. Christianity consistently taught the slave about spiritual freedom in the midst of physical servitude. Romans 16 demonstrates that early on many of those who were slaves came to a saving faith in Jesus Christ. Influenced by the witness of changed lives, their masters often became Christians as well.

The Characteristics of Christian Obedience

In the Western world today, the institution of slavery has been outlawed. However, the clear teaching of obedience within appropriate limits lives on. Such teaching lies at the heart of a solution to Julie Fredericks's dilemma. Paul says that the servant or employee must be obedient to the master or employer. Based on Ephesians 6:5–9, Paul identifies four characteristics of obedience. The Christian obeys:

"With Deep Respect and Fear" (v. 5)

Paul uses this same phrase in 1 Corinthians 2:3, 2 Corinthians 7:15, and Philippians 2:12. This favorite expression of the apostle does not imply cringing before the master, as the wording of several translations might imply ("fear and trembling"). Instead, it commands a respect or reverence for those who are in authority.

"Sincerely" (v. 5)

The word translated "sincerely" is found throughout Paul's writings (e.g., Ephesians 6:5; Colossians 3:22). The Greek word literally means without hypocrisy or divided loyalties. Sincerity of heart stands in direct contrast to double-mindedness. The employee should be focused and unswerving in loyalty to the employer.

Not Just "When They Are Watching" (v. 6).

Some translations, including the King James, use the expression "not with eyeservice." This is the flip side of singleness of heart. Obedience is not something that an employee should turn on and off as the situation warrants. It is a quality that is internalized, a sincere seeking after the employer's best interest. Watching the clock or looking busy when the boss is around reflects hypocrisy and double-mindedness.

"With Enthusiasm" (v. 7).

Paul demands Christian respect in the servant-master relationship. How much more would he insist on such wholehearted goodwill in the modern employee-employer context? The idea here is that the service must be enthusiastic, not grudging. An employer has a right to expect dedicated enthusiasm in the workplace.

Summarizing Ephesians 6:5–9 reveals that Paul believes an employer has the right to expect three things from employees:

- respect
- loyalty
- enthusiasm

While this is the nature of obedience, it is important to remember that obedience to an earthly employer has limits. Paul says slaves must obey their earthly masters. However, he implies that a higher master takes precedence. The older translations are instructive in this phrasing: "Servants, be obedient to them that are your masters according to the flesh" (KJV). There is a limit to obedience in the workplace. The commands of God in the spiritual realm are never to be disobeyed in the name of obedience to an earthly authority. For example, one would not expect an employee to murder or steal because an employer gave instructions to do so. One might respond to such a suggestion by saying, "Well, of course not! It is against the law of the land."

Paul would respond, "There is a better reason. Such behavior is against God's law."

This biblical teaching stands in stark contrast to what Alex C. Michales refers to as the "loyal agent's argument," which basically says that a manager's duty is to serve the employer in whatever way is possible to advance the employer's self-interest.[2] This is a type of exchanging of one's moral code for blind loyalty and in the process becoming the property of the company. It is ironic that this modern attempt to deny the appropriateness of stressing ethics in the workplace actually reduces managers to a type of slave relationship with employers.

Is it right to eliminate this employee?

Julie Fredericks must decide whether or not eliminating an employee from her staff will be a violation of God's moral law. If she feels that such a change will seriously threaten the care and well-being of patients in the Alzheimer's unit, she has an ethical obligation to refuse the instruction of her superior. If the matter is not quite that serious, she has an ethical obligation to serve her employer with obedience.

Ask the Pro

John Carmichael is executive vice president of an international missions organization. Following graduation from college in 1968, he served as a missionary in Haiti. He later became field director for the missionary effort in that country. For nearly twenty years, he has held a variety of administrative and managerial positions in the organization's home office. His responsibilities as executive vice president include serving as chief operating officer.

The authors asked John for his input on the dilemma facing Julie Fredericks at Sunset Manor. His candid assessment follows:

Q: What is your take on the Sunset Manor case? Whom should Julie let go?

Carmichael: This is a tough situation. I believe we must address two issues before we even consider whom to let go. First, Julie found fulfillment in her job because of the quality care Sunset Manor provides. I wonder if she can cut staff and still be true to herself. But more important, can she cut one person and still provide adequate care for the patients who depend upon it and deserve it?

Q: But the supervisor is already saying to let someone go. Doesn't she have an ethical responsibility to her employer?

Carmichael: Of course, but the greater moral issue involves providing adequate care for the patients. First, I would try to find a way to manage, through a restructure, to do an adequate job. In that case, I would recommend terminating the person who had been there for only a few months. However, if I believed Sunset Manor could not provide adequate care for its clients, it then would become morally wrong to try to operate with one less person. In that case, I would go to my boss and say, "I can't be true to myself and do this. I recommend I be the one you let go."

Q: What about providing for her family and paying her bills? Julie probably needs this job. Should she quit over the company's understaffing problems?

Carmichael: I have to stand before God one day. He is the One I ultimately have to answer to. One of my guiding principles is: "It is never wrong to do what is right." In this case, that means if I lose my job because of a moral issue, then I have thrown myself back upon God—and he will take care of me.

Q: You spent seventeen years in Haiti and have been exposed to a variety of cultures around the world. How much of ethics is culture based? Is there a universal right and wrong?

Carmichael: There are some things that never change, but culture has a great deal of impact. For example, when I first arrived in Haiti, there were things I labeled as bribery, things I would not do. After I had been there long enough to learn the culture, I did not use that term at all. I did those things.

Q: Can you be specific?

Carmichael: Suppose you are stopped by a policeman for some minor infraction. Haitians will give the policeman three or four dollars. He gives them back their licenses, and they go on. I used to think that was wrong. It was bribing a policeman. Today I see it differently. That policeman, if he gets paid at all, is three or four months behind in his salary. If I go downtown to follow procedures, it costs me half a day of work in addition to the ten- or fifteen-dollar fine that will go into the pockets of those sitting in the office. That night, however, the policeman's kids would still be hungry.

Q: Would you try to slip a policeman in Miami a few dollars?

Carmichael: There is no way I would even consider doing that here in the States.

Q: So, are all ethics culturally based, or are there universal limits?

Carmichael: For me the limits are found in Scripture. I would not violate the Bible, as I understand it. I would not steal, though many Haitians find stealing acceptable. Similarly, I would not lie in any culture. I won't cheat someone. Those scriptural standards are universal.

You Be the Consultant

Help Julie decide on the most appropriate course of action by responding to these key questions:

1. Is the second-shift supervisor's decision to refuse to dismiss an employee an ethical decision? Why or why not? Under what circumstances would refusing the order of a supervisor be ethical?

2. Is it possible that Julie is too close to the employees to make a good decision in this manner? Should upper management of Sunset Manor have instructed someone else to make the decision? What should have been Julie's role in the decision-making process?

3. What procedure do you think Julie should follow to make her decision?

4. How would you make this decision? Defend your answer. How would a follower of utilitarianism inform the person to be dismissed? How would the rest of the work group find out about the decision? Whom would a follower of utilitarianism dismiss? Whom would a Kantian dismiss? Whom would a follower of biblical justice dismiss? Give reasons for your answers. If you were making the decision, what impact would your personal statement of ethics have on your decision?

Endnotes

1. Len Marella, *In Search of Ethics: Conversations with Men and Women of Character* (Sanford, FL: DC Press, 2001), 33.
2. Alex C. Michales, *A Pragmatic Approach to Business Ethics* (Thousand Oaks, CA: Sage Publications, 1995), 44–53.

The Christian Manager as Ethical Planner

May he grant you your heart's desire and fulfill all your plans.

— Psalm 20:4

Chapter Challenges

A careful examination of Chapter 7 should enable the reader to:

- Recognize and identify the two components of a business plan.
- Define core values.
- Explain the elements and purpose of a mission statement.
- Identify the importance of planning in ethics.

Case Study

Hur Ministries

Allen Ford slipped wearily into his chair in the interview room at Hur Ministries. He had lost count of how many hours he had spent in this chair through the week. Yesterday he had interviewed potential mentors until 10:00 p.m. The three previous days, he finished after 9:00 p.m. It was now 7:45 a.m., and the first candidate of the day would arrive shortly.

Allen sipped from his coffee mug and closed his eyes in contemplation. Ironically, the heavy demands and long hours evidenced the tremendous success of Hur Ministries. Yet the demand for candidates—mentors—by far outweighed the number Allen could match with youth on his waiting list. When he had established Hur Ministries three years ago, he could not have dreamed of such phenomenal success. But his success had come at a price. The tremendous pressure of his job and his increasing fatigue were signs that the past few years undoubtedly had been the single most difficult time in his fifty years of life.

Lost in the Battle

It began with the divorce. In retrospect, there was no one to blame but himself. He and Joan simply drifted apart. She developed interests of her own while he worked sixty and seventy hours a week at the plant. She appealed repeatedly for more of his time. He called it nagging. Eventually she met "someone who appreciates me," as she put it. She filed for divorce a few months later.

Joan and Allen battled fiercely both in and out of the courtroom, primarily over property issues. Allen's twenty-year history of very lucrative positions, coupled with their frugal lifestyle, yielded significant assets.

Somehow, in the midst of the battle, no one had noticed that the couple's only child, seventeen-year-old Steven, had distanced himself from the family chaos and withdrawn into a private world of drugs. When he died of a drug overdose, the authorities ruled his death suicide. Both Joan and Allen knew they had missed the warning signs of Steven's drug abuse. Although Steven's death temporarily brought them closer, Joan left town with her new husband. Allen had no idea where she now lived.

Lifting Up Hands to the Lord

Allen reacted differently than his wife to the upheaval caused by his divorce and the death of his son. He returned to the faith of his childhood. He found a strong church, recommitted his life to Christ, and set out to help other families avoid the mistakes he had made. He wanted his life to make a difference.

One Sunday Pastor James preached from Exodus 17:8–15. In this passage, Aaron and Hur held up the hands of Moses while the Israelites battled the Amalekites. As long as Moses held his hands high, the Israelites gained on the enemy. When Moses lowered his arms to rest, the Amalekites began to dominate. "Aaron and Hur held up his hands—one on one side, the other on the other side. So his hands were steady until the going down of the sun. And Joshua overwhelmed Amalek and his people with the sword" (vv. 12–13).

Allen wept bitterly when he discerned that if someone had been there to hold up Steven, he would no doubt still be alive. If only someone had listened to Steven, counseled with him, and become a friend when he needed one. That marked the beginning of Hur Ministries.

Managing Growth

Shortly after that Sunday, Allen founded Hur Ministries. The focus of the ministry was to act as a clearinghouse, matching Christian young adults with elementary and high school students whose parents were in the process of divorcing. As mentors, the young adults would hold the kids up during this difficult period.

In the first six months, Hur Ministries was a one-man operation. Allen Ford managed everything. Later, as courts and social agencies began to refer clients to Hur Ministries, Allen found it necessary to hire a recruiter whose job was to locate mentors. He also hired a staff to help with administrative work. Soon after, he hired a trainer to teach volunteers the techniques of peer counseling, proactive listening, and friendship evangelism.

Still, only Allen Ford selected mentors. The process required his reading a detailed application and conducting a personal interview. As a way to lighten his workload, the staff had encouraged him to hire an interviewer. But Allen was convinced that he was the most qualified person to select a mentor—the kind of mentor who would have made a difference in Steven's life. "I can't teach what it is that I'm looking for," he argued. "But I know it when I see it."

Last year Hur Ministries had matched more than three thousand young people with suitable mentors. Unfortunately, another twenty-five hundred had been turned away because there was inadequate time to conduct the candidate interviews. Now, a social service agency in a distant city had offered Hur Ministries a contract to expand to their area. Allen had explored the possibility of traveling one day each week to conduct the interviews. It seemed too promising an opportunity for the ministry to turn down.

A church friend who operated his own business offered some advice. "Allen," he said, "you have to decide where you intend the ministry to be in the future. If you want to continue growing, you will have to develop different procedures."

"It's not my business," Allen responded. "The Lord will send us the right clients, the right mentors, and the right opportunities. I intend to remain faithful and do this work the right way."

A knock at the door jolted Allen back to reality. "Mr. Ford," the receptionist announced, "your first interview is here."

On Background

The Business Plan

On the surface it appears that Allen Ford's problems involve time and procedures. Using current operational procedures, there simply are not enough hours in the day to foster Hur Ministries' growth. The efficient, effective, and ethical management of a business, church, or a family does not occur by chance. It requires planning by those involved. A business will have several types of plans. The plan that gives direction to the organization is the *business plan*. Nickels, McHugh, and McHugh define *business plan* as "a detailed written statement that describes the nature of the business, the target market, the advantages the business will have in relation to competition, and the resources and qualifications of the owner(s)."[1] The business plan is fleshed out through two other plans, the strategic plan and the operational plan.

> *Business plan*: detailed written statement of a business; the plan comprises a strategic plan and an operational plan.
>
> *Strategic plan*: process of identifying major goals, policies, and strategies for an organization.
>
> *Operational plan*: composed of short-term and specific goals of an organization designed to meet the strategic plan over time.

Careful inspection of Hur Ministries' operations reveals a deeper problem than lack of time. Allen has no business plan. He doesn't know where Hur Ministries is headed. He continues to make business decisions with long-term implications without the benefit of a strategic plan. This adversely affects the meeting of important goals, and very well may set the stage for unethical decisions to be made. When managers are in new terrain, lack clear well-thought-out direction, and are under extreme pressure from various stakeholders, the situation is ripe for panicked or hasty decisions that are more reactionary and protective than rational and proactive.

The Strategic Plan

Ethical managers agree that the absence of a strategic plan usually yields ineffective decision making on a day-to-day basis. Many realize that such a deficiency sets the stage for possible unethical decision making.

Consider the case of a small computer programming business that hired a programmer. The new employee was excellent with computer work but seriously lacked social skills. "No problem," concluded the business owner. "All we need this employee to do is program. He never has to meet the public."

Two years later, an unexpected downturn in business made it necessary for management to combine positions. The programmer now had to serve as a telephone receptionist during a portion of the day. Ultimately the programmer was released because he lacked even basic skills in dealing with the public. Many criticized the dismissal as unethical. The company's management believed it had no other choice. An effective strategic plan would have allowed management to anticipate the business turn and possibly avoid the ethical dilemma.

The strategic (long-range) plan is defined as "the process of determining the major goals of the organization and the policies and strategies for obtaining and using resources to achieve those goals."[2] Strategic planning is a first step in fleshing out the business plan. Experts use a variety of tools to develop a strategic plan. Most approaches employ at least four elements:

- a statement of core values
- a mission statement
- a vision statement
- a statement of operational goals

Core Values: The Heart of the Organization

Core values are those principles around which a business is established and maintained. They serve as the compass to guide managerial decision making in five basic managerial functions. For example, a business might make a commitment to "never sacrifice quality for price." Other core values might be "integrity at every level," "customer satisfaction," "lowest cost," "fastest growing," or "low employee turnover." Since the core values of a business become the basis for its future plans, it is essential to invest sufficient time and gather broad-scale input from key stakeholders to identify the core values that will best exemplify the attributes of the company.

The Mission Statement: A Guiding Light

The *mission statement* provides the stakeholders with a succinct statement of the fundamental purposes of the company. An organization's mission statement should be brief enough to be known by all members of the team. One industrial facility adopted this mission statement: "Come, grow with us." Every employee knew the statement and recognized that personal growth and business were the heart and soul of the organization.

> *Mission statement*: succinct statement of the fundamental purpose of the company, which becomes the guiding light for every organizational decision.

The mission statement also should be comprehensive enough to provide a clear, thorough guiding light for every organizational decision. For example, the authors adopted a mission statement early in the research/writing process of this textbook:

To seek ways to bring about positive, ethical changes in the structures, functions, and cultures of American businesses by challenging managers to grow cognitively and spiritually.

The mission statement gives team members an easily remembered summary of the organization's core values—its reason for being.

The Vision Statement: An Eye to the Future

A *vision statement* usually expands upon the organization's mission. It seeks to answer the strategic question, how will we know whether or not we have accomplished our mission, our reason for existing as a company? Planners develop a vision statement with an eye to the future: as an organization, where are we trying to go? A three-year or five-year vision is common in many businesses. Some believe that a vision statement, like the mission statement, should comprise only a sentence or two. However, most believe that at the very least a one-page statement more adequately allows for vision explanation and development.

A vision is an important ethical statement of the company's perceived, achievable, and measurable future. It is in striking contrast to a dream, which represents where a company's leaders might like to be in three years—but they have no realistic hope of seeing the dream realized.

For example, the manager of a fledgling used car lot declared to the local bank that the company's vision was to be the largest dealership in the county within five years. The bank refused to participate in the venture, explaining that the company instead should adopt a more modest, yet realistic business plan of 7 to 10 percent growth per year.

Vision keeps its feet on the ground, melding the "what might be" with the "how to." At the same time it reinforces why the company exists by translating the core values into measurable goals for the employees, managers, and other stakeholders to see. It gives stakeholders a yardstick to evaluate a company's fit with their goals and aspirations. Unethical decision making potentially increases when there is no clearly defined operational plan for the attainment of the company's strategic plan.

Operational Goals: Steps on the Path

Once an organization establishes an ethical vision that reflects its core values and implements its mission, the management team is ready to establish *operational goals*. Operational goals break the long-term vision into short-term specific plans.

For example, one company divided its five-year plan into manageable goals for each of the five years. The chief executive officer (CEO) declared, "This is what we must accomplish this year in order to achieve our vision in five years." Another firm referred to its operational goals as "quarterly aims." The shorter duration of the operational goals forced the management team to revisit the vision statement more frequently to determine its validity in light of current trends and market conditions.

Mike Krzyzewski, the highly successful coach of the Duke University men's basketball team, insists that goals need to be attainable, but cautioned that improper goals can be limiting. For example, he never sets a precise number of wins as a goal, because such a goal might inadvertently prevent a team from winning more games than that. Instead, he opts for goals like, "to become the best defensive team in the history of the school." That goal he believes is attainable but not limiting.[3]

Operational goals are fleshed out in the operational *plan* that not only gives day-to-day direction for the meeting of the operational goals but also defines the rewards-and-punishments system that provides for the effective and efficient implementation of the operational and strategic plans.

Experienced managers sometimes develop their own approach to strategic planning. Some may use different names for the basic elements of the plan. Others may expand upon the four components. Nevertheless, an ethical manager always has a strategic plan. At a minimum, that plan should include statements of core values, mission, vision, and operational goals. The ethical manager also reduces the opportunity for unethical decision making by management and employees by aligning the strategic plan, the operational plan, and the rewards-and-punishments system of the company.

Toward an Ethical Christian Worldview

Luke 14:28–32

For which of you, desiring to build a tower, does not first sit down and count the cost, whether he has enough to complete it? Otherwise, when he has laid a foundation and is not able to finish, all who see it begin to mock him, saying, "This man began to build and was not able to finish." Or what king, going out to encounter another king in war, will not sit down first and deliberate whether he is able with ten thousand to meet him who comes against him with twenty thousand? And if not, while the other is yet a great way off, he sends a delegation and asks for terms of peace.

Counting the Cost

Before making this tower-building analogy, Jesus tells the crowd that there is a cost to discipleship and that the cost is extraordinarily high. Jesus notes that discipleship may preempt business activity, family joys, or other pleasures. He then offers a parable designed to encourage his listeners to carefully consider these high costs. The parable assumes the importance of planning.

Often wealthy landowners built a tower at the corner of the vineyards or other estate lands. As a defense mechanism, the tower could be used for observation, giving the landowner an advantage over an approaching enemy. Building such a tower required enormous resources in material and labor. Imagine the embarrassment—not to mention the financial loss—that a landowner might endure were he to run short of resources prior to completing the tower. As a matter of good business, the landowner certainly would want to plan his project carefully.

In a more recent example, a development company began to build a large motel complex along a busy interstate highway. Before the project reached completion, it became obvious that the company could not withstand the cost overruns. As a result, the company declared bankruptcy. Subsequent development of that particular interchange proceeded very slowly, primarily because of the eyesore known as the "ghost motel." Part of planning ahead includes counting the cost.

Planning Ahead

Following the building example, Jesus turns to an analogy of the threat of war. Here he makes the same point about the cost of discipleship. He stresses common-sense planning and advance analysis. A military leader who fails to prepare adequately for battle can create a deadly disaster with lasting implications.

While historians disagree about the circumstances surrounding the defeat of George A. Custer at the Battle of Little Big Horn, at least one viable theory involves the possibility that Custer failed to adequately estimate the size of the Indian force. Inadequate information and planning may account for Custer's "last stand" and the deaths of more than two hundred of his men.

Within God's Will

One Christian businessman failed to develop the business plan recommended by consultants. He argued that it was a spiritual matter. Since planning (as he saw it) limited the work of the Holy Spirit, the serious Christian should avoid it. He viewed trusting the Lord to be in direct opposition to planning. He even backed up his argument with this scriptural passage from James 4:13–15:

"Come now, you who say, 'Today or tomorrow we will go into such and such a town and spend a year there and trade and make a profit' — yet you do not know what tomorrow will bring. What is your life? For you are a mist that appears for a little time and then vanishes. Instead you ought to say, 'If the Lord wills, we will live and do this or that.'"

Ethical Dilemma

Should Allen Ford of Hur Ministries adopt a business model?

However, A. F. Harper notes, "The sin of these men was not in planning for the future, but in failing to consider God in their plans."[4] The tower builder in Jesus's parable, who plans yet ignores God's clear teaching, is undoubtedly worse off than his nonplanning counterpart. James teaches that Christians should plan with a careful eye to the will of God. He uses the metaphor of mist or fog to make his point, noting that life is brief like a fog under the influence of the morning sun. In only a moment, all the best of earthly plans can come to naught. Therefore, the wise manager plans for both the temporal world and the eternal world.

Ask the Pro

Mike Dates has served as executive director of a family YMCA for ten years. He brings more than twenty-five years of leadership in nonprofit organizations to this position, having served as athletic director, dean of men, principal, and marketing director for a variety of Christian institutions and organizations. Mike holds degrees from three universities. He has been active in his community and church, has served on the church board, and as a Sunday school teacher.

The authors asked Mike to apply his many years of managerial experience in the nonprofit sector to the Hur Ministries case. He agreed to sit down in his office for the following interview:

Q: Before we get to Hur Ministries, let's just take a moment to discuss ethics in general. How would you define ethics?

Dates: Ethics means deciding ahead of time what you are going to do in a given situation. I believe there must be some really firm rules, but not too many of them. They are your nonnegotiables.

Q: What are they for you personally?

Dates: I have to be honest and fair. I can't cheat, lie, or steal. Actually, I guess the Ten Commandments are a good place to start. I don't struggle in those nonnegotiables. They are fixed. The gray areas are much harder.

Q: Can you think of an example?

Dates: Some time ago, our Board here at the YMCA decided to get a license to operate a bingo hall to raise money. I don't personally play bingo. I don't gamble. I didn't really want to do it, but I wouldn't leave my job because of it. Maybe someone who felt more strongly than I did about gambling would see it differently. In fact, we had a board member resign over the issue. It ended up that we never used the license, and I was glad. For me, that was a gray area.

Q: Given your definition of ethics, what ethical issues do you see in the Hur Ministries case?

Dates: Allen's refusal to adopt a business model is unethical in itself.

Q: Explain what you mean.

Dates: He is unrealistic in his expectations. It is good to depend on the Lord, but there are business techniques that could help Allen. He seems oblivious to that. He reminds me of Moses trying to do everything. His father-in-law advised him, "Look, you need to appoint a management organization rather than kill yourself by continuing to do it all." [See Exodus 18.]

Q: What about Allen's opinion that if he doesn't do it, it won't be done right?

Dates: That is clearly unrealistic and demonstrates inexperience in management. He needs to hire some interviewers to take notes. He can still make the decisions, but someone else could do the legwork. His attitude leads to the kind of ineffectiveness far too common in nonprofits and some businesses. In the business world, if you don't make a profit, you're gone. Nonprofits sometimes limp along for years without being effective. Hur Ministries is not nearly as effective as it could be if he adopted some sound business practices. Twenty-five hundred potential customers are not being served because he won't do it right. I believe he will have to answer for that one day. It is not entirely about being proud that we ministered to three thousand; it is about accepting responsibility for the ones we failed to serve.

Q: How can a nonprofit manager avoid that pitfall?

Dates: There are a lot of times when I could just go ahead and do something, but I have decided to take it to the YMCA board for approval. I choose voluntarily to be accountable. Allen needs a board to establish some policies and protect him from his own ego. I see him as selfish and egotistical, reflecting this attitude, "I'm the only one who can do the job well."

You Be the Consultant

Help resolve the problems at Hur Ministries by answering the following questions:

1. Hur Ministries operates without a strategic plan. Why? What ethical problems have developed as a result?

2. Suppose Allen Ford hired you to serve as a planning consultant. What core values and mission would you suggest for Hur Ministries?

3. One advisor suggested that Hur Ministries adopt the mission "supporting our city's youth." Another liked the phrase "mentoring the next generation." How would the differences in these mission statements influence the vision of Hur Ministries?

4. Suppose that the three-year vision Hur Ministries adopts includes expanding to the extent of matching mentors with twelve thousand at-risk clients each year. What operational goals would you suggest for the first six months?

5. Aside from the lack of planning, what ethical problems do you see at Hur Ministries? What is the best way to address them?

6. In what ways (how) does your personal statement of ethics support the need for adequate planning? Does answering this question reveal weaknesses in your statement of ethics? If so, what would you add to or how would you clarify your statement?

7. Is Allen Ford most likely operating from utilitarianism, ethical egoism, or Kant's categorical imperative? Give reasons for your answer.

Endnotes

1. Williams G. Nickels, James M. McHugh, and Susan M. McHugh, *Understanding Business,* 5th ed. (Boston: McGraw-Hill, 1999), G2.
2. Nickels, McHugh, and McHugh, *Understanding Business,* G17.
3. Mike Krzyzewski, *Leading with the Heart: Successful Strategies for Basketball, Business and Life* (New York: Warner Books, 2000), 64.
4. A. F. Harper, *Beacon Bible Commentary* (Kansas City, MO: Beacon Hill Press, 1967), 10:236.

Notes

8

The Christian Manager as Ethical Implementer

Work with enthusiasm, as though you were working for the Lord rather than for people.

— Ephesians 6:7 (NLT)

Chapter Challenges

A careful examination of Chapter 8 should enable the reader to:

- Distinguish between ethical and unethical goals.
- Recognize the ethical limitations of implementing some operational goals.

Case Study

Oak Dale Bed and Breakfast

Joanna Williamson smiled with satisfaction as she signed her name to the employment agreement. Even her new title—Oak Dale Innkeeper—carried a satisfying ring. The responsibilities matched her abilities perfectly.

Mr. Fred Keller, owner of Oak Dale, agreed that the new relationship held great promise. Oak Dale had been Fred's boyhood home. Recently he had remodeled the ground floor of the old farmhouse to create a quaint five-unit bed and breakfast facility. The lower level provided a newly redecorated apartment for the innkeeper.

Solid Christian Principles

Fred viewed Joanna's interest in the position as an answer to prayer. He wanted his innkeeper to share his Christian faith, someone who could adjust readily to the demanding schedule of a small bed and breakfast. He met Joanna after explaining his need to the admissions director of a nearby evangelical seminary. Both Joanna and her husband, Roy, were students at the school.

In exchange for scheduling, cleaning, and cooking a hearty breakfast for the guests, the employment package provided Joanna and her husband the apartment and utilities. In addition, Joanna earned 10 percent of the gross revenue. The agreement enabled Joanna and Roy to stay in school until graduation, and it gave Fred the innkeeper he was looking for.

Fred proved to be well organized. From the earliest days of the business, he had carefully crafted the ethical framework of Oak Dale Bed and Breakfast. "The mission of Oak Dale is to provide a quality bed and breakfast operated on solid Christian principles," he declared. "I know we can't exclude all non-Christians, but I intend for our clientele to be exposed to the gospel, even if they don't know Christ when they arrive. Further, one of our operational goals is to refuse to rent to unmarried couples. There will be no shacking up on my property."

A Special Offer

Joanna started to raise a question about the propriety and legality of refusing to rent to people on the basis of their marital status then thought better of it. She really did enjoy her innkeeper's job and wasn't willing to challenge Fred's ultraconservative views. Fred continued, "I'm sure the occupancy rate will be low at first. But we will do plenty of advertising and build up some repeat business over time. This area has a good number of summer visitors due to the nearby lakes. The winter months may be more of a struggle."

"What we really need is a winter promotional incentive," Joanna enthusiastically offered. "Something to encourage people to come during the off-season."

"Excellent idea!" Fred responded. "How about a discount for pastors, missionaries, and others in full-time Christian service? I would like to limit it to conservative evangelicals but I suppose it would be hard to sort out liberals. We could make that discount apply only in the winter months."

After some discussion, the pair agreed on a 30 percent ministry discount during December, January, and February. The arrangement promised to provide some additional cash flow during those months and also offer an inexpensive time of renewal for those in Christian ministry. During the first month as innkeeper, Joanna drafted the following letter:

OAK DALE BED AND BREAKFAST
100 Four Seasons Drive
Middleville, Pennsylvania

Dear Ministry Professional:

At Oak Dale Bed and Breakfast, we recognize that the demands of your ministry allow little time for personal rest and relaxation. However, during the slower winter months, we have an offer that should allow you that opportunity.

During December, January, or February, you are invited to stay at Oak Dale with a 30 percent discount off our regular rates. Of course, these rates include spacious rooms with private baths, as well as a full breakfast.

Even if you cannot join us at Oak Dale this season, we hope you will spread the word of this great opportunity. I encourage you to pass this letter on to another ministry professional in your community.

The enclosed brochure includes a detailed description of the facilities, a map of our location, and our e-mail address and phone number to assist you in making reservations. I hope to hear from you very soon.

In Christ's service,

Joanna Williamson

Joanna Williamson
Innkeeper

Joanna used phone books and denominational district directories to develop a mailing list. Soon callers began mentioning the letter, and occupancy dramatically improved. By late February, Joanna was feeling comfortable in her new role.

An Unexpected Contingency

On one particular Friday, she glanced at the schedule and realized that for the first time during the winter, all five rooms were booked on the same night. Three of the rooms would be occupied by repeat customers who had visited during the fall season. The occupant of Room 4, Gary Grossman, had mentioned the promotional letter that a colleague had given him. This entitled him to the ministry discount. Room 5 had been reserved for Jerry and Norma Heitmyer. Norma had called to make the reservation, saying that they were celebrating their first anniversary and were anxious to use the discount program.

"Completely full," Joanna said with satisfaction. She called Fred to share her excitement. "That's marvelous," Fred responded. "I never dreamed Oak Dale would take off so quickly. God has indeed been good to us and to the business. Implementing our basic Christian mission has been the key, Joanna. And you are doing a great job as innkeeper."

Joanna hung up the phone with Fred's words of praise still ringing in her ears. The bell rang indicating that guests had already begun to arrive. Two women and a man, all strangers, stood on the front steps.

"Hello," the man said. "I'm Rabbi Grossman. I have a reservation for your inn. A Protestant minister in my home community shared a ministry discount letter with me. And," he said, turning to the two women, "this is Norma and Jeri. We all just met as we came up the walk."

"Hi, I'm Norma Heitmyer," one of the women said, extending a hand. "This is Jeri."

Joanna stammered, "Reverend . . . I mean Rabbi . . . Norma and Jerry . . . ah, Jeri . . . Oh my!"

On Background

Implementation

Joanna has just confronted a hard reality that managers often face. She and Fred Keller have developed operational goals consistent with the vision and mission of Oak Dale. However, in implementing one of those operational goals, they have encountered an unexpected snag. Joanna must now decide quickly whether to implement the ministry discount by extending it to those outside the Christian faith. Further she must decide whether to implement Fred's "no shacking up" policy in light of the unmarried couple that stands before her.

The ethics of implementation revolves primarily around two key issues: (1) ethical limits and (2) unethical goals.

The Ethical Limits of Implementation

A manager must decide beforehand the ethical limits of implementation. Sometimes ethical operational goals cannot be effectively implemented aside from unethical processes and procedures. Suppose, for example, that a firm decides to increase its female representation at the upper levels of management. The goal—to reflect more accurately the diversity of the culture at large—is itself ethical. However, firing male senior managers in order to implement the goal would certainly stretch ethical limits.

In another example, a nonprofit organization establishes the operational goal of increasing membership by 5 percent during a particular fiscal year. Nothing appears unethical about this plan. By year's end, the chief executive officer (CEO) offers cash incentives to current members who recruit others. That practice directly violates the organization's charter. Hence, we see an unethical implementation of an ethical goal.

Unethical Goals

The second area of concern surrounds implementing operational goals that are themselves unethical. This is of special importance since "the managerial systems for planning, control, and motivation are interrelated within a company, both conceptually and pragmatically."[1] It is easy to see how the rewards and punishments for success or lack of success in carrying out the organization's strategic and operational goals can lead to the development of unethical operational goals or unethical implementation of sound operational goals. Since lower-level managers charged with implementation of the operational plan often have little input in the development of operational goals, this scenario occurs more often than you might think.

For example, a sales representative for a particular company believes that one item in the company's product line could prove to be unsafe to consumers. He feels ethically justified in not pushing that particular item. Because of his superior sales ability, he still excels in overall sales. A problem develops when the company makes the item in question the focal point of a massive sales appeal for one quarter. At that point, the sales representative is forced to consider the ethical limits associated with implementing what he views as an unethical goal.

Constitutional Dilemma

Many will view the dilemma Joanna faces as fitting into this second category of ethical concern. In their view, excluding non-Christians or those with particular sexual practices from Oak Dale is unethical. They will suggest that an ethical innkeeper would not implement the Oak Dale operational goals because to do so would deny the belief that all humans are created by God and therefore have value and deserve fair and just treatment.

Before you decide how to advise Joanna in this matter, you should be aware that the Fair Housing Act (Title VIII of the Civil Rights Act of 1968) prohibits any discrimination on the basis of race, color, national origin, religion, gender, familial status, and handicap. These groups of people, sometimes labeled *protected classes*, have the same rights to purchase or lease property as all others have.

> *Protected classes*: groups protected by the Civil Rights Act of 1968 including those classed by race, color, national origin, religion, gender, familial status, and handicap.

However, the Constitution clearly mandates freedom of religion as a fundamental American right. Fred Keller has a guaranteed right as an American citizen to practice his faith as he sees fit. Still, courts are divided on the question of whether religious freedom or freedom from discrimination takes precedent.

In the landmark case of *Thomas v. City of Anchorage et al.*, the Ninth Circuit Court of Appeals ruled in favor of two landlords who refused to rent a house to an unmarried couple. The owners justified this decision because they believed that cohabitation outside of marriage violated their religious beliefs. The couple sued, claiming violation of their civil rights. The court sided with the landlords' claim that enforcement of housing laws violated their religious rights.

However, this opinion was not popular with everyone, and in a number of states such as California, Illinois, and even conservative Georgia, movements developed to pass state laws to close what many view as an unjust loophole in the Fair Housing Act. Whether or not that loophole remains is a subject for serious debate. The Fair Housing Institute, a private, full-service training and consulting company whose mission is to educate and advise the housing industry, concludes, "the answer to the question 'can a landlord's religious beliefs trump the Fair Housing Act?' is probably 'yes' in Alaska, 'no' in California and 'maybe' everywhere else."[2]

It would appear that Joanna and Mr. Keller face ethical questions not definitively answered by the law. Further, ethical Christians may disagree about whether Oak Dale's leadership should revise its operational goals or forge ahead with implementation. Managers should not view vision, mission, core values, and operational goals as eternally fixed. Effective managers revisit these from time to time in an attempt to maximize business performance. They should also review these business plans as they relate to ethical implementation.

Toward an Ethical Christian Worldview

James 2:1–4

My brothers and sisters, do you with your acts of favoritism really believe in our glorious Lord Jesus Christ? For if a person with gold rings and in fine clothes comes into your assembly, and if a poor person in dirty clothes also comes in, and if you take notice of the one wearing the fine clothes and say, "Have a seat here, please," while to the one who is poor you say, "Stand there," or, "Sit at my feet," have you not made distinctions among yourselves, and become judges with evil thoughts? (NRSV)

On the surface, the words of the apostle James seem to contradict the behaviors of Oak Dale's management. James exhorts believers to avoid favoritism. He goes on to illustrate this principle by offering an analogy. Two visitors appear at the same meeting. One man is obviously wealthy and is given a choice seat. The poor man is told to sit on the floor. Discrimination toward other humans is a practice that Scriptures discourage. God has reserved the right to be the judge of a person's actions. How these biblical teachings fit with the belief that Christians should not support the unholy acts of humans is one that all believers struggle with at some time in their lives. As you develop and refine your ethical Christian worldview, you will want to examine multiple Scriptures related to interpersonal relations so that you synthesize the underlying principles and concepts. Is Joanna caught between operational goals and a contradictory biblical teaching related to the treatment of humans?

A Matter of Justice?

To better understand this scriptural passage, we need to look at the original Greek word for *meeting*. In Greek, it is used of a type of assembly held in a Jewish synagogue. However, this word typically describes assembling for the purpose of handing out justice, not worshiping. It would parallel more closely an American court of law than a church meeting for worship. The teaching dictates impartiality in matters of justice.

This clear call to justice compels us to reexamine the Oak Dale practice of giving preferential treatment to Christian sisters and brothers. One could argue that such a practice violates the command against favoritism. This person might reason, "To do business as they do at Oak Dale is unjust."

A Matter of Judgment?

In contrast, Fred Keller undoubtedly justifies his business practices on the basis of Scripture verses such as 2 Corinthians 6:14 "Do not be unequally yoked with unbelievers." He may on some level equate being yoked with offering discounts to a rabbi who has rejected Messiah or housing a couple with whose lifestyle he disagrees. However, a careful look may challenge some of Fred's assumptions. Paul explains the importance of not being unequally yoked by asking: "For what partnership has righteousness with lawlessness? Or what fellowship light with darkness? What accord has Christ with Belial? Or what portion does a believer share with an unbeliever? What agreement has the temple of God with idols?" (vv. 14–16).

How can Joanna determine the proper decision?

Unless Fred intends to equate Judaism with lawlessness or homosexuality with idolatry, he will need to re-examine his exclusionary business policies.

More immediately, however, Joanna must decide whether or not to extend business discounts to everyone in ministry regardless of their faith. Further, she must determine whether to welcome all guests or only those who demonstrate a particular lifestyle. These are ultimately decisions of implementation.

Ask the Pro

Julie Barns is broker/owner of a local franchise of a national realty company in a Midwestern manufacturing city of thirty thousand. She has operated this business with two partners for the past three years and has fourteen years of experience in real estate sales.

Prior to developing her career in real estate, she worked in the automobile-parts manufacturing sector for nearly twenty years. The last six years in manufacturing, she served as a production line supervisor, overseeing the work of more than one hundred production employees.

Julie attends a Missionary Baptist Church where she is involved in women's ministries. Through a Saturday morning prayer meeting via conference call, she also stays in close contact with her five brothers and sisters, who are now scattered across the eastern United States. The authors caught up with Julie over lunch and asked her to comment on the Oak Dale case.

Q: I suspect that as a real estate professional you have some strong opinions as to what is happening at Oak Dale.

Barns: I certainly do. I don't care what the owner's religious beliefs are; he cannot discriminate.

Q: Isn't it true that because Oak Dale is such a small operation, it may be legal for him to exclude certain people from the dwelling?

Barns: I think he would not be exempt because he has too many rooms, and because he isn't living on the premises. Regardless, I would not want to be associated with him or his business.

Q: It is really Joanna Williamson, the innkeeper, who has a dilemma. She is just trying to keep a good job. Her boss made the rules. What should she do?

Barns: In my opinion, she should quit and report him.

Q: You not only would give up the job, but turn him in as well?

Barns: Yes, it takes people who are willing to take a stand. She should have walked away from this job to start with.

Q: Does that mean when you make one unethical decision, it leads to having to make more?

Barns: The lack of ethics "snowballs."

Q: What about his right to his religious beliefs? After all, it is his property.

Barns: He has a right to hold those beliefs. In fact, I personally agree with his positions. Cohabitation is not biblical. But when you choose to work with the public, you agree not to force your faith on others. For example, I can't preach in the office or to my clients. I worship as I choose, but in the marketplace I have to sometimes overlook other lifestyles.

Q: At what point do you say, "Enough. As a Christian I refuse to be involved"? Obviously for you it is not cohabitation. What about the homosexual couple?

Barns: Same thing. I have sold property to homosexual couples. I disagree with their lifestyle, but as a professional I must get beyond that and provide the best service possible.

You Be the Consultant

Help to resolve Joanna's dilemma at Oak Dale by answering these questions:

1. Do you believe the Oak Dale decision to offer lodging discounts to Christians in ministry is an ethical one? Which ethical principles would support your answer and why?

2. Which ethical principles discussed in Chapter 4 ("Christianity and Ethics") would support excluding unmarried couples? Which would not?

3. Which secular ethical principles would support excluding unmarried couples? Which would not?

4. How would your response to Norma and Jeri differ if they were an unmarried heterosexual couple (Norma and Jerry)? Why?

5. Is it ever appropriate to behave unethically in order to keep a job? How would the answer of a Kantian ethicist differ from an ethical egoist?

Endnotes

1. LaRue Tone Hosmer, *The Ethics of Management*, 3rd ed. (Chicago: Irwin, 1996), 146.
2. "Can a Landlord's Religious Beliefs Trump the Fair Housing Act?" Fair Housing Institute, http://www.fairhouse.net/library/article.php?id=5, accessed June 3, 2011.

9

The Christian Manager
as Ethical Organizer

I have taught you the way of wisdom;
I have led you in the paths of uprightness.

— Proverbs 4:11

Chapter Challenges

A careful examination of Chapter 9 should enable the reader to:

- Recognize the importance of an organizational chart.
- Identify various forms of organization from their organizational charts.
- Understand the relationship between organizational structure and ethical decision making.

Case Study

Pirrman's Lawn Care

"Stacy, I have a special project for you," Dick Pirrman announced to his office manager, Stacy Schafer. The request seemed a little unusual, since for the most part Dick distanced himself from the office. In fact, he had turned over almost all the office aspects of his business, Pirrman's Lawn Care, to Stacy. Her duties included payroll, taxes, purchasing, billing, and anything else that required paperwork. "I'm into growing things," Dick once quipped, "and papers and pencils don't grow."

The business unofficially began during Dick's high school years when he mowed the lawns of several elderly people in his small hometown. Dick tried college for one semester but dropped out. He relocated in a thriving city with a growing number of retirees and went back to mowing. During the next six years, business grew "faster than grass in the springtime," as Dick liked to say.

Today Pirrman's Lawn Care has four separate crews of residential and commercial mowers. In addition, two trucks deliver and apply chemicals twelve hours a day during the summer months. Still another crew works strictly on landscaping jobs, which Dick bids and assigns. He manages it all from his pickup truck and often pitches in on one task or the other, doing the physical labor he enjoys so much.

The Special Project

"Hildebrand Nursery is for sale," Dick continued. "As you know, that is the best greenhouse and nursery in this area, and I intend to buy it."

"That's great," Stacy responded. "I know you've talked for a long time about eliminating the middleman in the landscaping work."

"More than that," Dick said. "Their retail sales appear to be very strong. It seems to me like a natural growth area for Pirrman's Lawn Care."

"I think so too," Stacy agreed. "But what does that have to do with me and this special project?"

Dick propped an elbow on the counter and adjusted his glasses. "I talked to the bank yesterday about the money to buy out Hildebrand. They seem to view it as a strong possibility, but before they go to their Board for loan approval, they want to see an organizational chart, along with a policies and procedures book. Draw me up something quick, will you?"

"I don't know about that, Dick," Stacy answered cautiously. "It's been a long time since my college class in organizational development. I'm not sure where to begin."

"Just make it look fancy," he said, chuckling. "Those people at the bank don't know anything about the lawn care business anyway. Once I get the loan, I'll run the expanded version of Pirrman's Lawn Care just like I always have."

"There *is* a purpose to those organizational tools," Stacy continued. "The bank people know that adding Hildebrand Nursery will double your number of employees and gross income. They simply want to know how you plan to manage it all."

"I guess I'll need some more business heads like you in the store, but my plan is to manage Hildebrand the way I do the rest of the business. I'll just do what makes sense at the time." He turned to the door as if to leave.

"The more you acquire, the more risky that approach becomes," Stacy pressed, rising from her chair and approaching the counter. "You need a clear chain of command to effectively handle that many more people and increased volume."

Opening the door, Dick paused and looked over his shoulder. "I guess you may be right," he agreed reluctantly. "So draw me up an organizational chart and sell me on it. I will in turn present the structure to the bank."

Later that day Stacy looked over the basic data as it related to employee count. She came up with the following list:

- eight employees on four teams for mowing
- two drivers with trucks on application
- two Pirrman "lawn doctor" landscapers
- the owner and one office manager
- four additional Hildebrand landscapers
- seven people in the store at Hildebrand

Additionally, she recognized that Mr. Hildebrand had operated a very hands-off business in contrast to Dick Pirrman's strong central command. Hildebrand had appointed one of his landscapers as manager of that division. His employee count for the store included a store manager and a purchasing agent. These three were the only ones who reported directly to him.

"This won't be easy," she mused. "Especially with Dick likely to continue to make all the day-to-day decisions himself."

On Background

Organizational Structure

A proper *organizational chart* for Pirrman's Lawn Care encompasses more than just lines and boxes. Stacy has correctly advised Dick Pirrman that the structure of his business may become vitally important as the business expands and develops, because the effective operation of a business greatly depends on the quality of its organizational design. Nickels, McHugh, and McHugh define organizational design as "The structuring of workers so that they can best accomplish the firm's goals."[1] A function of the organizational design is to define the span of control or "the number of subordinates reporting directly to a given manager."[2] In addition to its economic impact, the correct structure for a particular business sets the stage for sound ethical decisions in the future. Similarly, the absence of organizational structure may facilitate inefficient, ineffective, or unethical decision making that may lead to ethical dilemmas for employees and the business as a whole.

When Structure Is Missing

One company hired a new secretary/receptionist to accommodate its growing workload. The new employee immediately became overwhelmed with demanding special projects assigned by all six of the firm's key managers. She resigned in frustration after only a few weeks. This company failed to remember the important principle that every employee deserves to report to a single supervisor in a clear chain of command.

In another example, an industrial firm was barraged with questions from the press after the arrest of an employee in the workplace. The organizational structure failed to indicate who was to handle public relations in such a matter. As a result, several different managers gave conflicting reports to the media. This company discovered an important principle the hard way: an adequate organizational structure delineating corresponding responsibilities must take into account potential contingencies as well as regular organizational expectations. Failure to do so may set the stage for ethical dilemmas to arise.

> *Organizational chart*: visual representation of an organization's structure.

The Organizational Chart

An organizational chart visually represents a company's organizational design. It is "a diagram of an organization's structures, showing the functions, departments, or positions of the organization and how they are related."[3] This management tool shows at a glance the division of work, the various departments within the company, the reporting structure, lines of communication and chain of command, the coordination of functions, and what groups or individuals bear responsibility for the various aspects of the organization's performance. A well-designed chart is a useful management tool for the company's superiors and subordinates and a guide for interaction for those outside the organization.

Flat Organizational Structures

A flat organizational structure has few levels of management. It typically describes an organization that has decentralized management, and in which there are broadly defined jobs and general job descriptions. Decentralized or flat organizational structures might use cross-functional teams, relying on employee expertise from different parts of the organization to solve problems or develop new products or services. Employees might be cross-trained to facilitate sharing of knowledge, tasks, and responsibilities to ensure a relatively smooth operation of the company. Some would say that this organizational structure reflects top-management's view of human beings: their integrity, ability, worth, and so forth.

This organizational structure is often found in smaller organizations where cross-training allows for maximum use of the talents and skills of a limited workforce. Larger organizations striving to meet the demands of a more competitive marketplace may use this structure to improve efficiency. Eliminating levels of middle management cuts costs and decreases the time required to get innovations from the idea stage to the customer.

Flexibility and speed in decision making are typically strengths of flat organizational structures. However, there are some disadvantages. Employees must be trained to multitask, often an expensive venture. Because this approach to organization seems to place more confidence in workers' abilities to produce and to manage themselves honestly and with a high level of accountability, the ratio of managers to employees is much smaller, thus possibly reducing the frequency of communication between the workers and management. A flat organizational structure is found in Figure 9.1.

Figure 9.1. A Flat Organizational Structure

A Flat Organizational Structure

Tall Organizational Structures

Organizations such as the armed forces, diversified companies, and large corporations often use the more top-down management-structure approach known as the bureaucratic or tall organizational structure. This structure features highly specialized jobs and narrow job descriptions with many levels of management. Some would say that the tall organizational structure reflects a particular view of human beings: their integrity, ability, worth, and so forth.

Benefits of a tall structure include (1) a high degree of skill development in employees in a department, (2) corresponding advancement structures based on level of skill development, (3) use of the principle of economies of scale due to concentration of materials and skilled individuals within the department, (4) good coordination within departments, and (5) stronger control of the company's operations by top management.

In general, the weaknesses of the tall organization correspond to the advantages of the flat one: flexibility and speedy decision making. The amount of time and energy necessary to overcome the inertia within each level of management often makes it difficult to change poor policies quickly, to institute new initiatives, or to adapt efficiently to a changing business environment. This weakness was graphically illustrated in the armed forces during the war in Iraq. Early on, it was apparent that many of the vehicles transporting US troops lacked proper armor. It took months for officials at the Pentagon to decide on the proper decision-making structure to handle equipment complaints from Iraq before they began planning and implementing corrective action. During that lag time, many field officers took their vehicles to Iraqi metal shops to have the

Figure 9.2. A Tall or Bureaucratic Organizational Structure

A Tall or Bureaucratic Organizational Structure

doors fitted with armor. The smaller structure on the battlefield overcame inertia and resolved the problem while in Washington, the taller structure with its territory and rank issues was still trying to work out the protocol for problem resolution.[4] Figure 9.2 demonstrates a tall or bureaucratic organizational structure.

Stacy's Task

Managers have long recognized that an appropriate organizational structure sets the stage for effective organizational operations. Similarly, a structure that aligns the day-to-day operations of the company with operational goals that reflect the company's mission, core values, and vision will limit inconsistencies in the functioning of the staffing, planning, controlling, and rewards-and-punishments systems that can foster unethical decisions, processes, and practices. Stacy will need to be certain that she portrays the company's scope of operations and management philosophy accurately. Additionally, she will want to propose a structure that facilitates ethical as well as effective day-to-day operations by reflecting the interdependence of the various aspects of the business.

Toward an Ethical Christian Worldview

Exodus 18:13–23

The next day Moses sat as judge for the people, while the people stood around him from morning until evening. When Moses' father-in-law saw all that he was doing for the people, he said, "What is this that you are doing for the people? Why do you sit alone, while all the people stand around you from morning until evening?" Moses said to his father-in-law, "Because the people come to me to inquire of God. When they have a dispute, they come to me and I decide between one person and another, and I make known to them the statutes and instructions of God." Moses' father-in-law said to him, "What you are doing is not good. You will surely wear yourself out, both you and these people with you. For the task is too heavy for you; you cannot do it alone. Now listen to me. I will give you counsel, and God be with you! You should represent the people before God, and you should bring their cases before God; teach them the statutes and instructions and make known to them the way they are to go and the things they are to do. You should also look for able men among all the people, men who fear God, are trustworthy, and hate dishonest gain; set such men over them as officers over thousands, hundreds, fifties and tens. Let them sit as judges for the people at all times; let them bring every important case to you, but decide every minor case themselves. So it will be easier for you, and they will bear the burden with you. If you do this, and God so commands you, then you will be able to endure, and all these people will go to their home in peace" (NRSV).

The issue in Exodus 18, like the situation at Pirrman's Lawn Care, concerns organizational structure. Apparently, because Moses was in direct communication with God, he rationalized that he was to assume total responsibility as judge for the more than two million people of Israel.

Jethro, Moses's father-in-law, correctly points out that this lack of organizational structure will lead to negative results. "What you are doing is not good," he says, quickly assessing the situation. The practice is neither efficient nor effective. There promises to be a serious impact upon Moses personally. Further, the people have to wait for justice, from morning until evening. The lack of adequate organizational structure delays justice and thus is unethical.

Upon Jethro's advice, a structure is established in which judges preside over thousands, hundreds, fifties, and tens. The text does not indicate whether the numbers refer to family units or individuals. Either way, judgment is now meted out more swiftly. Presumably, a system of appeals is included, with Moses acting as a final arbiter and receiving only the "difficult cases."

In Deuteronomy 1 this organizational structure expands to include the appointment of captains and officers. Thus ethical organization moves from a strictly "courtroom" interpretation to influence other areas of Israelite life. Moses and the people learned that the lack of organization is itself a type of structure—all too often an unethical one. Although these examples deal mostly with the concepts of speed of action and due process, it is important to understand that Moses was forced to recognize the capabilities of the people under his control and to use those individuals in the most appropriate ways. Here we see the interrelatedness between the managerial functions of staffing and controlling and the organization's structure. The lack of properly functioning managerial functions sets the stage for possible neglect or mistreatment of people under the manager's control.

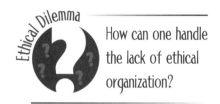

How can one handle the lack of ethical organization?

As Pirrman's Lawn Care expands, implementing a clear organizational structure will help meet the growing demands of the business, and also provide a structure for fair and adequate decision making in the areas of staffing and training, resource allocation, planning, control systems, and capital investment. As the presence of a well-developed organizational structure provides guidance for the managerial decisions in these areas, it reduces indecision and reactionary decision making that often unethically affects employees, suppliers, and customers.

Ask the Pro

Dr. Mary Jeter is a vice president for enrollment management of one of the fasting growing small colleges in the United States. During her ten years of service, the enrollment has increased nearly 400 percent. After completing her undergraduate work at a southern Bible and liberal arts college, she obtained a doctorate in higher education administration from West Virginia University.

In addition to the responsibilities of her position at the university, she teaches in the Master of Business Administration and the Master of Education programs. In the past, she worked in administrative and pastoral capacities in a variety of organizations and churches, including five years in nursing home administration.

In light of the rapid expansion at the college, the authors asked Dr. Jeter to discuss the Pirrman's Lawn Care case and provide insight into the structures necessary as businesses undergo expansion.

Q: There seems to be both managerial and ethical issues at work at Pirrman's Lawn Care. Would you agree?

Jeter: The ethical issue immediately jumped out at me in this case. To obtain a loan, this man will have to sign that what he represents about the organization is true. The owner is trying to fabricate a model for the organization that will never be used. This will be a misrepresentation of the business to the bank. That is a criminal offense. If the business has been a one-man show and he suddenly has four vice presidents show up on an organizational chart, there is misrepresentation.

Q: Do you see any managerial flaws in the case?

Jeter: Yes! He is asking an employee to be involved in a situation that is very unethical. If I were Stacy, I would question the manager's request.

Q: How should she handle the situation?

Jeter: If I were Stacy, I would say to Dick in private, "Dick, you know we cannot take false information to a bank. We need to represent the organization accurately." I would also document my conversation if I were Stacy. I would put right principles above my job.

Q: Might that cost her a job?

Jeter: If it meant losing my job, I would still confront him. It is unethical for the owner to put an employee in that situation.

Q: How realistic is this scenario?

Jeter: This happens every day, but it still is not right. Let me give you a real-life example. My father worked for a company for thirty years. One day, the president of the company asked him to do something which my father's ethical standards would not allow him to do. So he said to the president, "You know I really appreciate you. You are a great boss. I would do almost anything for you, but I can't do that."

The president responded angrily, but later my father was promoted to vice president. When he was dying, that president looked at his son and said about my father, "Son, I would willingly give this man the keys to the company because I know he is a man of principle."

My father had four children, but he took a stand on an issue even if it meant he would lose his job. It was more important for him to do the right thing. In reality, he didn't lose the job; he got a promotion and the respect of the company president.

Q: And Stacy might get the same results?

Jeter: She might, but I know I would like to see more employees take a stand for what is right.

Q: Does the organization's structure affect the degree of accountability that provides control over management decision making?

Jeter: Organizational structure definitely impacts accountability and managerial decisions. Organizational structure and accountability are correlated terms. I have found that a good organizational structure and operating systems often reduce pressure on senior executives to compromise.

However, many small-business owners view established structures and accompanying accountability for actions as a negative, because structures bring more control into the organization. They often do not understand that structure deals with span of control and its inherent accountability, both of which are necessary for the business to produce and sustain growth. The more the manager can instill his or her vision and the principles of accountability into the fabric of the organization, the more they will bring a sense of professionalism to the organization and the more likely the organization will grow. Investors will want to see appropriate structures in place, and good managers will see to it that they are.

Q: Can freedom from structural control set the stage for unethical decision making?

Jeter: My philosophy is that I need accountability to be an effective leader. Structure controls and safeguards my decision making by opening up my decision making to scrutiny, which in turn makes or encourages me to be an ethical leader.

Q: You have seen enrollment at your college triple in size over the past eight years. What relationships have you seen between its structures and its rapid growth?

Jeter: As businesses experience rapid growth they need to constantly be monitoring their structures and accompanying systems to ensure that they have adequate span of control and accountability systems in place.

In our college, we have changed our organizational structure several times over the past eight years in order to manage the present and also to manage for future growth.

Q: Dr. Jeter, in your experience in leading small businesses through rapid growth, have you seen a relationship between the type of structures in place and the type of managerial philosophy embraced by management?

Jeter: There has been a definite shift in managerial philosophy in our college. Eight years ago when our organizational structures supported a student enrollment of 2,500 students, our management philosophy was concerned more with keeping details in line and empowering the top management. Over the years as our structures have adapted to serve a student enrollment of seven to ten thousand students, top management's philosophy has shifted to one of empowering others to manage their departments and serve our constituency.

You Be the Consultant

Help to resolve Stacy's problem at Pirrman's Lawn Care by answering the following questions:

1. Dick Pirrman wants a mock organizational chart for the bank, yet he seems open to the idea of organizing Pirrman's Lawn Care in a new way. How should he proceed? Why?

2. What ethical problems may arise if the strong centralized leadership style of Dick Pirrman is applied to the Hildebrand organization?

3. Suggest an organizational chart for Stacy's proposal. Is your chart more closely aligned with the flat or tall charts described in the chapter? Explain how.

4. How would a Kantian ethicist view the issues surrounding the development of an organizational chart? Would this view differ from a utilitarian's or one who follows ethical egoism? Explain your answers, giving specific ethical principles involved in your answers.

5. Which elements of your personal statement of ethics would assist Stacy Schafer in completing her assigned project at Pirrman's Lawn Care? How would they assist?

Endnotes

1. Williams G. Nickels, James M. McHugh, and Susan M. McHugh, *Understanding Business*, 5th ed. (Boston: McGraw-Hill, 1999), G13.
2. James A. F. Stoner and R. Edward Freeman, *Management*, 5th ed. (New York: Simon & Schuster, 1992), 313.
3. Stoner and Freeman, *Management*, 313.
4. Michael Moran, "Frantically, the Army Tries to Armor Humvees," Brave New World, MSNBC, http://www.cfr.org/iraq/msnbc-frantically-army-tries-armor-humvees/p10170, accessed August 20, 2012.

Notes

10

The Christian Manager as Ethical Employer

Masters, treat your slaves justly and fairly, knowing that you also have a Master in heaven.

— Colossians 4:1

Chapter Challenges

A careful examination of Chapter 10 should enable the reader to:

- Recognize the elements of the managerial function of staffing.
- Become familiar with three steps in ethical staffing.

Case Study

White's Service Garage

Mickey White pored over the employment applications on the table in front of him. "Here we go again," he mused. "I have to find another new attendant."

For the past seven years, Mickey had owned and operated White's Service Garage, one of the few traditional service stations left in the city. Mickey serviced all automobile makes and models and offered full-service as well as self-service gasoline islands. A long-time fixture in the community, the garage was located on a busy intersection. Several chains had offered to buy him out and turn his place into a more modern convenience store, but Mickey enjoyed being a mechanic and assisting the public. However, he did not enjoy the problems associated with hiring and keeping quality help.

A One-Man Operation

For the most part, White's functioned as a one-man operation. Mickey did all the repair work himself, as well as purchasing inventory and supplies. Saturday afternoons and weekday evenings were reserved for record keeping and other bookwork. He hired one employee to staff the "front end," as Mickey referred to it. That employee's job consisted of answering the phone, scheduling appointments in the repair bay, selling accessories, collecting money from the customers, pumping gas and providing associated services for the occasional full-service customer.

Mickey paid minimum wage and expected his employee to work when the garage was open—8 a.m. until 8 p.m. Monday through Friday, and 8 a.m. until noon on Saturday. "That sixty-four-hour workweek means someone can earn a decent week's pay," Mickey reasoned.

Once again, for the fourth time in the last six months, the position was open. Mickey decided to select a new employee from the four applications he had passed over earlier. "After all," he thought, "the most recent one lasted only ten days. These four are probably still available."

Finding Decent Help

The first applicant was enrolled as a student at the local Bible college. He had held a similar position in his hometown during high school and offered references from that job. Because he was taking classes, he needed a flexible work schedule. He also refused to work on Wednesday evenings because that was his church night.

The second applicant, a high school dropout, had never held a full-time job. He liked cars and seemed interested in mechanics. "I got no work record," he had written on the application, "except part-time, since I just quit school last month."

The third applicant had retired as a factory laborer three months earlier. He had explained when he dropped off the application that he could work only twelve hours per week without jeopardizing his pension from the plant. "I'll work around the clock, though, if you pay me cash with no taxes taken out," he offered.

The fourth applicant had recently been released from the county jail for possession of narcotics. His work record until a few years ago appeared normal. "The drug thing really messed me up," he had explained to Mickey. "That's over now. What I really need is a second chance."

"What a bunch of losers," Mickey grumbled as his wife, Shirley, entered the room. "Why can't I find decent help?"

"Applications again?" she asked. "I thought you hired someone to run the front end."

"I did, just a few days ago. I had to let him go, though. He turned out to be another moron."

"What this time?" Shirley inquired.

"You remember old Mrs. Shepherd?" Mickey asked. "She's a regular customer at the garage."

"Of course. She's that sweet little lady who always buys from the full-service island."

"That's her. Except she wasn't so sweet when the boy genius didn't even wash her windshield, let alone check under the hood. Guess he thought full service meant pumping her gas and taking her money."

"Did he give any reason for the oversight?" Shirley asked.

"Not really. He said he just didn't think about what we meant by full service. Said he had never heard of the idea before."

Turning to the applications in front of him, Mickey continued, "Any idea which one of these might not have to be told every move to make?"

On Background

Staffing

Mickey is involved in the important management function of *staffing*. Staffing is generally considered to be one of the basic managerial functions by many writers in the areas of human resource management and organizational management (Hilgert and Leonard,[1] Mathis and Jackson,[2] Robbins and Coulter,[3] and Giordani[4]). It involves the three distinct tasks of recruiting, selecting, and training employees. Each of the three must be completed for the hiring process to be complete and ethical. However, it is evident that Mickey may not fully understand the principles of staffing. As a result, he has set himself up for disappointment again, and has also set the stage for unethical behaviors.

> Three Steps in Ethical Staffing
>
> *Recruiting:* process of encouraging people to apply for an open or potentially open position.
>
> *Selection:* the process of screening potential employees who have been recruited.
>
> *Training:* the process of orienting employees to their jobs and expectations for the positions.

Recruiting Employees

Recruiting involves encouraging people to apply for an open or potentially open position. Sometimes employers advertise a position. Sometimes they use word of mouth or professional recruiters. In other cases, managers may recruit through employment agencies or by networking with associates. Ethical managers recruit without regard to an applicant's race, nationality, gender, or age. They also take special care to avoid misrepresenting: (1) the company's values, mission, vision, and operational goals; (2) the position's responsibilities, place in the company structures, and accompanying compensations.

Mickey apparently has decided not to readvertise the opening at White's Service Garage. As a result, he places himself at a recruitment disadvantage by limiting the pool of potential employees. He may have decided that time does not allow for adequate recruitment or that the cost of recruitment exceeds the benefits. However, according to most employers a larger pool of candidates more than compensates for the cost of recruitment.

Selecting Employees

The second phase of staffing is *selection*. Selecting employees involves screening applicants who have been recruited. Some situations will require a manager to conduct extensive interviews or administer written tests. In other situations, a review of applications may provide the employer with the information necessary to make an appropriate selection. Ethical managers screen in a manner that is open and fair to every applicant. They recognize their ethical obligation to select the candidate who represents the best possible match to the current opening and the company's ethos. The ethical manager also must be certain that the decision to reject any candidate is based on that candidate's inability to meet the job qualifications, and not on age or another discriminatory factor.

In one situation, the principal of a large rural school campus (grades 1–12) sought to fill the position of assistant principal for the elementary grades. The principal was criticized for rejecting an applicant he believed was overqualified for the position. The applicant had many years of experience as a principal of large urban schools as well as higher academic preparation than any administrator in the entire school corporation. Some believed the principal's ethical responsibility should have been to find the most highly qualified individual. However, he correctly argued the value of matching the candidate to the position and considering all potential outcomes of that match. This manager thought an overqualified individual might become frustrated or divisive if the position required less than what the candidate had to offer.

Training Employees

The final phase of the hiring process is *training*. Although this phase involves additional time and expense, it pays rich dividends in improved employee performance, worker satisfaction, and employee longevity. Good managers willingly accept their responsibility to provide quality training for a new employee. They realize that it is unethical and unjust to assume that employees understand expectations.

Training will vary from one position to another. At a minimum, it must incorporate an orientation, which may take several minutes or several weeks. A comprehensive orientation should include an introduction to the work environment and co-workers, safety and quality control issues, and suggestions on how the employee can gain additional information when necessary.

Depending on the complexities of the job or the frequency of new regulations by regulatory agencies, regularly scheduled continuing education may be a part of an ethical orientation system. A key underlying question is: "Is it ethical to expect a given level of performance from an employee without providing the tools necessary to do the job?" Having adequate knowledge to succeed is a key tool for success.

Mickey faces what has become an all-too-familiar task at his worksite—hiring a new employee. Before he proceeds, he should ask himself, "Have I been ethical and effective in recruiting potential candidates? What ethical standards should I employ in the selection process? How must I orient and train a new employee to maximize his potential for success?"

Toward an Ethical Christian Worldview

Matthew 20:1–15

Jesus tells a story in Matthew 20 that Mickey White may find interesting. It involves the employer/employee relationship and some interesting things that can go wrong.

For the kingdom of heaven is like a landowner who went out early in the morning to hire laborers for his vineyard. After agreeing with the laborers for the usual daily wage, he sent them into his vineyard. When he went out about nine o'clock, he saw others standing idle in the marketplace; and he said to them, "You also go into the vineyard, and I will pay you whatever is right." So they went. When he went out again about noon and about three o'clock, he did the same. And about five o'clock he went out and found others standing around; and he said to them, "Why are you standing here idle all day?" They said to him, "Because no one has hired us." He said to them, "You also go into the vineyard." When evening came, the owner of the vineyard said to his manager, "Call the laborers and give them their pay, beginning with the last and then going to the first." When those hired about five o'clock came, each of them received the usual daily wage. Now when the first came, they thought they would receive more; but each of them also received the usual daily wage. And when they received it, they grumbled against the landowner, saying, "These last worked only one hour, and you have made them equal to us who have borne the burden of the day and the scorching heat." But he replied to one of them, "Friend, I am doing you no wrong; did you not agree with me for the usual daily wage? Take what belongs to you and go; I choose to give to this last the same as I give to you. Am I not allowed to do what I choose with what belongs to me? Or are you envious because I am generous?" (NRSV).

A Matter of Expectations

At first glance, the early workers in Jesus's parable of the vineyard have a legitimate complaint. Further examination of the passage reveals that each worker has been treated fairly.

In ancient times the marketplace was the central meeting place in every city. Here one could find the seat of judgment, men philosophizing, merchants buying and selling, and prospective employees willing to work. The employer in Jesus's story went to the marketplace early in the morning and hired all the workers he could find, agreeing to pay them a denarius, the going rate for a full day's work. He returned at 9 a.m., noon, and 3 p.m. and gathered up more workers, agreeing to pay them "whatever is right" for the partial day. Finally at 5 p.m., he returned one more time, hired still more workers and gave them the same promise.

The problem arose when he instructed the paymaster to give everyone a denarius, a full day's pay. Those who labored all day assumed they would receive more than they had previously agreed to. In short, they calculated a rate by the hour, while the employer paid each according to his need for a day's pay.

How can employment expectations reflect ethical principles?

Interestingly, the employer did not shortchange anyone. Ethically, he kept his original agreement. The dispute arose over the matter of expectations. Those hired first expected more than the agreed amount and became jealous and angry when others fared better.

The issue at White's Service Garage may also involve expectations. Ethical employers understand that employees expect reasonable hours, fair pay, and adequate training for the job. Mickey must decide whether he has provided adequately to meet these realistic expectations, or, like the early-morning workers in the parable, whether his employees expect too much.

Ask the Pro

Ralph Lawrence is the owner and operator of Ralph's Car Wash. He holds a bachelor's degree in business from the University of Southern Mississippi and has owned the facility for ten years.

Ralph, his wife and their two children worship at a United Methodist church. He has served on the church's administrative council, staff parish committee, finance committee, and has held other volunteer responsibilities.

Ralph's civic involvement includes service on the Board of the YMCA and occasional speaking engagements at local high schools on topics related to business and employment. Because he employs a staff of nearly thirty, about half being part-time and entry-level employees, the authors asked him for advice on the White's Service Garage scenario. We visited his office at the car wash. The results of that conversation appear below:

Q: We specifically wanted you to look at this case because you hire so many entry-level and part-time employees. How realistic is the White's Service Garage problem?

Lawrence: The service industry in general has a very high employee turnover rate. Whenever you have entry-level positions that don't pay at the highest scale, you automatically get a lot of transition. I have some hiring procedures that help, though high turnover is still a common occurrence.

Q: Would you tell us about the procedures that help?

Lawrence: I don't put a sign out front. I don't put an ad in the paper. I don't call the unemployment office. If someone drops in looking for work, I hand that person an application to take home and fill out. That's an initial screen to see if this person has the motivation to take it home, fill it out, and bring it back. I typically don't hire off the street because it doesn't work about 100 percent of the time.

Q: That's a pretty broad statement.

Lawrence: I have much better success when I either know the individual or that person's family. The other way I get employees is to ask someone already working here if they know someone who needs a job and is willing to work. They don't recommend someone who is lazy, because they have to work beside that person. As a result, I have people who have been with me for ten years. I have others who have left and come back. In general, we are doing better than average.

Q: Are there other areas where Mickey White is using the wrong approach?

Lawrence: He's putting too much of a workload on one person at that pay scale. That many hours should be divided among two or three people. Of course, that leads to other problems: you have two sets of problems from home, two cars that won't start, and two personalities to deal with. You compound the problems in some ways.

Q: What about his training program?

Lawrence: He certainly needs to write a job description and find a way to communicate it effectively. Perhaps a training video demonstrating how to do the job would help. He has to find some way to set policies and procedures and then abide by them. It is not ethical to expect performance that is not effectively taught and communicated.

You Be the Consultant

Answer the following questions to see if you can resolve Mickey's problem:

1. Mickey laments to you, "Why can't I get good help?" How would you respond?

2. How would you advise Mickey to recruit for the job opening? Which specific secular and scriptural ethical principles would apply?

3. Examine each of the four current applicants for the job opening at White's Service Garage. Which applicant would you select? Why? What ethical considerations have influenced your decision?

4. Design an orientation/training process for Mickey to use with his new employee. What aspects of staffing should be included in a fair and ethical program?

5. Explain how your personal statement of ethics allows for effective staffing. Support your answer.

Endnotes

1. Raymond L. Hilgert and Edwin C. Leonard, *Supervision: Concepts and Practices*, 8th ed. (Mason, OH: South-Western College Publishing, a division of Thomson Learning, 2001), chaps. 12–13.
2. Robert L. Mathis and John H. Jackson, *Human Resource Management,* 13th ed. (New York: South-Western, 2011), chaps. 3, 6–7.
3. Stephen P. Robbins and Mary Coulter, *Management*, 11th ed. (Upper Saddle River, NJ: Prentice-Hall, 2012), chap. 11.
4. Pattie Giordani, "Leaders in the Field: Where We've Been, Where We're Going," *NACE Journal* 66, no. 3 (Spring 2006): 14–22.

11

The Christian Manager as Ethical Performance Appraiser

You shall not render an unjust judgment; you shall not be partial to the poor or defer to the great: with justice you shall judge your neighbor.

— Leviticus 19:15 (NRSV)

Chapter Challenges

A careful examination of Chapter 11 should enable the reader to:

- Recognize the importance of ethical employee performance appraisals.
- Identify various types of performance appraisals.
- Use ethical performance appraisal.

Case Study

Tipton Manufacturing, Ruill Plant

Wayne Phillips had been on the job all of three months. It seemed like thirty years. When he signed with Tipton Manufacturing at a university senior job fair, the entry-level position seemed like a dream come true. Tipton offered a competitive salary and benefits. In addition, while other firms talked of training programs and a position as a production supervisor, Tipton offered Wayne the plant manager position at the Ruill, North Carolina, facility.

Involving only twelve production workers and an office assistant, the plant manager position at Tipton Manufacturing, Ruill, more accurately compared to frontline supervision at larger companies. Yet the company made a practice of moving plant managers every two to four years, usually to larger plants with more employees. The idea involved exposing people to the entire operation, leading up to more significant management opportunities.

Culture Shock

Right now Wayne doubted that he would last long enough even to visit other Tipton facilities. For one thing, Wayne and his wife, Jean, had not adjusted well to the move south. Raised and educated in Michigan, the preemployment visit to Ruill was the first opportunity for either of them to experience the South. "Just another small town," they concluded. "They're all alike."

Now, three months later, they questioned the wisdom of that conclusion. People moved slowly, made decisions slowly, and even talked more slowly. They sometimes used words that Wayne and Jean did not even understand. The couple became acquainted with very few of the town's folks and still felt like outsiders at the local community church. Wayne did not feel much more comfortable at the plant. He had to dig for any information on operations. People simply did what he asked—nothing less and certainly nothing more.

The Ruill facility made widgets. Each of the twelve production workers had a reputation as an accomplished production worker and typically managed her own work. For example, some workers completed a widget from start to finish, then began another. Others chose to cut out the product for part of their shift and then assemble for another block of time. The factory averaged a total of fifty units per day. Each week the completed products were sent to the packaging division located in Nashville, Tennessee.

Disturbing Data

Over the last several days, Wayne had contemplated production wages. Headquarters had issued a memo announcing a 4 percent increase in dollars available for production workers. Wayne was instructed to distribute raises as he saw fit and to make the increase effective in thirty days. As he investigated current salaries and his predecessor's recent history in handling such matters, Wayne discovered some disturbing data. Eight of the production staff earned minimum wage. Historically, they had received increases only when mandated by the federal government. The other four workers earned nearly $1.50 per hour more, although they performed exactly the same work as the other eight.

Wayne's investigation revealed that no one on the production floor was supposed to know anyone else's wage. Further, his assistant in the office seemed reluctant to discuss the matter, but Wayne sensed she knew more than she cared to reveal about the wage discrepancies. He could not tell if she simply did not want to update the "new guy from up north" or if she was protecting her beloved former boss.

Rather than press the issue with her, Wayne asked her to prepare a table showing each production worker, her hire date, the number of units she produced the previous month, the number of workdays she missed last year, and her current wage rate. The results of that study are shown below in Figure 11.1.

Figure 11.1. Tipton Manufacturing, Ruill, Employee Pay Scale

Tipton Manufacturing, Ruill, Employee Pay Scale

Employee	Hire Date	Monthly Production	Days Missed	Hourly Rate
1	6/22/97	87	12	$7.50
2	9/14/02	68	6	$7.50
3	8/12/04	66	22	$7.50
4	7/15/97	79	42	$8.98
5	6/10/09	83	30	$7.50
6	4/12/10	68	1	$8.98
7	2/14/11	85	5	$7.50
8	1/16/11	78	7	$7.50
9	3/31/11	74	25	$8.98
10	5/28/10	88	17	$7.50
11	7/2/11	76	22	$8.98
12	12/15/09	89	38	$7.50

Wayne saw absolutely no pattern to the pay scale inequities. His analysis of age and race factors indicated no evidence of illegal discrimination. Yet some explanation must surely exist for such a wide disparity in rate of pay.

An Unusual Business Practice

Finally, Wayne decided to phone George Jeffers, the recently retired plant manager. Wayne knew George as a local, well-respected member of the Ruill community. However, the corporate people who had hired Wayne had advised him not to rely too heavily on George's experience. "Not only is George anxious for retirement," Wayne's boss suggested, "but, frankly, his advice usually is not of much account. He was a 'good old boy' from that community down there who had some very unusual business practices."

George seemed genuinely willing to help when Wayne called. However, his advice left Wayne with additional questions about what course of action he should take.

"Well," George reported, "I always gave whatever raises were available to the same four. It truthfully was kind of a ministry for me, since those four attend the same church I do. I knew they were devout Christians and single mothers struggling to make ends meet. More important for you, those four are from families that have been in our community for a long time. They are people who can make you or break you in Ruill, son."

On Background

Legislation Governing Pay Practices

Wayne has uncovered a disparity in wage rates involving twelve production employees. He first must decide what to do about the current disparity. Then he must determine what to do with current and future additional funds allocated for employees. Several issues need to be a part of Wayne's thinking on this difficult ethical problem.

Checking for Discriminatory Behavior

Wayne seems to have dismissed the possibility of race or age discrimination in the disparity involving these twelve employees. His own research and George's comments seem to support that conclusion. Still, Tipton Manufacturing may be at risk with regard to Title VII of the 1964 Civil Rights Act. Provisions of this act include the following:

- It prohibits employers, public or private, who employ fifteen or more persons from discriminating in any aspect of employment.
- It prohibits discrimination of persons based on sex, race, religion, or national origin.
- The Age Discrimination in Employment Act of 1967 added persons ages forty or older to the list of protected individuals.

Establishing Performance Appraisals

In addition to solving the problem of possible discriminatory behavior against one or more employees, Wayne also must consider issues related to the need for adequate *performance appraisal*—a systematic review of an employee's job-related strengths and weaknesses.[1] The absence of an impartial performance-appraisal process and its equitable application provides opportunities for managers to make unethical decisions.

> *Performance appraisal*: systematic review of an employee's job-related strengths and weaknesses.

Firms often use performance appraisals to determine appropriate compensation for in-house job placement, for advancement determinations, or for discipline. An ethical performance-appraisal system is required by law to ensure that procedures are used to evaluate persons without regard to race, sex, national origin, religion, or age. An ethical system goes beyond the categories required by law to ensure that performance appraisals and other tools that measure the employee's value to the company and its mission are used in confidential and impartial ways in identifying the degree of reward or punishment employees are to receive. The *form and process* of performance appraisal should be known by all employees and should be a part of the company's orientation procedures. There should be no surprises.

The most ethical performance-appraisal systems avoid ratings on such nonquantifiable traits as dependability or attitude. Instead, raters evaluate employees on specific and measurable work dimensions. Often the process begins with a job analysis or job description. The rater then compares an employee's performance to clearly communicated standards of excellence. An appraisal system that fails to communicate expectations well in advance of evaluation would be considered less than ethical.

Types of Evaluation

Evaluation itself may take one or a combination of several forms or may use a specialized approach for a particular workforce.[2] For instance, a rater may use a preapproved checklist form or may write a narrative essay on each employee. Regardless of the process, care must be taken to emphasize both the strengths and weaknesses of each employee. Some companies use a process of self-evaluation in conjunction with the performance appraisal. This approach allows an employee to develop some ownership in the process and exercise a degree of control over what appears in the employment file.

Many firms also include an interview as an essential element of ethical appraisal. The interview allows for employee feedback to the appraisal and provides a measure of employee control over the process. Care must be taken that the performance-appraisal interview provides only one of numerous steps in the feedback process. Feedback in a variety of forms is part of an ethical organization's evaluating process.

In some firms, goal setting grows out of the performance-appraisal process. This procedure works especially well with self-directed employees who have a share in the responsibility for their task development. Some companies tie compensation to performance appraisal. This connection helps establish a pay structure that is consistent and equitable. The connection between performance appraisal and compensation works best in merit or incentive systems. Usually base-wage systems reflect only the value of the work performed and fail to differentiate between various employee inputs.

With this information as a guide, Wayne must decide which course of action is most ethical in light of the current situation. Before taking action, he will want to gain as much insight as possible from others who may have faced similar problems.

Toward an Ethical Christian Worldview

A surprising amount of space in Scripture addresses the relationship between employers and employees. Several passages speak directly to the issue of wages. In each case these verses support the need to pay workers a fair wage for their labors. Consider the following, for example:

- Woe to him who builds his house by unrighteousness, and his upper rooms by injustice, who makes his neighbor serve him for nothing and does not give him wages (Jeremiah 22:13).
- The laborer deserves his food (Matthew 10:10).
- For the Scripture says, "You shall not muzzle an ox when it treads out the grain," and, "The laborer deserves his wages" (1 Timothy 5:18).
- Behold, the wages of the laborers who mowed your fields, which you kept back by fraud, are crying out against you, and the cries of the harvesters have reached the ears of the Lord of hosts (James 5:4).

Are Wage Distinctions Biblical?

Paying people appropriately does not completely answer the question facing Wayne Phillips at Tipton Manufacturing, Ruill. Although his predecessor paid the workers, he reserved the highest wages for those who shared his faith. Deuteronomy 24:14 is instructive in this matter. It notes that there is to be no wage distinction between the children of Israel and the aliens living among them.

You shall not withhold the wages of poor and needy laborers, whether other Israelites or aliens who reside in your land in one of your towns. You shall pay them their wages daily before sunset, because they are poor and their livelihood depends on them; otherwise they might cry to the LORD against you, and you would incur guilt (Deuteronomy 24:14–15).

The term *alien* used in this passage refers to those from other ethnic groups or cultural backgrounds. Israel was also homogenous religiously. Even so, no distinction in wages was to be made to those outside the Israelite community.

How can an employer exhibit fairness (in business) for all employees?

Sadly, all too often one person's unethical behavior creates an ethical dilemma for others. Wayne Phillips must now decide how to respond to the fact that through the actions of his predecessor his company historically has made a distinction in wages between those within the confines of a particular religious group and those outside those confines.

Ask the Pro

Ramona Brown is administrator of an urban Christian college preparatory school. The school serves a variety of Christian families with 342 students in kindergarten through grade 12.

Before assuming her present responsibilities, she served the school for two years as assistant administrator. She also has experience as a classroom teacher in a variety of educational settings in New Jersey, Iowa, and Indiana. She holds an undergraduate degree from Asbury College in Wilmore, Kentucky, and a master's in education from Georgetown College in Georgetown, Kentucky. Along with her husband and their son, Ramona worships at a large Baptist church. They have assisted with many ministries in a variety of settings. The authors sat down with Ramona Brown in her office to discuss the Tipton Manufacturing case. Here are the results of that interview:

Q: Obviously the manufacturing setting in this case is very different from your area of expertise. Were you able to find a point of reference?

Brown: Absolutely. In fact, this case is very similar to something we went through here at the school a few years ago. A disparity in teachers salaries had developed in various subject areas. Certain subject areas were paid higher salaries in order to attract teachers in those areas. The reason was not unethical, like at Tipton Manufacturing, but over time it became unfair to other teachers who were making sacrifices to be here and contributing just as much.

Q: Was the issue addressed?

Brown: It's fixed. We established a base scale with increments for years of experience and professional development.

Q: To make that adjustment, did some get a cut in pay, or were you able to raise the pay for everyone?

Brown: Some took cuts, and some left. It was difficult, but it had to be addressed. Because our salaries are low anyway, there is always a temptation to pay a main breadwinner or a single parent more than others. But that is not fair. Now, we offer all benefits and supplements to everyone—the same across the board.

Q: You implied that you think Tipton Manufacturing got into this wage disparity as a result of unethical behavior.

Brown: Absolutely. As Christians we have to stand for what is right. The Tipton Manufacturing thing really bothers me. Hourly rates were awarded inconsistently. There seems to be no established policy. A personal agenda guided the salary process. The fact that he [George] was paying people more because they were Christians just screamed "unethical behavior and lack of integrity."

Q: How important is it for Christians to demonstrate ethical behavior?

Brown: It is absolutely essential. We try to teach this in disciplining students. We have worked hard to establish policy and include parents in student discipline. We guide students through a process of admitting mistakes when they are wrong and then making things right—restitution. We have thought that through, and we guide every student the same way through that process. It is especially exciting when solid Christian parents resist the temptation to take a son or daughter's part and support the school as we attempt to teach accountability and integrity.

Q: So you see integrity as a key to management ethics?

Brown: I do. Recently the Board's personnel committee and I had to dismiss an employee over a clear issue of integrity. That employee was involved in behaviors that violated the core values of our school. Many questioned our decision because we couldn't publicly say why the person was dismissed. On the other hand, if we didn't deal with the issue, what would it say to students? What would it say to other employees? We had to make a decision whether to "let it ride" or take a stand in favor of character and integrity. You just do what needs to be done and hope enough trust has been built with parents and other constituents that they believe you wouldn't take that kind of action unless it was absolutely necessary.

You Be the Consultant

Answer these questions as you consider the situation at Tipton Manufacturing:

1. Is the present wage scale at Tipton Manufacturing equitable? Explain your answer with specific examples. Is it ethical? Which secular and scriptural ethical principles support your assertion?

2. George gave more than one reason for the wage scale. Are any of the reasons ethical? Citing specific secular and scriptural ethical principles, explain why or why not.

3. How would a plant manager in Wayne's situation respond if he or she operated from these ethical systems?

a. utilitarianism

b. Kant's categorical imperative

c. ethical egoism

d. your personal statement of ethics

4. Develop an ethical performance-appraisal system for use at the Tipton Manufacturing plant at Ruill. Which secular and scripturally based ethical principles support your plan?

Endnotes

1. James E. Neal Jr., *Effective Phrases for Performance Appraisals: A Guide to Successful Evaluations* 12th ed. (Perrysburg, OH: Neal, 2009).
2. See, for example, Rosio de Andres, Jose Garcia-Lapresta, Luis Martinez, "A Multi-granular Linguistic Model of Management Decision Making in Performance Appraisal," *Soft Computing—A Fusion of Foundation Methodologies and Applications* 14, no. 1 (January 2010): 21–34. Also Sandra G. Leggat, "A Guide to Performance Management for the Health Information Manager," *Health Information Management*, 38 no. 3 (2009): 11–17.

Notes

12

The Christian Manager as Ethical Leader

Whoever would be great among you must be your servant.
— Matthew 20:26

Chapter Challenges

A careful examination of Chapter 12 should enable the reader to:

- Differentiate between theory X and theory Y leadership styles.
- Explain the concept of servant leadership.
- Implement effective and ethical leadership styles in various circumstances.

Case Study

West Park Apartments

Twenty-four-year-old Karen Lane sat in the manager's office of West Park Apartments. Even after being on the job for three months, she still felt very much alone in her position as manager of the complex. She had been hired from a field of six applicants. The fact that she already held a real estate broker's license, required for property management by her state, had been a huge factor in her selection.

As manager of the West Park Apartments, Karen managed the general operation of the two-hundred-unit complex. She received a base salary, in addition to free rent on-site in a two-bedroom unit. In exchange, she kept the apartment complex as full as possible, collected rents, and supervised the work of an office manager and three maintenance technicians.

Seeking Respect

The maintenance area had proven to be Karen's greatest challenge. She had little understanding of maintenance and repair work, but as the apartment complex manager she felt responsible for properly leading the maintenance staff. Perhaps because of her lack of technical knowledge, or because all three male employees were older than Karen, their relationship had been strained almost from her first day on the job.

Sometimes a disagreement developed over whether to repair or replace appliances or equipment. For example, the fan motor on the forced-air gas furnace in one unit failed last week. Joe Bowersox, the technician assigned to the job, recommended replacing the entire furnace. "Given the age of the unit and the high cost of replacement parts," he suggested, "I'd say just call the furnace people and have them install the whole unit."

Karen suspected Joe was thinking that if the whole furnace was replaced, the job would be contracted out. On the other hand, replacing the fan motor would be Joe's responsibility. "No," she insisted. "Buy the parts and repair it yourself. It's not a big deal." Joe had "milked" the job an entire eight-hour shift and still continued to grumble about Karen's "poor decisions."

Kenny Puegot, the second maintenance technician, was even more outspoken in his assessment of Karen's leadership. Kenny had worked at West Park for several years since retiring from a nearby assembly plant where he had served as union steward. In addition to odd jobs, he landscaped and maintained the grounds. Residents often commented on the well-manicured lawns and weed-free flowerbeds at West Park.

Soon after taking the manager's position, Karen had asked Kenny to take an expanded role in painting vacant apartments for the next occupants. "I always help out on painting," Kenny responded, "as long as the mowing is caught up."

"This time the painting is a priority," Karen pressed. "It won't hurt to let the grass grow a few extra days in order to get these units ready and occupied."

"Kids running the show won't work," Kenny had growled under his breath. "Especially female kids." Karen had let his jab go, but she concluded that the real issue was not about lawns, but about Kenny's unwillingness to accept her leadership.

Now she faced a confrontation with the third member of the maintenance staff. At twenty-seven, Gary Kessler was the youngest of the three. He had not been particularly friendly to Karen but had simply done what he was told, nothing more or less. At least that seemed to be his behavior pattern when he *came* to work. Over the past three months, Gary had missed eight days and had reported late for work six additional days. After the sixth absence, Karen had talked to Gary. "You simply have to be at work more regularly," she stated firmly. "We count on your being here."

"Well," Gary had started, "I have this problem that . . ."

"I agree, Gary," Karen interrupted. "You have a problem. One more missed day, and it will be a bigger problem. I expect you on the job and on time every day. Any questions?"

"Nope," Gary mumbled, shrugging.

"That's all then," Karen said, dismissing Gary to return to work.

Karen was troubled as she prepared for today's confrontation with Gary. Her repeated warnings hadn't seemed to faze him. "Somehow I have to find a way to help these people understand that I am in charge here. They simply have no respect for my leadership," Karen thought.

On Background

Leadership Styles

Karen is frustrated because she seems to lack the respect she would like to have from her employees. She is understandably anxious to be the recognized authority on the job. She would do well to "not underestimate the power and value of moral authority. It is essential and it depends on trust. Leaders earn that moral authority by their behavior, by straight forward communication of vision and objectives, by adherence to the shared values of the group, by fair and equitable treatment of all the organization's stakeholders, and by setting an example of genuine and ethical decision-making."[1]

As Karen contemplates what approach to use in dealing with Gary's attendance record, she may want to consider some leadership basics. In 1960 Douglas

McGregor wrote a landmark book on leadership techniques. In *The Human Side of Enterprise*, McGregor outlines what became known as theory X and theory Y management.[2] Figure 12.1 notes the basic differences in these two approaches to leadership.

Much of what has been written in the decades since McGregor's monumental work builds upon the theory X-theory Y assumptions. *Theory X* generally views people in a negative light. Employees are not motivated intrinsically by commitment to doing quality work, loyalty to the company, or pride in being a part of an organization. Instead, they are lazy, must be closely supervised, and are incapable of making decisions on their own or making contributions to the organization, processes, and improvements of their work responsibility. Theory Y tends to view employees as persons who are capable of self-management. They are thinking individuals who can contribute individually or as group members to improvements in their work areas. Theory Y employees respond to intrinsic motivations as well as to extrinsic motivations such as pay incentives, company stock options, and promotion opportunities.[3]

McGregor's Leadership Theories

Theory X: in theory X, employees are viewed as lazy and incapable. They must be closely supervised.
Theory Y: in theory Y, employees are viewed as capable of self-management and self-motivation.

The structure of the company may be better suited to a particular leadership style. For instance, a company with a flatter organizational structure may work better with a less autocratic leader in line with theory Y. If this is true, is it unethical to decide to hire an autocratic leader for a flat organization or vice versa? When hiring a member of the leadership team, the owners should consider how the proper match of leadership style and organizational structure would affect all aspects of the organization and its fiduciary responsibilities. Karen seems to have equated leadership with theory X management.

Robert Earl Kelly relates a real-life story that may call into question Karen's universal application of the assumptions of theory X to employees like Gary. According to Kelly, Kathleen Betts gained national attention when she discovered an irregularity in the way state and federal governments calculated hospital costs. Her efforts saved her employer, the Commonwealth of Massachusetts, nearly $500 million. Governor Weld rewarded Betts's initiative with a governor's bonus. Weld noted that Betts's work was totally a result of her own initiative, maybe more remarkable because she worked only three days per week as a processor of Medicaid claims. Betts provides a wonderful example of a theory Y performer on the job.[4]

The Christian Side of Leadership Style

Genesis 1:27 tells us that humankind is made in God's image. This imputes infinite value to humans, demonstrated by the price that God paid through the sacrificial death of his Son to redeem humankind. Being created in God's image gives us the right to be treated with respect and dignity. It also means that human beings possess the godly attributes of creativity, trustworthiness, inspiration, initiative, and satisfaction in a job well done.

Jesus's leadership style in preparing his followers for the task of founding the Christian church after his ascension is an example of putting this principle into action. He recognized the God-like hidden gifts and talents in this diverse group of men and women and cultivated the development of those attributes. At times he was stern in holding his followers accountable for their progress in developing their servant leadership skills and dispositions, but that is a reflection of the importance of these individuals and not an application of theory X principles.

Karen's mind-set about the nature of human beings finds ultimate expression in her approach to management. The same is true of any Christian manager. What they have already determined about their employees is expressed in their leadership styles. For example, not fostering employee input, not recognizing employee accomplishment, or not being willing to listen to employee concerns may say more about what Karen believes about the value and potential of human beings than what Joe, Kenny, or Gary believe about leadership.

That does not mean that Christian managers must always operate according to theory Y principles. In fact, some theory X assumptions are supported by Scripture. A study of Moses's leadership style in leading the Israelites out of Egypt and the forty-year journey in the desert or of Nehemiah's style in the rebuilding of Jerusalem reveals the use of some theory X assumptions. Some circumstances are best handled by a strong central-command structure. For example, in confronting a raging fire, a fire chief will not poll the workers and allow for employee feedback on the correct course of action. The fire chief is less worried about being considered a tyrant than in making an expeditious command decision to save lives. To do otherwise would be unethical. That leadership style should match individual circumstances is the mandate of Christian ethics.

The Servant Leader

For this reason, many Christian managers have adopted the leadership style Jesus suggested as a model for greatness. He said, "Whoever would be great among you must be your servant" (Matthew 20:26). Servant leadership allows the manager to be flexible in style, adapting to the needs of the situation, as in the example of the fire chief. However, it is crucial to note that this flexibility is in *style* of leadership only. Ethical principles must be upheld even in an emergency. This flexibility should never be confused with situational ethics, in which hypocrisy, dishonesty, immorality, and other actions done for personal or corporate gain are made to seem ethical.

Servant leadership generally rejects the "top-down" mentality of a theory X manager. It assumes that the role of a leader is to facilitate the work of followers. However, a servant leader also may respond authoritatively when the situation calls for decisive action for the good of employees or the organization.

> *Servant leadership*: assumes that the role of a leader is to facilitate the work of followers who are generally self-motivated. The servant leader generally engages in participatory management.

Servant Leadership in the Workplace

A servant leader managed the care of several patients in a nursing care facility. The majority of the time she behaved in a very gentle and caring manner with those under her care. When Mr. Jones refused to take his medication, however, she exercised her authority firmly and strictly. "Because I care for my people," she explained, "I have no choice but to insist that he take his medication."

Similarly, a factory supervisor modeled servant leadership and became known for his participatory style among the workers. Because he cared for people and wanted the best for them, he listened attentively to his employees' personal and job-related problems. When it was necessary to correct them, he did so gently and compassionately. However, when tornado alarms sounded at the plant one afternoon, his concern for the well-being of others caused him to bark orders, ignore questions, and demand immediate action.

An office manager usually exercised a participative style of leadership and accommodated the input of those under her supervision. Her supervisor informed her that the company risked losing an important customer if the employees could not complete a difficult and time-consuming task ahead of schedule. Because her servant leadership style had gained the respect of employees, she was able to organize the work, announce the plans, and complete the task in record time without employee objection.

Charting a Course

The key to ethical leadership thus involves flexibility of approach for the ultimate good of others. The servant leader constantly searches for ways to assist employees in the effective performance of their tasks. Some servant leaders prefer to invert the traditional organizational chart in order to remind themselves of their ultimate responsibility (see Figure 12.1). In the inverted chart, the leader's role as servant to managers and employees is emphasized by placing the servant leader below those being led. The leader has the responsibility to listen to the input of subordinates and to facilitate their success in their part of the company's enterprise.

Figure 12.1. Inverted Organizational Chart

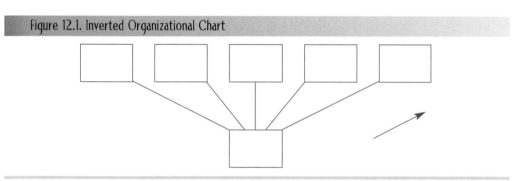

The arrow on the right side of the chart reminds servant leaders to consider mentally rotating the chart from time to time. This prompts servant leaders to remember their roots as ethical Christian managers by adapting their leadership style to best suit the circumstances.

The servant leader generally assumes a participatory leadership role (see Figure 12.2). The leader becomes the quarterback on the team, not the team's coach or general manager. The leader motivates the team, gets dirty in the processes of give and take with the team, and does whatever task is necessary for the team to win. The leader understands the role of each team member and that all roles contribute to the success of the team. At times, the servant leader may go alongside various team members and assist them in becoming successful team members. In short, the leader gets her hands dirty in the real work world of her subordinates.

Figure 12.2. Participatory Organizational Chart

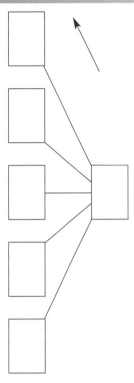

Occasionally the servant leader may face a crisis calling for immediate and decisive action (see Figure 12.3). The rotation of the chart demonstrates the servant leader's response. The leader has assumed a directive leadership posture, making decisions based on data from subordinates but with less direct participation by those subordinates. The leader becomes the coach on the stand, high above the practice field that sees the big picture, makes decisions, and calls out orders to the assistant coaches for implementation by the team's offensive or defensive players.

Figure 12.3. Directed Leadership Organizational Chart

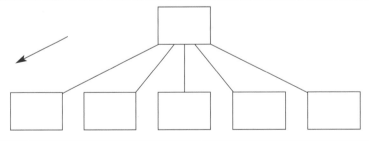

Once the servant leader has built quality employee relationships for the long term, employees willingly respond to directives in the midst of crisis. These employees realize that the servant leader will return to the more characteristic style of management as soon as possible. Ethical behavior demands it.

Toward an Ethical Christian Worldview

Mark 10:35–44

> *James and John, the sons of Zebedee, came up to him and said to him, "Teacher, we want you to do for us whatever we ask of you." And he said to them, "What do you want me to do for you?" And they said to him, "Grant us to sit, one at your right hand and one at your left, in your glory" (vv. 35–37).*

Examining Jesus's teaching on the nature of greatness in biblical context yields an even clearer insight into the nature of servant leadership and the ethical responsibility of Christian managers to practice the servant style. This conversation arises when two of the disciples, James and John, ask Jesus for a "blank check" with regard to their role in his future kingdom. "We want you to do for us whatever we ask of you."

Immediately it is clear that James and John see themselves and their needs as the primary issue. Jesus points out that the real issue is service to others: "whoever would be first among you must be slave [servant] of all" (v. 44).

The teaching of Jesus in this situation is reminiscent of Paul's instruction in Romans 12:3: "For by the grace given to me I say to everyone among you not to think of himself more highly than he ought."

Clearly, James and John's lofty self-image establishes an unethical view of their role as kingdom leaders. Jesus encourages James and John to adopt an attitude of servant leadership. What if they were to refuse? Ironically, if they were to continue to interpret leadership as a vehicle for elevating their own status, they ultimately would find themselves even lower than before. Wise King Solomon observed centuries earlier, "A person's pride will bring humiliation" (Proverbs 29:23 NRSV).

How important is it for a manager to be a servant-leader?

Karen's leadership style is ethically important to her employees and to the organizational structure of West Park Apartments. It is also important to Karen and her managerial future.

Ask the Pro

Mark Yoder is shift manager at an urban McDonald's restaurant. He has worked at this McDonald's location for three years, the last two as a manager. In addition to his job, he is a student at a local community college, studying toward a degree in computer-aided drafting. He is active in a local non-denominational church.

When he was promoted to manager at seventeen years of age, he was the youngest person ever to hold this position among the state's nine northern McDonald's stores. The authors believe that experience makes Yoder uniquely qualified to discuss the West Park Apartments case. The results of our conversation appear below:

Q: Karen's age seems to be undermining her ability to lead at West Park Apartments. Do you have any thoughts on that problem?

Yoder: When I first started as manager, I was only seventeen. I was with older employees who had been working here longer. Some of them didn't like the idea of me telling them what to do.

Q: Would that be worse for Karen as a female?

Yoder: I suppose that would have an effect. At least in my situation, some of the guys kind of looked up to me.

Q: Is Karen handling the leadership role correctly?

Yoder: When you have people who don't really respect you, you have to find ways to gain their respect. She doesn't have to beat on folks all the time. Eventually, they will come around if she just keeps doing what it takes to get the job done.

Q: Is there a particular place Karen should adjust?

Yoder: I think she was hard on Gary. She should have listened to him. When people have been here longer than I have, I try to give them the benefit of the doubt because of their experience. I would try to listen to him.

Q: Is it hard being a Christian in management?

Yoder: Sometimes. For example, the other day I had to send a woman home. She has two kids to take care of. But I get paid to follow the rules. It's sometimes hard to decide what is the right thing to do.

You Be the Consultant

Answer the following questions in light of Karen's difficulties:

1. What ethical concerns do you have about Karen's leadership style? How might they be addressed? What course of action could Karen take to salvage her relationship with the maintenance crew in general?

2. Karen believes that adopting a servant style of leadership would be viewed as weakness by her staff. She fears that they will run roughshod over her. How do you respond?

3. What are the problems with servant leadership? Will it work in every situation? Is it possible to be an ethical Christian leader without being a servant leader? Support your answers.

4. Which elements in your personal statement of ethics would you recommend for Karen to use in the upcoming meeting with Gary, and how should she use them? If your ethical statement is not comprehensive enough to apply to Karen's dilemma, what would you add and how would it apply? What specific action would an ethical egoist suggest? What specific actions would a Kantian suggest?

5. Which of the secular ethical positions discussed in Chapter 3 most closely parallels Karen's attitudes? Explain why.

Endnotes

1. Len Marrella, *In Search of Ethics: Conversations with Men and Women of Character* (Sanford, FL: DC Press, 2001), 184.
2. Douglas McGregor, *The Human Side of Enterprise* (New York: McGraw-Hill, 1960).
3. McGregor, *The Human Side of Enterprise*.
4. Robert Earl Kelly, *How to Be a Star at Work: Nine Breakthrough Strategies You Need to Succeed* (New York: Times Business, 1998), 49–62.

13

The Christian Manager as Ethical Record Keeper

Lying lips are an abomination to the LORD, but those who act faithfully are his delight.

— Proverbs 12:22

Chapter Challenges

A careful examination of Chapter 13 should enable the reader to:

- Recognize the importance of ethical record keeping.
- Define the managerial function of control.
- List the five characteristics of ethical record keeping.

Case Study

Ace Production Company

Jon gazed in amazement at the tub of parts. He estimated the tub to be 80 percent full. He had found the finished cams in a construction zone just east of the cam finishing area where one would not expect to find production parts. The tub had been covered carefully with cardboard to shield it from the view of passersby. "Buzz on the day shift is hiding cams," he whistled to himself. "So that's how he does it."

Jon Warren supervised the twenty-three hourly employees on the second shift in the cam finishing area of Ace Production Company. Buzz Johnson held the same position on the first shift.

Cam finishing involved finish-grinding and heat-treating the cams in preparation for shipment to the assembly division. At the completion of the process, workers placed each cam in a shipping tub. Tubs uniformly held 250 cams. The labor-intensive nature of the work meant that the cam finishing area produced only three tubs or 750 cams when it ran at 100 percent efficiency for an entire eight-hour shift.

Production control calculated efficiencies based on ready-to-ship completed tubs rather than individual parts. As a result, Jon's area might produce seven hundred parts on a given evening, but since those completely filled only two tubs, reports revealed a dismal 67 percent operating efficiency. Just fifty more parts would have completely filled another tub and yielded 100 percent efficiency.

The Efficiency Battle

For several months Jon had been under pressure from his general supervisor, Karen O'Neal. Karen had reminded him that over the past year his shift's efficiency had averaged only 82 percent.

"Look, Jon, I know it can be done. Buzz has a 97 percent efficiency for the same period," Karen challenged. "Your efficiency is declining, while his is increasing. You have simply *got* to get out more tubs of finished cams."

"Karen, those reports are misleading," Jon argued. "Night after night I leave a tub half or two-thirds full for Buzz to begin with in the morning. Yet consistently he has just finished a tub near the end of his shift. He leaves only a few dozen parts in the bottom of the next container for my people."

"It may seem like that," Karen said, her voice reflecting compassion. "But we have been through this before. The number of parts remaining at the end of each shift will average out. Over time, you gain as many as you lose."

Jon tried to convince the production control staff to devise a single–part-count measure of efficiency. However, the engineers saw no need to tamper with the current accounting procedure. "If it ain't broke, we ain't got time to fix it," one production controller had declared with finality.

So the situation remained the same, with Buzz consistently winning the efficiency battle between the two shifts. "I just know something is wrong," Jon told his lead man and truck driver, Joe. "But, I haven't been able to figure out what is going on. I think that Buzz has found some way to fudge the numbers."

Now, with the discovery of a nearly complete and apparently hidden tub of cams, Jon believed he had discovered how Buzz developed such a strong efficiency report.

"I finally figured out what the first shift crew is up to," Jon told Joe later that same evening. He described finding the nearly completed tub hidden in the construction zone. "In the morning, he will bring his work—the partial tub— back in and finish off the tub. Then he will run what he needs to complete the tub we have left him. By midmorning the first shift will have two tubs complete with six hours production time remaining."

"That sly old fox!" Joe said with a degree of admiration. "You've got to hand it to him for figuring a way to beat the system. But what are we going to do now that you've caught him, Jon?"

"I'm not sure," Jon admitted. "We could just go pick up that partial tub and get a great efficiency today."

"But tomorrow, he will find another hiding place for his partial," Joe finished the thought. "And unless we find them every day, the problem isn't solved."

"That's right," Jon said. "I suppose we could just find a hiding place of our own. Two can play this game—except it's not a bright move if the general supervisors find out."

"We only have three hours of production time left," Joe mentioned. "What do you want me to do?"

On Background

Edward Zinbarg points out that Moses recorded a list of contributors along with the details of their contributions as the Israelites embarked on the project of building a tabernacle. He further suggests that rabbinic commentaries pose the likelihood that independent audits of those funds were performed. "The Rabbis believed that even a man who spoke directly to God felt an obligation to keep accurate financial records and have them independently audited."[1]

Keeping Accurate Records

The managerial function called *control* embraces many aspects of the company's operations, such as performance appraisals, production statistics and standards, and the budgetary systems. In all of the control functions, the collection, storage, and use of clear, accurate, and appropriate information is vital. Arguably, no single function consumes more of a manager's day-to-day activity than record keeping. And no other task poses such ethical challenges — challenges that are not always met by executives.[2] At times, the records track accumulated production, as in the dilemma facing Jon Warren. On other occasions, the manager may be called upon to account for expenditures on an expense report. At still other times, personnel records must be maintained, including documentation of training sessions or discipline. Hence effective management requires the collecting and storing of accurate records. These records will demonstrate whether the institution is meeting its mission and core values. Failure to plan and provide for these aspects of record keeping creates "gray areas" of decision making that may lead to unethical decisions.[3]

> *Control*: managerial function that includes performance appraisal, production statistics and standards, and budgetary systems.

One manager reportedly interviewed a representative from several accounting firms before selecting one to perform bookkeeping functions for his fledgling business. A colleague inquired, "What was it in the interview process that convinced you to select this particular accountant?"

"Well," responded the manager, "I ask each accountant the same question: What does one plus one equal? All but one interviewee gave the answer as two. The accountant I hired was the only exception."

"What was that accountant's answer?" quizzed the surprised colleague.

"He responded with a question of his own. He asked, 'What do you need it to equal?'"

Similarly, another accountant who served as treasurer of a nonprofit corporation once boasted to the executive officer, "I can make the monthly report reflect whatever you want me to. Just let me know."

Perhaps there is some truth to this adage, "Figures never lie. But liars sometimes figure."

The Five Characteristics of Ethical Record Keeping

The same ethical standards apply to every record-keeping situation. We have summarized these as the five characteristics of ethical record keeping.

Records Must Be Understandable

The first characteristic of ethical record keeping is that records must be understandable. When an ethical record keeper is responsible for an organization's records, those records can be properly interpreted without undue difficulty. This characteristic relates to the transparency of data standard of the accuracy of information corollary discussed in Chapter 4 (see Leviticus 19:35–36).

One company's personnel files included an intricate coding system. This allowed officers to compile quickly the racial statistics for the quarterly affirmative action report required at division headquarters. Despite the fact that the data served a positive purpose, the procedure raises ethical questions. The data included in those personnel files was not readily understandable to observers.

Records Must Be Verifiable

The second characteristic of ethical record keeping is that records must be verifiable. In today's office, backup files are essential in the event of a computer malfunction. Backups also serve the secondary purpose of verifying the accuracy of records in the event the ethics of record keepers are called into question. This is supported by the credibility of data standard of the accuracy of information corollary (see principle of veracity in Chapter 4; see also Leviticus 19:35–36).

While receipts for certain purchases or fees may not be required with an employee expense report, they do provide necessary verification in the event of an inquiry. Ethical managers will attach such documentation to file copies, to demonstrate accuracy in record keeping.

Records Must Be Timely

In addition to being understandable and verifiable, ethical records must be timely. While a manager may occasionally fall behind in record-keeping tasks, records generally must be produced in an expeditious fashion.

For example, consider the manager who is required to keep a mileage log. The Internal Revenue Service (IRS) and others consider these logs most accurate when they are kept in the vehicle and created on a trip-by-trip basis. Logs generated in the office at the end of the month are considered to be less reliable.

One sales manager who was required to file an annual report of business activity failed to keep the records necessary to complete the report accurately. In response to each question, he would do the best he could to recall twelve months' worth of activity and fill in the report while thinking aloud, "I reckon about seven calls made," or, "I reckon about three hundred parts ordered." He jokingly referred to the document as his "reckon about" report.

The ethical record keeper avoids "reckon about" reporting by making timely data entries. There's a side benefit to timely reporting: it requires much less of the manager's time than attempting to re-create the facts later and from memory. The accuracy of information corollary in Chapter 4 supports this characteristic.

Records Must Be Complete

Fourth, ethical records must be thorough and complete. Record keepers create a "paper trail" of data and activity. Incomplete records leave holes in that trail and open the door to moral compromise.

The production control authorities at Ace Production have established a flawed system that invites fraudulent and incomplete record keeping. Since Jon and Buzz can count only full tubs of completed parts, the actual production count is misleading. On any given shift, from 1 to 249 parts may be unaccounted for. Such a hole in the documentation system has set the stage for Buzz's unethical behavior and Jon's current dilemma. Again, the transparency of data standard of the accuracy of information corollary supports this characteristic (see Leviticus 19:35–36).

Records Must Reflect Accountability

Ethical record keeping occurs when the record keeper is accountable. The basic management principle that every worker must be accountable to one— and only one—superior applies especially to record keepers. One nonprofit corporation hired a local firm to perform basic accounting duties, including ledger activity and check writing. As a safeguard, an employee of the nonprofit performed banking operations and delivered deposit slips to the accountant. On a day-to-day basis, the procedures worked efficiently, effectively, and ethically. However, at the end of the fiscal year, the same accounting firm performed the nonprofit's annual audit. The public record of the nonprofit's good performance essentially was the result of the accounting firm's self-audit. While this procedure is legal in the strictest sense, the practice lacks the ethical characteristic of accountability.

Ethical records are always understandable, verifiable, timely, and complete. They reflect the record keeper's accountability. The ethical record keeper will always record that $1 + 1 = 2$, not "whatever you want it to equal."

> ### Ethical Records Are Always
>
> - understandable
> - verifiable
> - timely
> - complete
> - reflective of accountability

Toward an Ethical Christian Worldview

Acts 5:1–10

The believers of the early church had agreed that they would hold all property in common. They had even gone so far as to bring the proceeds from the sale of property to the common purse. Many Christians surmise that the death of Ananias as recorded in Acts 5 teaches the importance of proper stewardship. However, a closer look reveals an even deeper issue at work.

> *But a man named Ananias, with the consent of his wife Sapphira, sold a piece of property, and with his wife's knowledge he kept back for himself some of the proceeds and brought only a part and laid it at the apostles' feet. Peter said, "Ananias, why has Satan filled your heart to lie to the Holy Spirit and to keep back for yourself part of the proceeds of the land? While it remained unsold, did it not remain your own? And after it was sold, was it not at your disposal? Why is it that you have contrived this*

deed in your heart? You have not lied to men but to God." When Ananias heard these words, he fell down and breathed his last. And great fear came upon all who heard of it (vv. 1–5).

Ananias's judgment stems not from his refusal to give, but from his dishonest report of the income he received from the sale of property. The phrase "kept back for himself some of the proceeds" in verse 2 is actually a single Greek verb sometimes translated "embezzled." It usually implies a secret theft from a much larger total. This word also appears in Titus 2:10 where slaves are commanded not to pilfer or steal from their masters. Interestingly, in this context the opposite of stealing is demonstrated with the phrase "showing all good faith."

Ananias sinned not because of his inadequate stewardship, but because he gave an inaccurate report on the sale of the property—he lied. In this case, the lie is magnified because it was directed toward representatives of the body of Christ, the Church, as well as the Holy Spirit.

The improper reporting stemmed from a conspiracy between Ananias and his wife Sapphira. She is judged to be as guilty as her husband and meets an identical fate.

After an interval of about three hours his wife came in, not knowing what had happened. Peter said to her, "Tell me whether you sold the land for so much." And she said, "Yes, for so much." But Peter said to her, "How is it that you have agreed together to test the Spirit of the Lord? Behold, the feet of those who have buried your husband are at the door, and they will carry you out." Immediately she fell down at his feet and breathed her last. When the young men came in they found her dead, and they carried her out and buried her beside her husband (vv. 7–10).

Whether these deaths resulted from divine judgment or natural causes has prompted a great deal of speculation through the centuries. Some believe that Sapphira died of shock from the combined loss of her husband and the revelation of her own evil intent. Others argue that her death was the result of the immediate and decisive wrath of God. Either way, the accounts reveal the clear position of the early church on the issue of ethical reporting.

While the deaths of Ananias and Sapphira are among the first references in the early Christian church to the vital importance of ethical reporting, the Old Testament places consistent

Ethical Dilemma

How important is accountability in operating a business?

emphasis on this topic. God's preference is that his people use ethical and honest accounting in all of their dealings. How Jon decides to respond to his real-life industrial dilemma will reveal the importance he places on God's standard.

Ask the Pro

James Wilson is plant manager of the largest of the Midwest popcorn processors. He is a graduate of the Purdue University School of Agriculture with a degree in food business management. James has seventeen years of experience in the food manufacturing industry.

James's company is a world leader in popcorn production and has been a privately held, family-owned business for seventy-five years. In addition to the Midwest plant, the company has a plant in Rojas, Argentina.

Along with his wife, James attends church regularly where he teaches children occasionally and volunteers frequently. The couple has three daughters in elementary school.

The authors asked James to discuss the Ace Production case and business ethics in general from the perspective of a Christian in industrial management. The results of our conversation are below:

Q: Jon at Ace Production has a problem with a co-worker. How should he handle that problem?

Wilson: He needs to engage Buzz face to face. I think I would find him now, even at home and asleep. I'd get in my vehicle and drive to his house if necessary. "We have to talk."

Q: That sounds confrontational.

Wilson: It doesn't need to be. In fact, if handled properly, Buzz could become an ally to get the system changed appropriately. I would encourage him to work with me to get management to find a better way to track efficiency.

Q: What better ways would you recommend?

Wilson: We use five key performance indicators that ensure accountability and become a template for success. Every person, every work group, every shift, every department—is measured by the same quantifiable standards. They are quality, safety, machine efficiency, labor efficiency, and scrap.

Q: So this scenario could not happen in your organization?

Wilson: It better not!

Q: Do you believe the production control engineers are ultimately responsible for this situation?

Wilson: Only partially. Jon did not engage his superior properly to present his ideas. A good manager must impact the business in a positive fashion by making sure his thoughts are heard. He should have made sure his ideas on calculating efficiency were considered. A dynamic leader gets heard.

Q: Does being a Christian in the industrial world influence any of that?

Wilson: I am proud of who I am. A big part of that comes through my walk with Christ. I express that at work in a variety of ways. The key components include engaging people. That's what Jesus did. He went to the lost wherever they were. Also, one must be consistent. I am so grateful to work for a company that allows me to be consistently Christian.

You Be the Consultant

As you consider Jon's dilemma, answer the following questions:

1. How would you advise Jon to respond to Joe's question—what do we do now? What longer-term plan would you advise Jon to implement following his discovery of the hidden cams? How would they reflect secular tools from Chapter 3 and Bible-based tools from Chapter 4?

2. Would the elements of the truthful communications corollary and the accuracy of information corollary in Chapter 4 assist Jon in his decision to inform or not to inform production control or Karen, the general supervisor, of his find? How would the secular positions of utilitarianism, Kant's categorical imperative, and ethical egoism found in Chapter 3 assist Jon?

3. Should he mention it to Buzz? Why or why not? Support your answer with Kantian ethics and biblical ethics.

Endnotes

1. Edward Zinbarg, "What Can the World's Religions Tell Us about Ethics?" in *Leaders on Ethics: Real World Perspectives on Today's Business Challenges,* ed. John C. Knapp (Westport, CT: Praeger, 2007), 35–40.
2. See, for example, Dianna B. Henriques, "A. R. Baron's Top Salesman Admits Guilt and Will Assist Inquiry," *New York Times,* June 6, 1997; "Chase Manhattan Bank Agrees to Pay $1 Million to Settle SEC Allegations," *Wall Street Journal* Eastern Edition, September 25, 2001.
3. James E. Copeland Jr., "The Ethical Crisis in the Accounting and Auditing Profession," in *Leaders on Ethics: Real World Perspectives on Today's Business Challenges*, ed. John C. Knapp (Westport, CT: Praeger, 2007), 43–50.

Notes

14

The Christian Manager as Ethical Disciplinarian

Poverty and disgrace come to him who ignores instruction,
but whoever heeds reproof is honored.
— Proverbs 13:18

Chapter Challenges

A careful examination of Chapter 14 should enable the reader to:

- Understand the purpose and principles of employee disciplinary action.
- Develop an ethical approach to employee discipline.

Case Study

Sagamore County Mental Health Association

"What is this trash?" Sue Yaton angrily demanded as she stormed into the office of her supervisor, Paul Novak.

"Now Sue, calm down and we will discuss the matter rationally," Paul responded.

"You calm down if you want to," Sue continued. "But I'm furious, and someone is going to hear about this." She slammed a memo from Paul down on the desk. "This is garbage, and you know it!"

Paul's memo to Sue indicated that he had placed a written warning in her file for insubordination. While the memo and the written warning did not indicate the circumstances, Sue knew the matter stemmed from an incident with Ivan Westmore, one of Sue's clients.

A Legal and Ethical Obligation

As case manager for Sagamore County Mental Retardation and Developmental Disabilities Association (MRDD), Sue managed a caseload of twenty-two adults with developmental cognitive disabilities. Her responsibilities involved making sure clients received the benefits available to them from state, county, and local agencies. She worked with these agencies to ensure that her people were granted full citizenship rights. Her task also included making sure the clients functioned as nearly as possible at their full capacity.

Some of her clients had severe disabilities and required close supervision. Others, like twenty-six-year-old Ivan Westmore, were only mildly challenged. Ivan held a regular full-time job and lived in his own apartment. He struggled with money management. Thus, he qualified for five hours of assistance each week to make sure he was not cheated during such activities as banking and shopping.

Ivan had developed an infatuation with a sixteen-year-old girl who lived in his neighborhood. Although he referred to the girl as "his woman," most observers doubted the seriousness of the relationship. The girl's father, had become sufficiently alarmed to ask a judge to issue a restraining order against Ivan. The court granted the father's request, and it had fallen to Sue to explain to Ivan that he must stay away from the girl or face contempt-of-court charges. She was confident that Ivan understood the court order and its implications.

A few weeks later during a routine interview, Ivan revealed to Sue that he and the girl had recently gone together to a movie. He discussed their date with enough clarity that Sue became convinced that not only had he violated the court order, but the two had become involved in a consensual sexual relationship.

As soon as she had reason to believe that Ivan had violated the restraining order, Sue believed she had a legal and ethical responsibility to notify the authorities. "Ivan," she said, looking steadily into his eyes, "do you understand that what you are doing is wrong and that I have to notify the sheriff?"

"Go ahead, Miss Sue," Ivan responded. "I'm willing to get in trouble, and my woman will wait for me until I get out."

A Heated Disagreement

While Sue's legal obligation seemed clear enough to her, Paul argued that Sue should look the other way on the matter. "Look, Sue," he instructed, "we have a MRDD levy before the voters in less than thirty days. Something like this in the papers could get blown all out of proportion and threaten all of our jobs. Quit asking the kid about his sex life, and forget what you already know."

"You're suggesting I violate the law," Sue argued. "I have no choice but to report what I know. If the voters can't sort out right from wrong, we'll just have to find alternative funding."

"No!" Paul demanded angrily. "I'm not *suggesting* anything. I'm giving you a direct order. Forget Ivan's sex life."

Later that same afternoon, Sue filed a report with the Sagamore County Sheriff's Office. As required by office procedures, she put a copy of the report in Paul's mailbox. Now she stood red-faced with anger in Paul's office.

"A written warning for following the law and doing my job correctly is a cheap shot!" she shouted.

"If you continue to raise your voice to me, I'll increase your discipline to a day off without pay," Paul responded.

The battle over disciplinary action at Sagamore County MRDD Association was heating up.

On Background

Progressive and Positive Discipline

Both Sue and Paul have made and/or are about to make ethics-related decisions. Paul believes he has used *disciplinary action* appropriately to deal with an insubordinate employee. Sue finds Paul's instructions inappropriate. She feels justified in her behavior and would argue that Paul's disciplinary action falls outside the bounds of propriety. The two disagree on several ethical fronts. Better understanding of the process of employee discipline may provide a starting point toward finding common ground.

Reasons for Employee Discipline

Experts generally group employees requiring disciplinary action into four categories: employees who are ineffective, employees with personal problems, employees involved in on-the-job criminal activity, and employees who violate company policy.

Ineffectiveness

Sometimes supervisors must deal with employees whose skills are inadequate for the jobs to which they are assigned. In other cases employees have the necessary skills, but use them in an ineffective manner. The ethical manager carefully analyzes each situation to make sure that discipline does not take the place of coaching and adequate training.

Personal Problems

A second category requiring disciplinary action involves employees with off-the-job personal problems that directly or indirectly affect job performance. Alcohol abuse may create an attendance problem; drug abuse may lead to unsafe work habits; marital difficulties may cause on-the-job lapses of concentration or overall ineffectiveness. For the Christian manager, this area touches the key concept that all individuals, regardless of their personal actions, have true value because they are God's creation and are made in his image. To discard employees with personal problems as if you were throwing away yesterday's newspaper is denying human value. The real ethical question for the manager is: "How do I provide Christian discipline, which includes corrective measures as well as punitive ones, while protecting the interest of fellow employees and fulfilling my fiduciary responsibilities to the company's owners and suppliers?"

In dealing with these kinds of employees, the ethical manager must make certain that discipline does not become a substitute for appropriate counseling. One manager made no distinction between an employee who failed to report for work because he was in the county jail for drunken and disorderly behavior, and another employee who failed to report for work in order to attend a family member's funeral nearly two hundred miles away. "If they're not here, they're not here," he growled. "I got no use for them." Most of us would agree that disciplining without regard to an employee's circumstances or record is unethical. In this regard, note the interdependence of the record keeping and disciplining aspects of a managerial control function; failure to recognize that interrelatedness can set the stage for inappropriate and often unethical decisions.

On-the-Job Crime

A third category requiring employee discipline involves the growing problem of on-the-job crime. Stealing from employers, embezzling funds, disclosing trade secrets, and misusing expense accounts or company credit cards all fall within this category. Often law enforcement authorities intervene, relieving the employer of disciplinary action. Ethical managers recognize the employer's responsibility to minimize opportunities for illegal behavior. Increasingly, companies use industrial security techniques, including security education, fraud control, and appropriate checks and balances.

Company Policy Violations

A fourth reason for employee discipline often is the most difficult to administer: violation of company policy or supervisor instruction. Paul believes Sue fits into this category. To determine appropriate discipline for such violations, the ethical manager must be certain that company policies and instructions have been clearly communicated. For example, when orienting new employees, many managers take a proactive approach. This goes beyond giving the typical walking tour of the facility, introducing key personnel, filling out tax and insurance forms, and handing out a policy manual. The proactive manager invests company time giving an in-depth new-hire orientation to policies and procedures and periodic reviews of policies throughout subsequent months or years of employment. Special attention is given to inform employees of any and all new policies and procedures.

This proactive approach helps the honest employee not to make mistakes through ignorance, and it gives management firmer ground to stand on in case of employee or union appeal or court action challenging management's disciplinary actions. This practice (or similar ones) intentionally addresses the question: "Is it ethical to discipline employees for violating policies or procedures that have not been taught to them?" Such an approach also complies with the philosophy that quality management equips its employees with the knowledge, skills, and resources to successfully do their required task. Is it ethical to do otherwise?

Progressive Discipline

Progressive discipline is a process that is not intended as a punishment for an employee, but to assist the employee in overcoming performance problems and satisfying job expectations. Progressive discipline is most successful when it assists an individual to become an effectively performing member of the organization.[1] When employee discipline becomes necessary, the ethical manager generally uses a four-stage progressive discipline approach.

Verbal Warning

First violations often result in a verbal warning or disciplinary discussion. This is the most common of all disciplinary actions and often brings about the necessary correction.

Written Warning

When verbal warnings fail to create the necessary changes in behavior, the ethical manager may issue a written warning. A copy of the warning is placed in the employee's personnel file and presented to the employee. This form of discipline is most effective when the written warning is presented as soon as possible after the infraction. Various policies may allow for multiple written warnings.

Disciplinary Layoff

If the two steps above fail to produce the intended change, some firms use a third step, the disciplinary layoff. Ranging from a few hours to a week or more, a disciplinary layoff means the employee is ordered to take time off without pay. Sometimes this step is divided, allowing for progressively longer periods of layoff reflecting the severity of the infraction or of repeated offenses.

Termination

The final step in the progressive discipline process (after other efforts to produce changed behavior have failed) is termination. Work guidelines and rules, including those instituted by the government and collective bargaining agreements, make disciplinary discharge extremely difficult to implement.

Where these safeguards do not exist, unethical managers may see termination as the solution to every employee problem, whether it for one or multiple infractions or some other nondiscipline-related issue.

Positive Discipline

A relatively new approach to employee discipline focuses on future behavior rather than past infractions. Called *positive discipline*, it recognizes that people do make mistakes, yet it de-emphasizes the use of punitive action in favor of written reminders, proactive interaction with the employee, and positive reinforcements for appropriate work-place behavior. The ultimate discipline, discharge, may still be necessary when circumstances warrant.

Positive discipline suggests that employees wish to be positive, contributing members to the society within their company. This results in more frequent and voluntary compliance with company policies and procedures, leading to worker satisfaction and positive worker contributions toward meeting the company's goals and vision. A key belief is that this intrinsic desire can be activated, leading to more appropriate employee behavior and productivity.

In this approach, management might establish a rewards system to reinforce appropriate employee response to company policies and practices. For example, cash bonuses or a company banquet may reward employees who have perfect attendance for the year, have committed no violations of company policy during the year, and have exceeded minimum annual productivity expectations. These activities are designed to prevent undesirable behavior from occurring.

When an employee is guilty of behavior that violates company policy or procedures, the company looks at the causes of the behavior as well as the cost and effects of the behavior. For example, if an employee has a chronic absenteeism problem, counseling for an identified root cause such as a drug problem may be the appropriate company response instead of termination. This is a human approach to discipline that is in part based in economic reality. If the company has a capable employee in whom it has made a major investment in training, positive discipline with related expenditures may be the cost-effective way to meet company needs.

This approach to discipline also respects the employee as a person of dignity and both personal and professional potential. Positive discipline does not "wink at" inappropriate behavior. It identifies inappropriate behavior, confronts it, records it, and even uses data collection for employee termination. However, it also looks for positive remedies and emphasizes the belief that human beings will respond in appropriate ways when they are treated as persons of dignity with both personal and professional potential. There is an underlying belief that when employees are managed and disciplined in a positive, proactive way, both the employee and the company benefit.

Systems in the company can set the stage for more opportunities of either ethical or unethical decision making, as evidenced in the area of employee discipline. Kant's concept of treating people with dignity while upholding several universal rights and various contractual rights, such as due process and fair and accurate data, requires management to develop well-defined and functional systems. When managed by administrators who (1) view people as being made in God's image, and (2) practice a redemptive philosophy of discipline designed to respect the dignity of employees, these systems can help employees overcome personal problems, destructive attitudes, and ineffective work habits.

Toward an Ethical Christian Worldview

Hebrews 12:5–11

Consider the following verses from the book of Hebrews, which start with a quotation from Proverbs 3:11–12:

> *"My child, do not regard lightly the discipline of the Lord, or lose heart when you are punished by him; for the Lord disciplines those whom he loves, and chastises every child whom he accepts." Endure trials for the sake of discipline. God is treating you as children; for what child is there whom a parent does not discipline? If you do not have that discipline in which all children share, then you are illegitimate and not his children. Moreover, we had human parents to discipline us, and we respected them. Should we not be even more willing to be subject to the Father of spirits and live? For they disciplined us for a short time as seemed best to them, but he disciplines us for our good, in order that we may share his holiness. Now, discipline always seems painful rather than pleasant at the time, but later it yields the peaceful fruit of righteousness to those who have been trained by it (NRSV).*

A Goal of Improvement

The Greek word *paideia*, translated "discipline" in this passage, has the same root as the English word *pediatrics*. This word implies the training or instruction a caring parent might give to a child. Interestingly, the passage suggests that discipline from God should be considered as evidence of his love. Just as a loving parent disciplines a child, so God disciplines in order to help his children improve.

Similarly, disciplinary action by a caring employer who desires to train, instruct, and improve the performance of an employee meets the scriptural parameters of ethical discipline. By contrast, revenge or reprisal, while often confused with discipline, are much different and are by definition unethical.

One manager sought some way to dismiss a person he perceived as a problem employee. He went through the progressive discipline steps, but his mind had been made up before he even began the process. "This troublemaker has to go," he declared. His preconceptions meant that the discipline he administered was only intended to fulfill the demands of a rulebook, not to improve the employee's performance. Such discipline does not meet a scriptural ethical standard. Looking again at Sagamore Valley MRDD, we must first determine whether or not Paul intended to bring Sue to a place of improved performance. Was his motivation caring? Did he want to make Sue a better employee, or did he have a different agenda?

A Teachable Spirit

Proverbs 13:18 suggests that even ethical discipline may not have the desired effect. Much depends on the attitude with which that discipline is received. "Poverty and disgrace come to him who ignores instruction, but one who heeds reproof is honored."

How can an employer's disciplinary action be above reproach?

One manager concluded that this verse points to the importance of a teachable spirit. Ethical discipline designed to gain an improvement in performance has neutral or even negative results in the life of an employee who lacks a teachable spirit. Whether or not Paul's discipline met the requirements of propriety, Sue had a responsibility to receive the discipline in an ethical manner.

Ask the Pro

Nancy Quan is a family case manager in the Child Protection Division of Family and Children, a governmental agency that is called upon to investigate allegations of abuse or neglect. In that capacity, she is called upon to investigate allegations of abuse or neglect. Prior to coming to the Child Protection Division, she worked for six years in private foster care. For more than four of those years, she was a supervisor.

Nancy graduated from Taylor University with a bachelor's degree in psychology. She has attended a Wesleyan church her entire life. At her church, she has served as secretary, board member, Sunday school teacher, and worship leader.

Nancy agreed to review the situation at Sagamore County MRDD from her perspective as a social-work practitioner, and also from her experience as a supervisor. The authors sat down with Nancy at her office for the following exchange.

Q: Paul thinks Sue made a poor decision. Do you agree?

Quan: I struggle deciding what she should have done. In my state, sixteen is the age of consent. There actually would be no crime in this situation. If I were Sue (knowing there had been no crime, but aware of the restraining order), I think I would have called the girl's father and let him know that his daughter had made a bad decision, and that the restraining order may have been violated. On the other hand, if the child were fifteen instead of sixteen, Sue would have had an obligation to report what she knew — because in that case a crime had been committed.

Q: Where do the supervisor's instructions come in?

Quan: The law is a higher standard than what a supervisor says. I would try to talk it out with Paul. I might even go to his administrator so that I wouldn't surprise anyone when I did what would have to be done.

Q: Let's look at the case from the supervisor's position. Did Paul act appropriately?

Quan: I can't imagine a supervisor telling an employee not to report something like this. That is wrong. But Sue certainly overreacted. She didn't demonstrate the right attitude in the way she told her supervisor that she didn't agree with his decision.

Q: But Paul is concerned about the levy. Does he really have any choices?

Quan: Since the levy is an issue, what still raises an ethical dilemma—but is much more likely to occur—is an attempt to get Ivan off the caseload, so that the office is no longer associated with the entire mess. That is still unethical if he needs the services. Personally, my value system would just cause me to say, "Tough. Forget the voters. Turn him in."

Q: You mentioned your value system. Tell me about values. What role do they play in your work?

Quan: For me, it is very hard to separate my life values from what I do at work. I have had co-workers who believe church life is church life, and work life is work life. They never combine the two. That is impossible in my life. All my decisions include my values. I can't imagine making a decision separate from values.

Q: Are there ever times when you are tempted to compromise those values?

Quan: I didn't realize when I started in this work how many times I would be put in a situation where I *could* compromise. You have to know clearly and in advance what you believe and then stand up for what's right, regardless of the cost. You might get a reprimand. You might even lose a job. You need a support group of people who share your values and help hold you accountable.

You Be the Consultant

Examine the ramifications of this ethical dilemma in light of these questions:

1. What are the specific principles in your statement of ethics that would support the ethicality or the unethicality of the way Paul handled employee discipline? Explain your conclusion.

2. Do you find Sue's report to the sheriff on Ivan's sexual behavior ethical? Explain using secular and Bible-based ethical tools.

3. Paul's concerns about a funding levy are not at all uncommon in government-funded agencies. What role should ethical concerns play in gaining public support? What are the limits?

4. Assume the role of a mediator. How should Paul and Sue handle their current differences? Would your mediator role be different if you were a Kantian? Explain your answer.

5. Compare and contrast employee discipline from the points of view of ethical egoism and utilitarianism.

6. How do you view the positive discipline approach used by some firms? Is it more or less inherently ethical than traditional approaches to discipline? How would one who uses Kant's categorical imperatives respond? How would one who is committed to utilitarianism respond?

Endnotes

1. "The Purpose of Discipline" *Fire Engineering* 160, no. 1 (January 2007): 12–16.

15

The Christian Manager as Ethical Communicator

From the same mouth come blessing and cursing. My brothers,
these things ought not to be so.

— James 3:10

Chapter Challenges

A careful examination of Chapter 15 should enable the reader to:

- Define communication.
- Explain six principles of communication.
- Identify four rules for ethical communication.

Case Study

Samoya Enterprises

Herb Walker left Mr. Samoya's office and walked toward the production floor with a smile on his face. At last, the years of long hours and loyal service were about to pay off. Herb had worked for Samoya Enterprises for ten years, having hired in as a night watchman while still a student at the local community college. Once he had earned his degree, he joined the twenty-five employees who made up the Samoya hourly production staff. Two years ago Mr. Samoya had promoted him to production manager. In that capacity Herb's responsibilities included supervising his previous colleagues on the assembly floor. However, what Herb had just learned in a private meeting with Mr. Samoya promised to be the biggest career break of his life.

"Herb," Mr. Samoya said, "what I'm about to tell you must stay in this room. If our employees get wind of it—well, frankly, it could unravel the whole deal. I've decided to sell the business to Widget Industries, our biggest competitor. They have made a very attractive offer that will allow me to retire comfortably."

Herb spoke frankly. "Of course, I'm happy for you, Mr. Samoya, but what about the rest of us?" he asked.

"That's why I wanted to see you, Herb. Widget intends to transfer you to Capital City as plant manager of their operation up there. Congratulations! It's a great move for you, and you deserve the opportunity."

Herb stammered a bit, but finally found the words to respond, "Me? Plant manager? Thank you, sir! I appreciate the opportunity. I am sure that your recommendation carried a lot of weight. I won't disappoint you, Mr. Samoya."

"I know you won't, Herb," Mr. Samoya said. "Now remember not a word of this to anyone."

"Of course, sir. Mum's the word. By the way, what does this mean for the rest of the people here at Samoya?"

Mr. Samoya shifted uncomfortably. "A few will have jobs if they are willing to transfer to other Widget Industry plants. Most will be dismissed, I'm afraid. But Widget has plans to grant a severance package of a full month's pay."

"One month?" Herb answered. "But, Mr. Samoya, some of these people have been with the company more than twenty years, and—"

"I realize this won't be easy," Mr. Samoya interrupted. "But, that's business, isn't it, Mr. Plant Manager?" he said with a wink. "Now, remember, no one is to know about any of this until the papers are signed."

Between a Rock and a Hard Place

Once on the production floor, Herb could scarcely contain himself. His thoughts tumbled boisterously in his head. "Imagine me, Herb Walker, Plant Manager!" The excitement must have shown on his face, because several people commented on how happy he seemed.

"You look like the cat that swallowed the canary," Joyce Wilson, Herb's office clerk, commented.

"Just having a great day," Herb responded cheerfully. Joyce had become a close personal friend of Herb and his wife, Mindy, over the past year. When Joyce and her husband had gone through a rather nasty divorce, Herb and Mindy had befriended Joyce. They had helped her make the transition to a single lifestyle. She had even stayed at their house for a few weeks until she could find an affordable apartment. Herb and Mindy helped her be involved in their church and were beginning to see some remarkable changes in Joyce's life. Herb and Mindy agreed that Joyce had become like a sister to them.

"I'm pretty excited today, too," Joyce continued. "I'm taking a very big step this week."

"What step is that?" Herb asked, his mind still on the plant manager position.

"I've decided that you and Mindy are right. It is time for me to move on emotionally. I'm going to take your advice and get on with my life."

"That's great," Herb responded sincerely.

Joyce continued. "So tonight I'm meeting with a real estate agent after work to take a second look at a little house just a couple of blocks from the plant. I've carefully calculated a budget, and my paychecks here at Samoya Industries total just enough to meet the monthly payments. I'm going to buy a house!"

"You're what?" Herb exclaimed in a voice that was louder than he intended.

"I'm going to buy a house!" Joyce repeated, grinning. "Isn't it marvelous?"

Facing her, Herb bent slightly and braced his hands on Joyce's desk. "Joyce, you can't," he said in a solemn, strained tone.

"Why not?" Joyce asked with a puzzled look.

On Background

The Principles of Interpersonal Communication

On the spur of the moment, Herb might dismiss Joyce's question. He could say, "Just surprised, that's all," and move the conversation to another topic for the time being.

Very soon, however, Herb must make a serious ethical decision. Should he keep Mr. Samoya's confidence, ensuring that he is given the plant manager position? Or should he tell Joyce what he knows and prevent a friend from making a potentially devastating personal financial mistake?

As Herb contemplates his options, he will want to consider some important facts related to organizational ethics and to organizational communication. Simply defined, *communication* is the interaction between two or more individuals. When only two individuals are involved in the communication process, such as the meeting between Herb and Mr. Samoya behind closed doors, *interpersonal communication* takes place. Increasingly communication skills are being taught by organizations in an attempt to formalize organizational patterns of communication.[1]

Most often in a workplace or organization, groups of people gather together and develop patterns of interaction. We refer to these patterns and the social collectives in which they occur as *organizational communication*. Sometimes the formal or informal rules for interpersonal interaction within an organization shape the way communication takes place.

> *Interpersonal communication*: interaction between just two individuals.
>
> *Organizational communication*: formal and informal rules within an organization that shape the way interaction occurs.

Regardless of the organizational rules for communication in place at Samoya Enterprises, Herb would benefit from understanding six basic principles of interpersonal communication.[2]

Principle 1: Communication Occurs over Time

Reading about Herb Walker's dilemma, examine the events as if they occurred in a vacuum—as if this particular interaction is the only one that has ever occurred between Herb and Mr. Samoya. In reality, an ongoing process of interaction has led up to this verbal transaction. Herb likely will evaluate the current situation by looking back over the process that preceded it, perhaps asking himself these questions:

- Has Mr. Samoya ever asked me to keep secrets before?
- How did he react when I challenged him in the past?
- Is he likely to be open to input from a subordinate?

Similarly, Herb may need to evaluate the process of communication he has established over time with Joyce. His questions might include:

- How much does Joyce trust me to give her good advice?
- How well can she keep a secret?
- How flexible is she in her decision-making style?

Realizing that communication is not about a single isolated conversation, but is instead a process, Herb can better decide on an ethical course of action.

Principle 2: Personal Motives Are Significant

Herb undoubtedly will have to do some self-analysis. He will want to explore how he feels about the pending promotion, and how much he is willing to sacrifice in order to gain it.

- Would he willingly sacrifice his friendship with and ministry to Joyce?
- Would he sacrifice his personal integrity?
- Would he sacrifice his reputation with the other employees at the plant?
- Would he sacrifice his relationship with Mr. Samoya over issues of integrity?

In the final analysis, only Herb can answer these questions. On a personal level, every manager ultimately has to answer these and similar questions.

Principle 3: Effective Communication Reduces Uncertainty[3]

Joyce undoubtedly has come away from her conversation with Herb Walker more confused than ever. Based on earlier conversations, she thought that Herb and Mindy felt she was ready to exercise a new independence. Now, based on Herb's facial expressions and his exclamation at her announcement, she wonders if he really believes she should buy a house. Maybe she misunderstood. Maybe Herb and Mindy don't think she's ready to handle that kind of responsibility.

In part, Joyce's confusion stems from the fact that Herb has not communicated very effectively. Effective communication decreases rather than increases the level of uncertainty. Consider two people who meet for conversation on a particular subject. In Figure 15.1, each person is represented by a circle. The figure demonstrates in the overlap of the circles a "meeting of the minds" prior to their conversation.

Figure 15.1. Meeting of the Minds

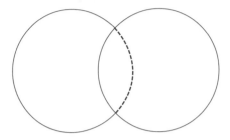

Figure 15.2 shows that the area of mutual understanding has grown as a result of effective conversation. Notice that when communication is effective, the area of overlap increases. The commonality has grown. There is a greater "meeting of the minds" than prior to conversation.

Figure 15.2. Effective Communication

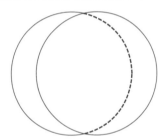

Figure 15.3 demonstrates what may have taken place between Joyce and Herb as a result of their conversation. Their common area of understanding has decreased because ineffective communication has left them uncertain about their standing with each other.

Figure 15.3. Ineffective Communication

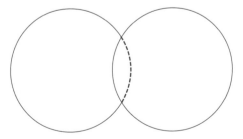

Principle 4: Communication Is Nonreturnable

Two children playing war in the backyard may trade insults. One child yells, "You take that back!"

The other finally admits, "Okay, I take it back."

The problem is solved. In the minds of children, it's as if the insults were never uttered.

By contrast, most adults recognize that it is impossible to "take back" that which has been uttered. Words, like thick smoke in a strong breeze, quickly cover a large area in a community or organization. Herb will need to proceed very carefully as he addresses either Joyce or Mr. Samoya. Little room exists for error in this communication; while communication can be amended or explained, it cannot be returned.

Principle 5: Communication Includes Both Content and Relationship

Herb will do well to realize that every communication event includes aspects of *content* and *relationship*. For example, suppose a student walks into a business ethics class and announces, "Take out a sheet of paper. We're going to have a quiz." Members of the class likely will jeer or simply ignore the student. They figure the student either misunderstands his role or is attempting to entertain them.

Imagine the totally different response of the class when the professor enters and makes the same announcement. There may be groans and mild objections: "You never told us," or, "It's not in the syllabus." But even as the groans are uttered, the sheets of paper come out.

How could two people get such strikingly dissimilar reactions to exactly the same words? The answer involves the relationship aspect of communication. While the content of the communication is identical in both cases, the relationship of the speaker to the hearer differs. The response depends upon both the content and relational aspects of the communiqué.

Herb will need to analyze two relationships as he decides what course of action to follow. His relationship with Mr. Samoya is that of a subordinate to a superior. However, additional aspects factor in. How have the two gotten along in the past? Have they ever socialized? If so, do they share a friendship as well as a professional relationship? Does Mr. Samoya share Herb's faith?

Similarly, Herb's relationship with Joyce will make a great deal of difference in how she responds to him. Does she see him as a coequal friend or a powerful superior? Has he given her good or bad advice in the past? Has the year of peer counseling she has received from Herb and Mindy helped her become independent, or does she find herself dependent on them?

Principle 6: Ethical Communication Is Never Risk Free

Regardless of how he decides to solve this dilemma, Herb is about to take some risks. Because it is impossible to determine how all parties involved will receive or interpret what is being communicated, it is impossible to determine all the possible short-term and long-term consequences of a communication. On the one hand, he may risk his job and a promotion. On the other hand, he may risk his friendship with Joyce and the ministry he and Mindy have developed toward her. Despite the risks, Herb has an obligation to look for an ethical approach. Joyce has the universal right to be told the truth and to be treated with dignity. The Christian ethic calls for fair and honest actions between the Christian and others. The mandate to do unto others as you would have them do unto you requires that a solution must be found that treats all parties in an ethical way.

Ethical Communication: Four Rules

As Herb seeks a solution to his dilemma, he may benefit from considering four general rules for ethical communication.

1. Never Intentionally Deceive[4]

Every member of an organization always has a responsibility to tell the truth. Certainly, Herb is not honor bound to tell all that he knows. He has a responsibility to protect the confidentiality of information shared by others. A common managerial dilemma revolves around protecting the confidentiality of one party while properly informing other interested parties. In the case of personal information, this is given legal force by privacy laws. However, if he is ethical, he cannot tell falsehoods either to Joyce or to Mr. Samoya.

2. Do Not Purposely Harm Others[5]

Herb has an ethical obligation to those with whom he communicates to ensure that he does not intentionally do them harm. Added to this is the principle of malfeasance, the carrying out of a task that one has no right to do. These conflicting important principles established the dilemma in the Herb Walker case. If he reveals what he knows about the pending sale, Mr. Samoya's sale could be jeopardized. If he remains silent, Joyce could find herself facing serious financial harm.

3. Practice "Golden Rule" Communication

Herb must sort out what he would want to have happen if he were Mr. Samoya. Similarly, he will need to "put himself in Joyce's shoes." How would he want her to communicate if the circumstances were reversed? Finding a solution that satisfies the "golden rule" of communication in both relationships will not be easy.

4. Consider the Organizational Culture[6]

Like all organizations, Samoya Enterprises, has a unique organizational culture. For example, in some organizations there are unwritten but expected dress codes at various management levels. In some there are expectations that employees will speak up or raise questions, and other organizations expect silent acquiescence to authority.

Often the organizational culture involves ethical issues. In some organizations, an employee is rewarded for standing on principle and insisting on doing what is right. For example, a company may support an employee who discovers that a potential customer intends to sell the company's products in a way that is in opposition to the company's biblically based mission statement. Even at the risk of losing the potential customer's business, the company recognizes the long-term benefits of remaining true to its mission statement.

In another organizational culture, this same employee might be expected to "toe the profit line" instead. He could expect not to be rewarded for placing principles above profits. Since Herb has worked at Samoya Enterprises long enough to know the company's expectations, he will have to include that knowledge in his analysis of what course of action to take.

> Ethical Communicators
> - Never intentionally deceive.
> - Do not purposely harm others.
> - Practice "golden rule" communication.
> - Consider the organizational culture.

Toward an Ethical Christian Worldview

James 3:3–10

If we put bits into the mouths of horses so that they obey us, we guide their whole bodies as well. Look at the ships also: though they are so large and are driven by strong winds, they are guided by a very small rudder wherever the will of the pilot directs. So also the tongue is a small member, yet it boasts of great things.

How great a forest is set ablaze by such a small fire! And the tongue is a fire, a world of unrighteousness. The tongue is set among our members, straining the whole body, setting on fire the entire course of life, and set on fire by hell. For every kind of beast and bird, of reptile and sea creature, can be tamed by mankind, but no human being can tame the tongue. It is a restless evil, full of deadly poison. With it we bless our Lord and Father, and with it we curse people who are been made in the likeness of God. From the same mouth come blessing and cursing. My brothers, these ought not to be so.

What Makes a Person Perfect?

In this passage, James implies that the tongue is the key to Christian perfection. A person who learns to control the tongue has learned to please God. That person is considered to be a perfect being.

The structure of this passage is similar to the structure Jesus uses in Matthew 5. The command to use direct speaking is followed a few verses later by his encouragement to please God by means of perfection:

Let what you say be simply "Yes" or "No"; anything more than this comes from evil (Matthew 5:37).

You therefore must be perfect, as your heavenly Father is perfect (Matthew 5:48).

To make his point, James uses three illustrations. The first is a bit in a horse's mouth. A bit is a small thing compared to the overall size of the horse, yet that small device controls the entire animal. James then turns to the maritime world. A rudder is a small part of a sailing vessel, yet that small part determines the course of the entire ship. In yet another illustration, James asks his readers to consider a tiny spark that has the ability to set an entire forest ablaze. The tongue, like a bit, a rudder, or a spark, is small, but it can cause big things to happen, either good or bad. While it is a small part of the body, it's control shows one has control of his entire body.

Having established the importance to the believer of direct conversation, James then declares that "no human being can tame the tongue" (v. 8). Were this the last word on the matter, the reader would be discouraged indeed. However, James continues with a solution to the communication problem.

Who is wise and understanding among you? By his good conduct let him show his good works in the meekness of wisdom. . . . the wisdom [that comes] from above is . . . (James 3:13, 17).

James implies that while human beings cannot tame the tongue, God's working in and through human beings can facilitate a change in the use of their tongues. James offers additional illustrations designed to demonstrate the absurdity of trying to tame the tongue through self-will. Fresh water and salt water do not come from the same source. Olives cannot grow on fig trees, nor figs on grapevines (vv. 11–12). Similarly, righteousness does not emanate from an unrighteous being. Only those totally controlled by God have the ability to use the tongue in ways that please him (vv. 15–18).

Ethical Dilemma

What happens when interpersonal communication runs the risk of harming others?

As Herb searches for the best course of action in communicating with Mr. Samoya and Joyce Wilson, he will want to consider the importance of godly communication.

Ask the Pro

Before retiring, Clarence Southcutt served as a high school principal for twenty-four years. Prior to that, he was an assistant principal for four years. Currently he chairs the board of directors of a local state bank.

Clarence and his wife have been active in a local Nazarene church for forty-five years. He has served the church on a variety of committees and in other leadership roles. The authors asked Clarence for his insights on the Herb Walker case. Our conversation follows:

Q: Before we talk about the solution to this dilemma, let's discuss the case itself. How "real life" is this scenario in your estimation?

Southcutt: There are tremendous parallels to real life. I have certainly been asked to keep secrets. And, sometimes, you can do that. But when it affects people's lives, their income, or their retirement, that's a totally different story. For example, I believe the severance package in this case is totally inadequate. People need time to prepare for a thing like that.

Q: Are you suggesting that if Herb doesn't talk, he is a part of that inadequacy?

Southcutt: Yes.

Q: How would you analyze Herb Walker's dilemma?

Southcutt: Remember, Herb came up through the ranks of this business. He has worked with people at all levels. He probably was raised in the local community. He has an obligation to the people he has worked with.

Q: You mean as a Christian?

Southcutt: No, I think he has that obligation whether he is a Christian or not.

Q: So, what should Herb do?

Southcutt: Herb needs to go to Mr. Samoya and say, "I can't keep this confidence under these conditions. I have too much at stake to remain silent. It's not just about my promotion to plant manager, but about all these people who are involved."

Q: Won't that cost him the promotion?

Southcutt: If it does, so be it. That's the downside. I think he would likely lose the position. On the other hand, no one can take away his education and experience. They can only take his integrity, if he allows it. I think it is possible that Mr. Samoya might have an even greater respect for Herb. He may call the new owners and say, "Wow, you really have something in that Herb Walker. Let me tell you about his integrity."

Q: Is there no in-between? Could he sit down with Mr. Samoya and say, "I need your permission to tell just one employee"?

Southcutt: Well, I suppose he could, but I don't think that is enough. All the people he has worked with trust him. I think he has an ethical responsibility to tell the people what he knows that is about to impact their lives.

Q: Did Herb overstep his bounds and get too close to Joyce as an employee? Did he violate a good ethic with regard to fraternization?

Southcutt: I don't think so at all. As a Christian, he was just reaching out to someone in need. That's what we are called to do.

Q: How about Mr. Samoya? Did he behave unethically when he said, "I'm going to tell you something, but you can't tell"?

Southcutt: That's harder to say. I'd like to know more about him and his motivations. I do think that when Herb heard those words, they should have acted as a red flag. As soon as he heard those words, he should have been on guard. Sometimes you can agree to abide by that, but sometimes you have to say, "Sorry, I can't agree to keep quiet." That's where Herb is now. He has to find a way to tell what he knows.

You Be the Consultant

Help Herb decide on the best course of action by studying and answering these questions:

1. Is Herb's relationship with Joyce appropriate? What are the ethical limits of employee fraternization?

2. What are the ethical limits of receiving or keeping secrets? Should Herb have stopped Mr. Samoya before he ever received the information about the sale of the business?

3. What do you see as Herb's best course of action at this point?

4. How might a follower of utilitarianism advise Herb to handle this situation? Compare and contrast that advice to what might be expected from two relevant scriptural principles from Chapter 4.

5. Is your personal statement of ethics adequate to deal with this situation? If yes, what parts and how? If no, what might you add to your personal statement of ethics to address this situation, and how would the revision address the issue presented here?

Endnotes

1. Greg Alger and Jessica Bunette-Lemon, "Ethics in the Real World: An Upcoming Training Program Will Help Communicators Understand and Develop Ethical Business Practices," *Communication World* 23, no. 5 (September–October 2006): 28–29.
2. Emory A Griffin, *Making Friends and Making Them Count* (Downers Grove, IL: InterVarsity, 1987), 18–24.
3. Charles R. Berger and Richard J. Calabrese, "Some Explorations in Initial Interaction and Beyond: Toward a Developmental Theory of Interpersonal Communication," *Human Communication Research* 1 (1975): 99–112.
4. Gary L. Kreps, *Organizational Communication*, 2nd ed. (New York: Longman, 1990), 250.
5. Kreps, *Organizational Communication,* 250.
6. Wilma Mathews, "What Should I Tell Them?: Why Every Organization Should Have an Official Policy for Communicating," *Communication World* 21, no. 3 (May–June 2004): 46–60.

Notes

16

The Christian Manager as Ethical Team Builder

Two are better than one, because they have a good reward for their toil.

— Ecclesiastes 4:9

Chapter Challenges

A careful examination of Chapter 16 should enable the reader to:

- Understand the concept of a work team.
- Identify several characteristics of a work team.
- Recognize four important rules of ethics for work team leaders.

Case Study

Pit Stop Northeast

"We think it would just be fairer to Randy, and we're all willing, so we propose to start tomorrow and rotate on a daily basis." Al Jenson spoke for the group, addressing regional manager Fred Bayon during the weekly staff meeting at Pit Stop's northeast branch.

Pit Stop operated five establishments at various locations throughout the city. Each location offered ten-minute oil changes and a variety of services and automotive accessories to busy auto owners. As regional manager, Fred provided general supervision for all five locations. He visited each of the five on an as-needed basis, ordering inventory and dealing with any personnel issues or customer complaints.

Pit Stop Northeast operated without a site manager. A team made up of four employees handled day-to-day operations. Fred suggested the team approach when the site manager quit nearly a year ago. Although the other four Pit Stops continued to have a single site manager in charge of the daily operation, Northeast had gotten along well using Fred's model. In fact, the success of the team approach at Northeast had captured the attention of corporate management. The team idea was now being tried in other cities. Fred believed he was in line for a promotion as soon as there was an opening at the corporate headquarters.

Fred encouraged the team concept at Northeast. For example, he paid a monthly bonus to the manager of the store that did the most volume that month. At Northeast, he split the bonus among the four members of the team. He constantly reminded the four employees at Northeast to think like a team.

A Perplexing Proposal

Listening to Al and seeing the looks on the faces of the other Northeast team members, Fred found himself thinking, "My teamwork idea is about to backfire for the first time."

At Northeast, each employee had specific job responsibilities. The same was true at all Pit Stop locations. Fred believed this concept worked especially well at Northeast. Since there was no site manager, each employee was personally responsible for one of four specific areas.

Operator 1 was the pit operator, whose job included all of the undercar duties. He pulled the oil plug and performed the greasing work. Of the four jobs, the pit operator's job was the dirtiest and most unpleasant. On a busy day, operator 1 often did not come up to ground level for several hours at a time. Randy Temple worked the pit at the Northeast location.

Bruce King was the second operator at Northeast. He swept the inside of the vehicle and cleaned the windows inside and out. It was also operator 2's job to check the tire pressure on each vehicle.

The third operator performed the underhood functions, which included checking fluid levels and belts. In addition, operator 3 put oil back in the vehicle. Al Jensen worked this job at Northeast.

The key to sales at all Pit Stop locations was the fourth member of the team. Operator 4 interacted with the customers. In addition, operator 4 completed all the necessary paperwork and sold additional services to customers. The real profit at any Pit Stop location came through the sale of such accessories as wiper blades, bulbs, belts, hoses, and filters. Operator 4 noted the need for these items and gained the customer's approval for replacement.

A few months earlier, Fred hired Stacy Jaggers to work as operator 4 at Northeast. Since Stacy had joined the team, sales jumped significantly. She worked well with customers, knew automobiles, and projected both a positive and confident image. While he was careful in not saying so, Fred believed he had demonstrated a stroke of genius when he hired a female to sell to the predominantly male customers at Pit Stop Northeast. In fact, Fred had been working on plans to replace the sales/services operators at his other stores with the most knowledgeable and attractive female employees he could find.

However, for the moment those plans took a "backseat" in Fred's thinking. The Northeast team had just made a proposal at the weekly staff meeting to begin a daily rotation of the four operators. That meant that three out of four days, Stacy would not be with the customers. Fred feared plummeting sales.

"Randy has such a dirty and nasty spot," Al said. "You have always emphasized that we are a team and should think creatively, with everyone being responsible for the whole operation. Well, we just think daily rotation would work well for us."

"Another benefit," Bruce added, "is that everyone will know every position. Remember last month, when Randy called in sick? It took us a couple of vehicles to get up to speed, because we weren't used to doing his job. This way, everyone will know every job."

Put on the Spot

"I don't know," Fred hesitated. "It seems to me that, by rotating, no one will be responsible for anything."

"Just the opposite," Randy corrected. "Since we're a team, everyone will still bear responsibility for the entire operation. Besides, we will feel more like we really *are* a team—not just hearing that word from you all the time." The group smiled knowingly.

"You *are* a team," Fred bristled. "I just dislike tinkering with the most productive Pit Stop staff in the city. Also, you have earned the monthly productivity bonus the last three months. I hate to see you risk losing that extra income."

After allowing the potential loss of revenue to sink in for a few moments, Fred continued. "Stacy, you're the best at what you do in the entire Pit Stop organization. Do you really want to rotate to the pit?"

"I'm willing," Stacy responded. "Not that it is my life's goal to work down there, but you *have* stressed teamwork. I'm willing to do my part for the team."

"What do you say, boss?" Al challenged. "Can we rotate starting tomorrow?"

On Background

Work Teams

Fred's reluctance to wholeheartedly endorse the Pit Stop Northeast employees' idea for rotation may indicate a potential ethical problem. His reluctance also may demonstrate a misunderstanding of the *work team* concept.

> *Work team*: basic production unit that builds tasks and organizations around processes instead of functions.

Harvey Seifter tells the story of team building at the San Diego Zoo.[1] When Douglas Meyers took over as executive director of that organization it had more than fifty separate departments—each with unique responsibilities from building maintenance to animal care. Meyers began to integrate the people into teams and train team members to do all of the necessary tasks. The result was a much more efficient overall organization.

In *Human Resource Development*, Jeff Hornsby says, "The basis of work teams is that jobs and organizations should be designed around processes instead of functions, and that the basic production unit should be the team, not the department."[2] Work teams build tasks and organizations around processes, leading to the achievement of organizational goals instead of functions within a department. At Pit Stop, the individual functions of four operators have remained the primary focus in spite of "team talk." Al, Bruce, Randy, and Stacy now propose shifting to a process orientation. They want to begin to view processing vehicles as paramount to each individual doing a particular task. Further, they believe the adjustment will increase their satisfaction level in the workplace.

How Work Teams Work

Fred must recognize several key characteristics of work teams as he makes what could become a very crucial decision with ethical dimensions.

Work Teams Build Synergy

Synergy is a term that grew out of the chemistry of medical science. It is the phenomenon that occurs when the effect of a combination of chemicals is larger than the sum of the individual effects of the chemicals. This is why your doctor may tell you not to take certain combinations of medicines or not to drink certain beverages and take certain chemicals at the same time.

This idea is applied to business when some type of team or cooperative approach is used. The synergetic result is that the people working together and building on each other's ideas and strengths will produce greater positive results than if these people had worked independently, assuming that the people are working toward a common, mutually advantageous goal. The strength of the combination is always greater than the sum of the strength of the independent parts. This concept is graphically demonstrated in a numerical formula. In highly effective work teams:

$$1 + 1 > 2$$

Work Teams Develop over Time

Fred should also consider that work teams take time to develop. No team becomes highly effective just because a manager orders it into being. Work teams develop over time through several distinct and predictable stages. Most teams demonstrate at least four stages:[3]

- Formation: in this stage, groups develop the rules for interaction and become accustomed to working with fellow team members.
- Conflict: in this stage, groups often grow tired of one another and threaten to unravel due to conflict.
- Integration: here work groups go back and forth between conflict and performance. Together, team members develop the standards for effective operation.
- Performance: in this stage, groups set their own work goals and maximize their potential for productivity.

Every highly effective group must pass through each of these successive stages on its way to maximum productivity. Managers must allow the process to "play out." For example, it may be tempting to abandon the work team concept during the conflict stage. This stage takes a great deal of time, and conflict resolution can seem to sidetrack the team from its main purpose. But highly effective work teams have learned to work through the conflict stage. Subsequently, they can anticipate and derail conflict better.

Perhaps Northeast has come closer to the performance stage than Fred realizes. He also should consider that the recent increases in productivity might be more directly attributable to group performance than to the gender or skills of one individual team member.

Work Teams Meet with Resistance

Finally, Fred needs to be aware that the most common barrier of work team performance is a lack of management commitment. Most managers verbally endorse the team approach but demonstrate a high resistance to change when organizational work groups are implemented.

In some cases, circumstances justify such resistance. Highly specialized functions, for example, do not lend themselves to cross-functional work teams that use cross-training among the various team tasks. For example, if one member of the Pit Stop team was required to read high-tech instruments or perform some other task requiring a high degree of training, the cross-functional team concept might prove less useful if not all team members had the same level of training.

Work Team Ethics

In addition to understanding this basic background on work teams, Fred needs to consider four important ethical aspects of work teams. Here we focus on the role of team leaders; they should:

Clearly Define the Parameters of Team Activity

"You will never have a dream team unless you have a blueprint for a dream team."[4] From the beginning, ethical team builders ask and answer these kinds of questions:

- Is the team ongoing or single issue in its breadth of operation?
- Is the team empowered to make changes or only to make recommendations?
- Does the team have product development authority?
- Can the team adjust current marketing strategies?
- Does the team have authority to alter work rules?
- Is the team permitted to discipline one of its own members?

All such questions should have clearly communicated answers early in a work team's development.

Exercise Patience

Since teams do not instantly attain high performance, management must allow for the development of work team effectiveness. Ultimately, synergy kicks in, but the development curve may be longer than the team leader intended.

Provide Empowerment Commensurate with Responsibility

Teams often are held responsible for certain job-related decisions or processes but are not provided adequate resources of time, money, or personnel to accomplish the task with maximum effectiveness. The ethical team leader acknowledges the need for an appropriate level of resources.

Recognize Their Personal Responsibility

Team building can become a hiding place for ineffective managers who declare, "I'm not responsible for that. I gave it to a team." With teams, as with individuals, managers may delegate authority, but not ultimate responsibility for the productivity and decisions of the team.

Characteristics of Ethical Team Leaders
- Clearly define the parameters of the team in advance.
- Exercise patience.
- Provide empowerment commensurate with responsibility.
- Recognize personal responsibility for the team.

Toward an Ethical Christian Worldview

Ecclesiastes 4:9–12

> *Two are better than one, because they have a good reward for their toil. For if they fall, one will lift up his fellow. But woe to him who is alone when he falls and has not another to help him up! Again, if two lie together, they keep warm, but how can one keep warm alone? And though a man might prevail against one who is alone, two will withstand him— a threefold cord is not quickly broken.*

The theme of the entire book of Ecclesiastes involves the futility of selfishness. Solomon found everything in life to be meaningless, or, as he put it, "Vanity of vanities" (1:2), until he discovered as the "end of the matter": "Fear God and keep his commandments" (12:13). In God, Solomon discovered purpose and meaning in life.

Ironically, as he struggled with his own selfish nature and the emptiness it brought to his life, he discovered something that brought temporary relief as he moved toward a more permanent solution in God. That temporary improvement involved teamwork.

The Threefold Cord of Teamwork

This passage points to how teamwork yields important positive results. These include accomplishment (v. 9), support (v. 10), warmth in the presence of cold (v. 11), and defense (v. 12). Each of these benefits comes in spite of the overall meaninglessness of life. In short, teamwork works.

How can a manager maintain an ethical teamwork atmosphere?

Solomon concludes that a "threefold cord" is not easily broken. If it is true that two heads are better than one, aren't three heads an even more beneficial arrangement? Solomon seems to think so.

Solomon's wisdom suggests the value of teamwork. What Solomon fails to address, however, are the limits of teamwork. At what point do the advantages of specialization and hierarchy of leadership outweigh the advantages of teamwork? That is the question that Fred Bayon must answer at Pit Stop. Apparently his answer must come very quickly.

Ask the Pro

Carmen Medina is in her eleventh year as head coach of a university volleyball team. Her lifetime record is 415 wins against only 110 losses. Coach Medina has led teams to the National Tournament four times, achieving an Elite Eight distinction. She holds a doctor of education degree from a mid-western University.

Carmen grew up in a small town, where she continues to play an active role. She has served in recent years on a variety of committees and has assumed a host of leadership responsibilities.

The authors sat down in the University Grill with Medina to discuss the team development concepts of the Pit Stop case. The results of that conversation follow:

Q: What are the issues of this case as you see them?

Medina: There is a conflict between allowing people autonomy to carry on, and having someone who is responsible for keeping the main goal or mission statement before them. It appears to me that rotating, as they perceive it, might put people in jobs for which they are not qualified. You might say this is an idea that threatens the quality control of the business.

Q: Does the team-building concept have natural limitations?

Medina: Of course. Ultimately, there has to be someone in charge. Decentralization is great, but all the goals have to stay in harmony, or it won't work.

Q: Since on the volleyball court the goal obviously is to win, is such a scenario unlikely?

Medina: Not at all. At Pit Stop the goal is financial gain. The problem is that employees, like players, have different perceptions of how they can best get to that goal.

For example, a freshman in our system usually takes very little leadership on the court. I had one a few years ago, however, who was a defensive starter and a very verbal leader. The captains took charge in an early match and simply told her to keep quiet. As leaders, they were attempting to instill proper respect for program process and getting a functioning unit in place. However, the results at half-time were devastating. She became timid and noncommunicative. We unraveled. I had to step in and say, "As a team we have some misunderstandings about leadership. Let's talk about how we lead and the best way to communicate with one another."

Q: So, like Fred Bayon, you had asked for a team attitude, then stepped in and said, "Wait a minute, that's not exactly what I had in mind."

Medina: Exactly! Now, the key for Fred is communication. *How* he says "Good idea, but we're not doing it" is very important.

Q: How would you suggest he approach that?

Medina: I would bring them all in, since they are all stakeholders in the decision. I would focus on the part of their recommendation that is good. Further, he needs to explain that he must retain enough decision-making power to accomplish business goals. I might suggest a compromise where they do dual roles rather than a full rotation. That uses the best of their idea within limits and keeps the rotation from allowing people to be in areas where they are not qualified.

Q: Do you see a gender ethics issue in this case?

Medina: I looked at that very carefully, because it seems to be on the borderline. As it stands, I don't see a gender ethics issue. I wonder if some of Stacy's co-workers aren't suggesting that she ought to do some of the dirty work, too. But if Bayon isn't asking her to dress a certain way in order to get the attention of the male customers, or something like that which is not discussed here, then I decided he's okay. It could be that she is just a good people person regardless of gender.

You Be the Consultant

As you consider Fred's concerns, examine them in light of these questions:

1. Which specific secular and Scripture-based ethical principles should Fred consider as he contemplates the proposal of the Northeast team? When might an ethical manager refuse to adopt a team proposal?

2. How would you characterize Fred's attitude toward Stacy and her performance? Is his attitude ethical? How would a Kantian agree or disagree? How about someone who applies utilitarianism?

3. Which stakeholders need to be considered as Fred makes the decision about rotation? What are the implications to each stakeholder?

4. Is your personal statement of ethics adequate for Fred to resolve this dilemma? Support your answer by explaining which principles in your statement relate and how. If your statement of ethics is not adequate, make necessary addition(s) to make it more comprehensive.

Endnotes

1. Harvey Seifter, *Leadership Ensemble: Lessons in Collaborative Management from the World's Only Conductorless Orchestra* (New York: Time, 2001), 123–25.
2. Jeff Hornsby, *Human Resource Development* (Muncie, IN: T.I.S., 2001), 98.
3. P. Buhler, "Group Membership," *Supervision* (May 1994): 8–10.
4. Dave Timmons, "The Art of Business Leadership: Truth, Truth, and More Truth," *Women in Business* 57, no. 1 (January–February 2005): 45.

17

The Christian Manager as Ethical Motivator

So we built the wall. And all the wall was joined together to half its height,
for the people had a mind to work.

— Nehemiah 4:6

Chapter Challenges

A careful examination of Chapter 17 should enable the reader to:

- Recognize the difference between motivation and manipulation.
- Understand the characteristics of ethical motivation.

Case Study

Workman's Benefit Insurance Company

Jim Johnson glanced at his watch as he pulled into the driveway at 1104 South Street. He didn't want to be late for his very first appointment. Last Friday afternoon he had finished the two-week orientation course with Workman's Benefit Insurance Company. This beautiful Monday morning marked his first day as a full-fledged claims adjuster. Workman's Benefit had assigned Jim to a five-state area to handle all of its disability claims.

Workman's Benefit specialized in low-cost disability insurance for blue-collar workers. Usually the policies were sold door-to-door in lower middle-class neighborhoods like the one in which Jim now found himself. Often the agents made weekly premium collection visits to the homes of the insured.

The policies were a specialized disability insurance that promised to pay only in the event of a work-related injury. The schedule of benefits varied depending upon the extent of the disabling injury. For example, the company promised to pay one hundred dollars per month for life for the loss of a finger. The benefits increased to a maximum of two thousand dollars per month for life in the event of a total and permanent disability.

Jim's task as claims adjuster included verifying the disability by means of personal interview and medical record research. In addition, he represented Workman's Benefit in an attempt to "buy out" legitimate claims by offering up-front cash settlements. Of course the buyouts cost the company less in the long run than the promised monthly benefits.

In his very first full-time job since graduating from college, Jim looked forward to handling several large buyouts very soon. The old-timers said that claim adjusters made a name for themselves in the company and increased their opportunity for advancement by arranging buyouts that saved Workman's Benefit huge sums of money. These buyouts also were advantageous to Jim. Besides his small cash salary, Workman's Benefit would pay him a percentage of the savings in the form of a bonus for each buyout. If he could favorably handle a few major claims, Jim hoped to repay the bulk of his education loans in just a few months.

An Up-Front Settlement

Jim knocked on the door of the little bungalow belonging to Moses Engels. Since the verification of total and permanent disability was not in question, during today's visit Jim hoped to convince the fifty-seven-year-old Engels to take significantly less than the two thousand dollars per month to which the policy entitled him. The actuarial outlook revealed that Workman's Benefit stood to pay Moses nearly four hundred thousand dollars in lifetime benefits.

Moses Engels's daughter, Sherry, greeted Jim at the door. "Thank you for coming, Mr. Johnson," she said as she showed Jim to a chair in the cramped and cluttered living room. "Could I get you some coffee?"

"No thanks," Jim responded. "If you don't mind, I'd like to get down to business with your father."

"Dad will be right in," Sherry acknowledged. "Actually, my father has only a sixth-grade education and is not very adept at business matters. I work with him on all but the most routine decisions. While I don't have power of attorney, my father and I get along very well in this relationship. Here he is now," she noted as Moses Engels entered the room.

Jim rose and greeted Mr. Engels. After some casual small talk, Jim stated his purpose in being at the Engels home. "Workman's Benefit has authorized me to offer you a very large sum of money right now as settlement for your injuries. We don't want to see you wait on those small monthly checks."

"There are a lot of medical bills right now," Moses responded. "One doctor charged me almost three hundred dollars for one office visit. Can you imagine a man making three hundred dollars an hour?"

"Ridiculous, isn't it, sir?" Jim readily agreed.

"Daddy," Sherry said, "we've already talked about all those bills. I understand that they are a worry to you, but if I take care of those and pay off the house, then you will have all you need from your monthly check."

"Girl, that's nearly fifteen thousand dollars," Moses interrupted. "It ain't right for a grown man to take charity, especially from his own young-uns."

"Daddy, we'll talk later," Sherry said, speaking with finality. Turning to Jim, she continued, "Mr. Johnson, we are really not interested in any up-front settlements, regardless of how generous. My father needs the monthly cash flow to manage more than ever since the accident. Thank you, though, for coming."

She stood and extended a hand. It was clear the meeting had ended. Jim made his way to the door. Not exactly the outcome he had hoped to report to Workman's Benefit in his first day's report.

Not one to accept temporary setbacks as permanent defeat, within a few hours Jim hit upon an idea. He stopped at a local department store and purchased a large two-suit suitcase. After a couple of calls to the home office, he received a wire from Workman's Benefit for fifteen thousand dollars, which he cashed in small bills. Carefully he placed the money in the suitcase. After calling ahead to confirm that Sherry had left her father's house, he returned to 1104 South Street.

"Mr. Engels," he greeted Moses, "I've been thinking about our earlier conversation, and your very honorable desire to not take charity from your children. Workman's Benefit would like to help. I think I have found a way that you can pay those bills yourself. In fact, one quick signature, and you could be debt free. May I come in?"

On Background

Motivation vs. Manipulation

The Workman's Benefit case describes the interaction between Jim Johnson and Moses Engels, two men who have very different goals and objectives with regard to a personal injury claim. At issue is ethical behavior in the area of *motivation*. Motivation comes into play when a claims adjuster meets a claimant. Of course, motivation is relevant in many other kinds of relationships; for example, between employer and employee, salesperson and customer, or parent and child. In fact, in any situation in which two people hope to convince one another of something, persuasion takes place. Therefore, motivation comes into play and ethics becomes an issue.

The Motivation Continuum

Before attempting to define ethical motivation, we first should look at motivation in general. The word *motivation* comes from the root word *motive*, something that moves or compels us to action. Motivation occurs along a continuum between the behavioral extremes of inner drive and manipulation. Figure 17.1 demonstrates this continuum.

Figure 17.1. Continuum of Motivation Possibilities

Continuum of Motivation Possibilities

Inner Drive				Manipulation
-10	-5	0	5	10

Inner Drive

We often associate motivation with varying degrees of natural inner drive. We sometimes say, "She is highly motivated," or, "The position requires a motivated self-starter." Such statements recognize an innate characteristic related to degrees of ambition. For example, Jim Johnson seems to be motivated by a drive to become a successful claims adjuster, one who intends to pay off educational loans in the process. On the other hand, Moses Engels appears to be motivated by the desire for independence. Presumably no one dangled these goals before either man. Instead, these goals are internalized as part of the individual's makeup.

Manipulation

At the opposite end of the motivation continuum is *manipulation*. In its most benign sense, to manipulate means to manage or use skillfully. However, the word *manipulation* today often carries negative overtones. We call someone who attempts to control a situation to his or her own advantage a manipulative person. At its most extreme, it becomes coercion. For example, contracts executed at the point of a gun have long been held to be invalid due to duress. One party *manipulated* rather than *motivated* the other to sign the contract.

A *New York Times* article describes manipulative bosses.[1] According to the article, such bosses usually fit into one of four categories. Snakes may smile to your face but will stab you in the back. Screamers are given to public displays of temper. They use these temper tantrums to keep subordinates in line. The third group of manipulators is called nitpickers. These bosses are constantly criticizing and undermining. Finally, the gatekeepers pick favorites and keep everyone else in line with frustration and abuse.

> *Motivation*: drive that compels a person to action.
> *Manipulation*: extreme form of motivation that is sometimes seen as coercion.

Ethical Motivation

It seems clear that manipulation is not ethical. What requires more careful analysis is determining which behaviors along the continuum of motivational possibilities are ethical and which fall outside the bounds of acceptable ethics. In *Communication Ethics: Methods of Analysis*, James A. Jaksa and Michael S. Pritchard say, "We want persuaders to be honest, disclosing important and relevant information for the case at hand."[2]

What constitutes ethical motivation? The following are guidelines for managers with high ethical standards:

Communicate Your Own Goals

In and of itself, the desire to be successful and to earn money is not unethical. In fact, Nobel laureate and economist Milton Friedman argues that earning profits may be the ethical thing to do in some circumstances.[3] Dr. Friedman has often stated that a primary fiduciary responsibility of managers is to make as much money as possible for the company's owners without breaking the law or violating moral standards. Making consistent profits is good for the economy and protects the jobs of the employees. However, attempting to hide profit-oriented motives behind more altruistic intentions is unethical.

For example, a used car salesman may say to a prospective buyer, "I really couldn't care less about the commission I make; I just want you to have the best car possible." That salesperson may be viewed with greater suspicion than a competitor who declares, "Of course I want to sell you a car! That's how I make my living. But I also hope to help you find the best car possible."

Consider the Goals of Other Stakeholderss

One manager's ethical statement declared that the key to leadership lies in finding out what people want and then helping them obtain those things. He felt that the nature of the things desired made no difference whatsoever. As long as he helped others achieve these desires, in his view he was behaving ethically.

That manager holds a rather extreme understanding of ethical behavior. Some people want things that are illegal. Others may want what is not in their best interests. This is an inadequate view in that it has no boundaries and does not require the manager to confront the issues at hand. The ethical motivator, however, considers the ethicality of the other person's goals as they relate to the greater good before developing a motivational strategy. The ethical motivator further recognizes that "Most people who succeed in significant areas do not succeed because of a desire for money."[4] Experts in motivation generally categorize people's desires according to levels of need. Maslow's hierarchy of needs, explained in his landmark 1954 work *Motivation and Personality*, is an example of this concept. It suggests that there is a hierarchy or ranking of importance of human needs. Maslow listed them, in order of importance, as these: physiological, safety, love and belonging, esteem, and self-actualization.[5] Until one level of need has been satisfied, the next level does not serve to motivate.

Our most basic needs are *physiological*—food, water, avoidance of pain, for example—which serve to keep our bodies healthy and alive. If these needs are not met, a person will typically be consumed with a desire to meet them and will be able to care about little, if anything, else. Those who have experienced the temporary trauma of "having the wind knocked out" of them know that in that moment of airlessness nothing matters but the desire to breathe. Homeless people will search restaurant dumpsters for leftovers, their need for food overwhelming any embarrassment they might feel.

According to Maslow, the next need is for *safety,* to have security and stability in what can be a chaotic world. Abused children often have developmental problems. They "freeze" at the point at which the abuse began, unable to seek satisfaction of their higher needs. Students living in high-crime areas often are more concerned with their day-to-day safety than with their teachers' urgings to "live up to their potential." What good is it to study for a test if I won't be alive tomorrow to take it?

Love and belonging needs follow safety. Humans crave interaction, acceptance, and membership in groups. Once the basic physiological and safety needs are met, humans reach out to other humans for validation and support. To what lengths did you go as a teen to be accepted by your peers? Think of the social groups to which you belong and how you would feel if you were rejected by one of them.

Next is the *esteem need*. Humans desire recognition for their abilities and achievements, both from within themselves and from others. Reaching a certain goal or mastering a particular skill makes us feel good about ourselves. We also want others to acknowledge our successes. A man who has received a promotion and a hefty salary increase may purchase an expensive car. The unspoken message to all who see the car is, I make a lot of money, and I am successful. I have power."

The final need Maslow discussed is *self-actualization*. This need drives people to seek their true purpose in life by "being all they can be" and by rising above the mass of humanity and being different. Robert Gwynne points out that "it is usually middle-class to upper-class students who take up environmental causes, join the Peace Corps, go off to a monastery, etc."[6] Their other needs are adequately met, and their motivation is to fulfill their maximum physical, spiritual, or intellectual potential.

To motivate employees, it is helpful to identify and address their levels of need. Doing so can prevent ineffective effort expended on false motivators — rewards that management erroneously believes to be of interest to employees. The higher needs of love, belonging, self-worth, and prestige are often ignored by approaches to motivation that rely solely on financial rewards such as pay increases, increased medical or retirement benefits, or child care. Maslow's thesis would say that these types of motivators lose their potency as employees' personal and family situations improve beyond the point of survival issues. When these basic needs of employees are met, managers must both recognize the need for and develop motivational strategies that address professional self-fulfillment issues.

The needs of an individual must be met at one level before that person is motivated to move to the next level. Recognizing another person's level of need helps the motivator be successful. Such awareness also increases the necessity for ethical persuasive or motivating behavior. An ethical manager will regard employees as God-created individuals and will exercise care in the use of that knowledge in open, nonmanipulative ways. This knowledge of employees can be used in negative ways, especially when company systems divide motivation into reward and punishment systems. To a person known to be having trouble providing the basic needs for her family, the threat of time off without pay may be a very effective motivational tool. But is that use of knowledge regarding need ethical?

Be a Skilled Listener

Most people agree on the importance of listening. Surprisingly, many managers fail to listen effectively. People's words and nonverbal communications provide clues to their goals. The careful listener can be well ahead of peers in determining whether or not communication is being properly understood.

One can learn to become a more effective listener. Learning and practicing these three listening skills can set the stage for more ethical motivational strategies:

- Listen with all of the senses. "Listen" to verbal communication; as well as body language and facial expressions. Someone may respond, "Oh, I'm fine," while wringing her hands and blinking nervously. These physical signs tell you that the person is *not* fine.
- Control *thinking speed*. We think three times faster than we speak. The good listener fills the available time with feedback that enhances communication. The listener may be analyzing the speaker's content, reflecting on the emotions evoked by the speaker's content or delivery style, or otherwise focusing on the speaker and the information being communicated. However, many people let their minds wander to other topics when someone else is speaking.

- Delay evaluation. Skilled listeners avoid jumping to conclusions about what the other person is saying. They postpone evaluation until after totally digesting the message.

Balance Rewards and Punishments

Experts agree that both rewards and punishments can serve to motivate effectively. For example, the reward of more money can motivate an employee to work longer hours. The fear of being fired can motivate an employee to avoid making personal phone calls during work hours.

Ethical managers use a combination of rewards and punishments to motivate. Using only punishment may serve to cheapen human life, and punishments lose their effectiveness over time. Using only rewards may ignore the original nature of every human being. The Bible is replete with examples of people such as Adam, David, and Solomon who illustrate this point. They received the positive rewards of God; even so, they deviated from desired behavior.

Wrap-Up

Even when using these four guidelines, managers often face difficult decisions in their motivational roles. Motivating people means exercising the power of persuasion. Walking the continuum between inner drive and manipulation can present great challenges to the Christian manager who seeks to apply an integrated ethic in his or her role as motivator.

Ethical Motivators

- Communicate personal goals.
- Consider others' goals.
- Listen.
- Balance rewards and punishments.

Toward an Ethical Christian Worldview

Nehemiah 4:6

So we built the wall. And all the wall was joined together to half its height, for the people had a mind to work.

Perhaps nowhere in Scripture is there such a powerful account of motivation than in the book of Nehemiah. According to the book that bears his name, Nehemiah, a Jew, served in the palace as cupbearer to the Persian king Artaxerxes. The walls of Jerusalem were still in ruins and the safety of those "back home" weighed heavily on Nehemiah. Once convinced of his God-appointed role to rebuild, Nehemiah gained the permission of the king to lead a work team to Jerusalem. Under Nehemiah's capable leadership, the monumental task of completing the wall was accomplished in just fifty-two days! (see Nehemiah 1–6).

A Mind to Work

Nehemiah acknowledged that the accomplishment was because the "people had a mind to work."

After a century and a half of inactivity, why did the people all of the sudden have a mind to work? The answer lies clearly in the superior motivational skills of Nehemiah. He caused the people to see the divine appointment under which they labored. He gave appropriate recognition and credit to those who achieved goals. He effectively divided the labor to facilitate incremental accomplishment.

How can a manager motivate employees while maintaining integrity?

He skillfully overcame obstacles, whether physical, mental, or emotional. In short, he proved to be a superior motivator.

As Jim Johnson seeks to motivate Moses Engels and others in order to accomplish his life goals, he should take a lesson from Nehemiah. One has to wonder how the godly Nehemiah would view Johnson's approach thus far.

Ask the Pro

Twenty years ago Randell Sweetser sold his first policy as an independent insurance agent. Today his office services more than five thousand policies for automobile, home, health, life, and business coverages and has grown to the second largest of its kind in his state.

Randell holds a bachelor's degree in business management from a Christian liberal arts university. He and his wife have four children. He attends a large Wesleyan church and serves on the board of directors of its private school.

The authors asked Randell for his perspective on the situation at Workman's Benefit Insurance Company. The results of that conversation appear below:

Q: How realistic is the Workman's Benefit scenario? Surely, what Jim Johnson is trying to do in this scenario would not be attempted in real life.

Sweetser: You'd be surprised. I'm not directly involved in the claims process, but there are certainly individuals and companies out there who search for ways to avoid paying a claim. One of the reasons I chose the company that I am with is that it is a fair company. This scenario would not develop.

Q: Is Johnson's behavior against the law?

Sweetser: No, but he has crossed a line of ethical propriety. The daughter made it very clear that Moses needs the monthly cash flow. For Johnson to go back later when the daughter is not there and blatantly appeal to Mr. Engels's emotions is wrong.

Q: Nevertheless, if it's not illegal, won't he get away with it?

Sweetser: If Johnson lived in my state and were turned into the Department of Insurance by the daughter, in my opinion he would very likely be suspended or at least put on probation.

Q: So this is such an ethical breach that it doesn't take a Christian worldview to identify it as wrong?

Sweetser: That's correct, no.

Q: Are there issues in your business in which being a Christian does lead to a different conclusion?

Sweetser: Being a Christian is not something you wear around on your sleeve. What would Jesus do? (WWJD) is all right, but the truth is you can bend the answers to benefit yourself. I get real tired of the hypocrisy I see among Christians in business. If you have to go around telling people you are a Christian, you are being a martyr. As a Christian in business, it is most important to treat people right. I think the Golden Rule is very important.

Q: Isn't that just good business?

Sweetser: Of course, but it is also a way of life. I deal with real human beings. Some folks in my business deal with computer screens or statistical tables. With human beings, you must add the element of compassion. Relationships become much more important for a Christian in business.

You Be the Consultant

As you consider Jim Johnson's actions, answer these questions:

1. How would the limits of ethical motivational strategies differ between those whose ethics are derived from utilitarianism and those whose ethics come from the Kantian perspective?

2. Compare and contrast Kantian ethical motivation with what the biblical principle of love would say about ethical motivation.

3. Has Jim Johnson behaved ethically in his offer to Moses Engels? Why or why not? Would his offer be more ethical if he had made it in the presence of Moses's daughter? Would the offer be more ethical if it were for more money? If so, at what dollar amount does propriety begin?

4. Is Workman's Benefit's "buyout" approach ethical? Why or why not? Provide biblical as well as philosophical evidence to support your answer.

Endnotes

1. Carey Benedict, "Fear in the Workplace: The Bullying Boss," *New York Times*, June 22, 2004.
2. James A. Jaksa and Michael S. Pritchard, *Communication Ethics: Methods of Analysis* (Belmont, CA: Wadsworth, 1985), 35.
3. Michael E. Hattersley and Linda McJannet, *Management Communication: Principles and Practice* (Boston: McGraw Hill, 1997), 211.
4. Summer Redstone, "What I've Learned," *Esquire*, January 2003, 64.
5. Abraham Maslow, "A Theory of Human Motivation," *Psychological Review* 50 (1970): 370–96.
6. Robert Gwynne, "Maslow's Hierarchy of Needs" (1997), http://cmapspublic3.ihmc. us/rid=1069526220354_1105967791_4524/maslow.htm, accessed August 21, 2012.

Notes

18

The Christian Manager as Ethical Marketer

Let the words of my mouth and the meditation of my heart be acceptable in your sight,
O Lord, my rock and my redeemer.

— Psalm 19:14

Chapter Challenges

A careful examination of Chapter 18 should enable the reader to:

- Understand and implement the five-question checklist of ethical advertising.

Case Study

Dupont Men's Wear

All Men's Suits **10% Off!**	**Back to School Special!** • • • • • • • • • • • • • **Boys' Jeans $19.95**
Get Ready for Fall! *Check Out Our Complete Line of Flannel Shirts*	**Baseball caps** *Reduced, Now Starting at Only $7.95*
DUPONT MEN'S WEAR *On the Courthouse Square • Downtown Doville*	

Ryan put the finishing touches on the ad for the Sunday paper as Karen, Ryan's wife and business partner, entered the office. "Working on the ad?" she asked, looking over his shoulder.

"Just finished," he responded. "What do you think?"

Karen studied the ad carefully. "Looks okay," she responded somewhat tentatively.

Ryan and Karen had recently taken over Dupont Men's Wear and were learning the retail business together. Karen's father, Ralph Dupont, had founded the clothing store and operated it for forty-five years. Three months ago, he had suddenly decided that it was time for him to retire.

Both Ryan and Karen had worked part time as sales associates at the store, but they had little experience in the details of operating a small business. Nor was Ralph any help. He verbalized only one stipulation when he handed them the keys and signed over the inventory. "Don't call me. I've done my time. Good luck!" He had not come into the store since.

In fact, not too many others had come into the store either. Dupont's was situated on the courthouse square of the small town of Doville, the county seat. Forty years ago Doville had been the area hub of activity. Today much of the traffic can be found at the outskirts of town, the site of several national chain stores. Ryan and Karen were learning that doing retail business in Doville's downtown area was a very difficult challenge.

An Advertising Question

"I certainly hope this ad generates some activity," Ryan mused. "Cash flow has become a major issue in the last few weeks."

"I realize things are tight," Karen said. "That's why I'm wondering about a 10 percent discount on men's suits. I'm not sure we can afford that much of a discount. After all, selling suits to Dad's repeat customers has kept us going so far."

"You're right," Ryan responded. "So we need to go with our strength. My plan is to price every suit at least 10 percent higher before we run this ad. That way, the advertisement will generate sales, but after we discount at the register, we will be right back to our regular price."

"I don't know," Karen said. "That plan sounds questionable to me. How does this idea fit into our ethics statement and our agreement to operate the business with genuine Christian values?"

Both Ryan and Karen had been Christians since their dating days. They were active in their local church and intently lived out their faith. When they had taken over the store, they had agreed to honor the Lord in everything they did.

They had carefully crafted a personal statement of ethics that served as their guide to decision making.

"I don't see any problem," Ryan replied. "As long as we get the suits marked up before we run the ad, it's just a routine price increase. Besides, we aren't twisting anyone's arm to buy at the new price. We just offer the suits, and the customer makes the decision to buy. What is unethical about that?"

"You make it sound so proper," Karen said. "So why do I feel like a kid sneaking a cookie from the cookie jar?"

Ryan shrugged. "Probably because it is business, and as we have agreed a hundred times before, you are just too sweet for the tough decisions of business." He gave her a quick kiss on the cheek. "Now, what do you say? Shall we get busy and mark those suits up?"

On Background

Ethical Advertising

In these early days of operating Dupont Men's Wear, Ryan and Karen have come face to face with one of the most controversial ethical dilemmas managers face. Some automatically consider advertising to be unethical. Others see it as just a necessary part of doing business. They argue that as a process, advertising is neither ethical nor unethical.[1]

Advertising creates a need. An ad works when it generates either consumer desire for something or a desire for *more* of something. Some Christians contrast the nature of advertising with Paul's testimony: "I have learned to be content with whatever I have" (Philippians 4:11 NRSV). Paul declares further, "There is great gain in godliness with contentment" (1 Timothy 6:6). Others would argue that advertising simply serves to inform potential customers. The advertising itself does not alter a customer's freedom to choose.

Some would argue that anything goes in advertising so long as it is legal. "Advertising is simply the exercise of free speech," they suggest. "An ad is no more or less ethical than any other information exchange, regardless of what that ad communicates."

Most managers who give thought to ethical practices fall between these two extremes. They will benefit, as will Ryan and Karen, from asking themselves five questions regarding advertising.

Is It Accurate?

Both ethical managers and the Federal Trade Commission agree that an ad must not be false or misleading. According to case law and federal regulations, total impression of the ad provides the key. To be considered ethical and legal, the total impression must not be false or misleading. For example, advertising a particular headache remedy as a cure for a headache may be improper advertisement if the product only temporarily masks the symptoms of a headache.

Is It True?

Marketers interested in an ethical approach will also consider whether an ad tells the truth. Here subtle distinctions become important. Generally the buying public anticipates and even expects a certain amount of "puffery" or puffing up to accompany a product's advertisement. A certain amount of speculation is considered acceptable and within the boundaries of ethical propriety. Misrepresentation, on the other hand, is both illegal and unethical.

Consider, for example, an advertisement that declares a particular briefcase to be "one of the finest leather cases made." If the case is made of imitation leather, the ad is untrue and unethical. If it is made of genuine leather, the "one of the finest" descriptive aspect will probably be viewed as puffery, but still ethical.

Is It Clear?

A general guideline in ethical advertisement is that the ad must be clear, even to those of a lower intellectual capacity. To intentionally confuse potential consumers in order to deceive them would violate the truthful communications corollary described in Chapter 4. A travel agency advertisement offered a free Florida vacation with every purchase of a teddy bear. When potential buyers investigated, they discovered that the teddy bear cost $2,500.00. In reality, the agency was offering a Florida vacation with a free teddy bear. While technically not illegal, most people would consider this ad to be unethical.

An advertising approach may be ethical if it is deemed to be so outrageous that no serious buyer would be confused. For example, those who drink a certain sports drink don't expect their perspiration to be the same color as the beverage—despite what the TV commercials depict. In cases like these, the advertisers are more interested in capturing the consumer's attention, creating humor, or exercising creative license than in attempting to confuse the consumer.

Is It Offensive?

Perhaps the most difficult item on the advertising ethics checklist involves the issue of offense. Since nearly everything is offensive to someone, the concept of community standards has been established to determine an ad's potential to offend. Community standards have certainly changed over time. Sometimes, advertising the majority of Americans found offensive thirty years ago often is considered harmless today (or vice versa).

Further, the concept of community standards requires geographic definition. Does a state university student body constitute an independent community? If so, does the school's newspaper determine the appropriateness of a particular advertisement based on that community alone, or does it consider the impact on the larger community outside the campus?

Perhaps the Christian manager would benefit from considering a biblical standard over a community standard. While community standards change and even scriptural interpretations change over time and geographic area, Scripture remains the same.

Is It Harmful?

Ethical advertisers acknowledge their responsibility to protect consumers. Of special interest in this category is the issue of potential harm to children. For example, some years ago the courts determined that advertisements for alcoholic beverages had the potential to harm children. As a result, such ads have been banned from those publications catering to persons under eighteen years of age. More recently, "watchdog" groups have raised questions about tobacco products carrying the same risk of harm to minors.

Some would argue that certain snack foods threaten the health of children. Should companies that manufacture these commodities be forbidden to advertise because of potential harm? When does interpretation infringe on the constitutional right of free speech? Free speech applies to advertisers, as well as to Americans in general. This right must be safeguarded.

Wrap-Up

While there may be other considerations that bear on the issue of ethical advertising, Ryan and Karen would certainly do well to begin with this checklist in determining the ethics of their newspaper advertisement. While applying these and other principles, they may also wish to consider this comment from LaRue T. Hosmer in *The Ethics of Management*: "It does not break the law is only the beginning point in making ethical decisions and not the ultimate standard."[2]

> Ethical Advertisers Ask:
>
> - Is it accurate?
> - Is it true?
> - Is it clear?
> - Is it offensive?
> - Is it harmful?

Toward an Ethical Christian Worldview

Matthew 21:12–13

And Jesus entered the temple and drove out all who sold and bought in the temple, and he overturned the tables of the money-changers and the seats of those who sold pigeons. He said to them, "It is written, 'My house shall be called a house of prayer,' but you make it a den of robbers."

The vivid details with which all four gospel writers describe Jesus's cleansing of the temple makes it one of the most dramatic accounts in all of the New Testament. Some misunderstanding of his motivation continues to create confusion in the modern church. Many conclude that Jesus's purpose involved the elimination of buying and selling in the temple area. Thus they strictly enforce a "no sales in the church building" policy in support of Jesus's attitude.

But in quoting Matthew 21:13, "You make it a den of robbers," Jesus seems to indicate a different purpose. His behavior is aimed at the elimination of dishonest commerce at any location, not so much at the elimination of commerce in the temple.

A Matter of Principle

In Jesus's day, the court surrounding the temple proper included a market where goats and sheep were sold for sacrifice. The law required that only animals declared by the high priest to be "without blemish" were appropriate for sacrifice. Everything purchased in the temple court, often at grossly inflated prices, was guaranteed for approval. By contrast, even the finest animals carried onto the premises from outside were certain to be rejected. Such abuse of power to achieve personal economic advantage stirred Jesus's ire.

Similarly, every adult male had to pay an annual temple tax of half a shekel. The tax had to be paid with a Phoenician coin. Since daily commerce operated in Greek or Roman coinage, most people had to get their money changed. Priests who operated the exchange tables were permitted to charge as much as a 15 percent fee for the exchange. Jesus objected to the impact of such unscrupulous behaviors on the common people.

Ethical Dilemma — How can a manager ethically meet the marketing demands of the enterprise?

Considering this background about honesty in business dealings, Ryan and Karen at Dupont Men's Wear should examine their advertising practices in light of Jesus's decisive action recorded in Matthew 21. They should ask themselves: "Does our intended advertising match the behavior of the temple priests in this passage, or does our behavior rise above such unscrupulous dealings?"

Ask the Pro

Bill Miller is the owner/manager of Miller's Do It Best Hardware. His grandfather began the business in 1924. Bill started working in the store in the mid-seventies after graduating from college. At that time, his father and mother owned the business. He has owned this two-employee operation for twenty-five years.

Bill and his wife attend a community church located in their small town where they team-teach a fourth-grade Sunday school class. The couple has four teenage children. The authors sat down with Bill at the store to discuss business ethics in general and the Dupont Men's Wear case in particular. Here are the results of that conversation:

Q: Ryan and Karen seem to be under enormous pressure because of their location. You operate in a very small town at a time when much larger high-volume stores seem to be the norm. Can you sympathize at all with them?

Miller: Oh, of course. We don't even have a grocery store here, so people shop in the larger county seat. It would be nice to have the traffic that is generated by a large department store next door. On the other hand, repeat customers return because of what you do, not because of where you are. We simply highlight the differences between our store and the chain competitors.

Q: What differences?

Miller: Service. Honesty. Integrity. Principles—like treating customers fairly and having what they want. I think it would be easy to sit and criticize Ryan for his mistake. After being in business for thirty years, I have made some similar mistakes. One thinks, "It won't hurt to do this. It's no big deal." Sometimes, one learns the hard way.

Q: So you do think Ryan's approach is a mistake?

Miller: I don't think it will work, for one thing. Whether it's right or wrong is another issue. But from a business standpoint, I don't think it will work. Most of his customers are going to be smart enough to figure this one out. It won't work, and it creates a bad precedent.

Q: What do you mean by a bad precedent?

Miller: Well, this appears to be a rather insignificant thing that doesn't really matter. That is a red flag. Scripture is clear that small things do matter. All one has to do is give the devil a toehold, and he will make himself at home in your life or your business. It's like a camel sticking his nose under your tent. What differences does a little nose make? But, in the long run, it can make a lot of difference. What starts out as a little insignificant thing can become much more than that. One must be very careful, because in business you face little things every day that have the potential of becoming large, direction-determining issues.

Q: Does a Christian in business face those little things differently than a non-Christian might?

Miller: I think it is just good business to follow Christian principles. The biblical worldview works. It is practical.

Q: That almost sounds like it is necessary to be a Christian to succeed in business.

Miller: I suppose you can be a perfectly good businessman and not be a believer, but you can also be a Christian and operate your business effectively.

You Be the Consultant

Examine Ryan and Karen's approach to advertising in light of these questions:

1. According to your personal statement of ethics, is Ryan's plan for generating sales ethical? Giving specific points from your statement, explain why or why not. If your statement is not sufficient to adequately address this situation, how would you amend it to be adequate? How would someone who has adopted utilitarianism respond? How would someone who operates from ethical egoism respond?

2. How would you evaluate Karen's statement, "I feel like a kid in the cookie jar"? Are feelings an adequate measure of ethical standard?

3. Suppose Ryan visits with others in the retail sales business and discovers that his plan is rather common. Would that change your answer to question 1? Why or why not? In which ethical positions would such information have an impact?

4. Which system of ethics would most likely consider community standards when determining ethical propriety? Defend your response with specific ethical principles from secular philosophy, Bible-based ethical principles, and/or your personal statement of ethics.

Endnotes

1. Films for the Humanities and Sciences, *Business Ethics: Truth in Advertising* (1997), 28-minute video.
2. LaRue Tone Hosmer, *The Ethics of Management*, 3rd ed. (Chicago: Irwin, 1996), 75.

19

The Christian Manager as Ethical Negotiator

. . . Esteem them very highly in love because of their work. Be at peace among yourselves.

— 1 Thessalonians 5:13

Chapter Challenges

A careful examination of Chapter 19 should enable the reader to:

- Recognize the circumstances that necessitate negotiation.
- Be able to compare and contrast win-win and win-lose negotiation strategies.

Case Study

Decker and Associates Real Estate

"You're staying late again," Tonya said, turning off her office light and heading for the front door.

"Just hoping the phone will ring after hours," Jay responded. "Everyone advises that that's the best way to make sales happen in the first few months."

The two visited near the reception desk and switchboard of Decker and Associates Real Estate. As licensed real estate agents, Tonya and Jay comprised part of the "and associates" who worked in the large real estate office of principal broker Tom Decker.

Tonya had been involved in real estate sales for more than ten years. During the first six years, she continued teaching fifth grade at one of the local elementary schools. She worked part time at real estate and built a large client base. As her experience and the number of referral clients grew, she eventually "took the plunge" and quit her teaching job, devoting herself full time to a career in real estate sales. She was the number-one agent at Decker and Associates and one of the leading salespeople in the area. Tonya had a reputation for tough, no-nonsense business. As a dedicated professional, she worked hard on behalf of her clients and, as a result, earned a six-figure income. Earning that much in commissions was no small feat, considering that she listed properties at only 6 percent of sales in a market where the average home sold for only seventy-three thousand dollars.

Jay had worked in real estate sales only three months. Though he had grown up in the local community, he had been away for five years earning a degree in business at the state university. Since returning, he had married his high school sweetheart and now rented a desk at Decker and Associates. Like all new agents, Jay enjoyed very little repeat or referral business. As a result, he spent a lot of hours knocking on doors in high-turnover neighborhoods or, like this evening, sitting at the front desk after hours waiting for the phone to ring.

"You're doing all the right things," Tonya encouraged. "It takes a few months to get rolling. Don't get discouraged."

"Thanks," Jay said. "Coming from you, that means a lot. I really am not discouraged. I had my first closing earlier this week and had a big break on a cold call today."

"Great!" Tonya responded sincerely. "What happened?"

"I was knocking on doors over on McGregor Avenue. You know the routine, 'I'm looking for a property in this neighborhood for a client. Do you know anyone in the area who might be willing to sell?'"

"Don't tell me that line actually worked?" Tonya said, chuckling.

"It may have," Jay answered. "I found a couple who said they were anxious to sell if I could find them their dream home on the south side."

"Marvelous," Tonya said, "What do they consider a dream home?"

"They need a four-bedroom, two-bath house. It looks as if they could be in the $150,000 range," Jay reported.

"Did you say McGregor Avenue?" Tonya asked. "I'm working with a couple on McGregor, too."

"Really," Jay responded with genuine interest. "What are your folks looking for in a move up?"

"They also want a four-bedroom, two-bath home," Tonya answered. "In addition, she is really big on an eat-in kitchen and prefers country style. He insists on a family room large enough for a pool table."

Jay could not disguise the shocked look on his face. "It can't be," he said, his voice expressing his confusion. "Are we both working for the same couple?"

"I wouldn't think so," Tonya said. "I've been helping the McCartys for nearly six months."

"But it *is* the McCartys I ran into today," Jay said with dismay. "Tonya, I had no idea. They never mentioned another real estate agent. I'm showing them a house later this evening."

On Background

Few Clear Industry Boundaries

Both Jay and Tonya make their living on commission sales. Gaining the McCartys' business is very important to them. While real estate agents can be very aggressive, there is a tacit, ethical understanding that under no circumstances should an agent solicit another agent's client.

Some in the real estate business would argue that Jay has done nothing unethical. "If Tonya had taken care of her buyers," they might say, "they would not even have responded to Jay's cold-call sales pitch."

Others suggest that Jay had an ethical responsibility to ask the McCartys first if they were involved with any other agents. They maintain that the highest ethical standards demand that Jay ascertain for certain that no competitor, certainly not one in the same office, be undercut by his sales techniques.

These differences in point of view have become severe enough that many states have adopted new licensing regulations allowing for a buyer's broker. Under these legal requirements, unless Tonya has a signed contract with the McCartys, she has only a prospect, not a full-fledged client. Most real estate professionals would continue to honor her link to the McCarty family as a matter of professional ethics and courtesy.

An Awkward Situation

Regardless of the legal requirements for maintaining a client-agent relationship in their state, Jay and Tonya now find themselves in an awkward but not uncommon situation with regard to their future course of action. Of course, at issue are any commissions resulting from the sale of a new home to the McCartys. In addition, listing and selling the McCartys' current residence could add thousands of dollars to the potential dispute. Jay and Tonya are about to enter into a period of negotiation necessitated by the presence of three circumstances:[1]

- Conflict of interest. When no conflict exists, there is no need for negotiation. In the Decker and Associates case, both Jay and Tonya have a keen interest in finding the McCartys a dream home and earning a sizeable commission. The personal interest of each creates a conflict—though unintended.
- No automatic solution. If Decker had a policy book covering such circumstances, then the outcome of this dilemma would be less ambiguous. In the absence of policies or an established set of rules negotiation remains a necessary next step.
- Opportunities for compromise. There are several possible solutions. These range from deciding that the first to work a case owns it. On the other hand, the proverbial response of "finders, keepers" may rule. Most of the potential solutions will result in some degree of dissatisfaction for Tonya, Jay, or both. To avoid conflict, a compromise seems necessary.

Negotiation Strategies

In the presence of any of the three circumstances above, parties who face potential conflict are in a position to negotiate. If Jay and Tonya have been trained in negotiation competence, they may recognize and implement an ethical course of action.[2] If not, they each automatically will adopt one of two possible negotiation strategies in the next few moments.

> *Win-lose strategy*: conflict negotiation strategy based upon the assumption that when one person gains a benefit the other must lose in corresponding fashion.
>
> *Win-win strategy*: conflict negotiation strategy based on the assumption that it is possible to maximize benefits for both parties simultaneously.

Win-Win Strategy

They might adopt a *win-win strategy*. Using this negotiation approach, the two believe that a solution exists, one that will maximize mutual benefits. Jay and Tonya will search for a solution that is good for both of them. To use a win-win approach, emotion will need to take a back seat to reason. Both Jay and Tonya will have to be open to persuasion—in being personally persuaded as well as in trying to persuade the other.

Win-Lose Strategy

More than likely, at least one of the Decker associates will adopt a *win-lose strategy*. Sometimes called zero-sum negotiation, the win-lose strategy is based upon the belief that only one McCarty commission exists. Who gets it or how to divide it up is the real issue. What one gains under this approach, the other automatically loses.

When a win-win strategy is employed, the common interests of both parties are pursued. As a result, trust and mutuality are enhanced and the relationship is strengthened. By contrast, in a win-lose strategy there is a strong tendency to allow emotions to interfere with objective discussion. The parties involved in the negotiation will usually allow competitiveness to rule their discussion as they demand more and more from one another. Usually the relationship suffers as a result of this negotiation style.

Some may argue for one approach over another. They may see one or the other approach as more ethical or more effective, regardless of the circumstances. However, experts in negotiation believe that the most appropriate strategy will vary from one circumstance to another. Negotiators also note that selecting an appropriate strategy depends to a great extent on the counterpart's choice of strategy. One can see the differences between diplomacy and war in the geopolitical world. This can also apply to the business world in the contrast between friendly mergers and hostile takeovers. In a hostile takeover situation, the aggressor may say that the forced acquisition is in the best interest of both companies, but the characteristics of the takeover are win-lose. The bullying tactics and the loss of independence of the acquired company are clear evidence of the lack of a win-win philosophy. The extreme example is when the newly acquired company is dissolved and its capital and other resources sold at a loss to provide tax benefits for the aggressor company.

Strategies and Outcomes

Consider the possible strategy choices for both Jay and Tonya, along with the likely outcome for each combination. If the senior agent, Tonya, claims her rights based on rank in the company and first contact with the customer, she might anticipate a big win for herself, but there are risks; she risks animosity between herself and Jay as well as possibly the homeowner. She could get all the commission or cause the homeowner to lose confidence in the agency and seek help from a competitor agency. If Jay sticks to his guns and bases his right to the listing on currency and the apparent fact that the homeowner has lost faith in Tonya's ability to sell the current house and find them another, he also faces risks; he will probably gain the commission—and a powerful adversary within his own company.

In a win-win scenario, the two agents would talk things through and develop an agreement that would not jeopardize the sale and would benefit them both financially as well as build cooperation between them instead of animosity.

This case is based on an actual situation that arose between two agents in Indiana. A win-win situation was adopted, and the results were beneficial to all three parties.

Jay and Tonya discovered they could adopt a win-win strategy leading to positive outcomes for both of them as well as for their shared client. On the other hand, if either of them insists on a win-lose strategy, one of them will undoubtedly lose a commission and their client is less likely to be effectively served.

Toward an Ethical Christian Worldview

Luke 12:57–59

And why do you not judge for yourselves what is right? As you go with your accuser before a magistrate, make an effort to settle with him on the way, lest he drag you to the judge, and the judge hand you over to the officer, and the officer put you in prison. I tell you, you will never get out until you have paid the very last penny.

Jesus's words in Luke 12 are designed to call attention to the spiritual rift that exists between God and humankind. In this case it is also advantageous to settle matters with God before entering the judgment hall. In an adversarial situation, this passage suggests that reconciliation is good common sense. To throw oneself at the mercy of the court or some other kind of arbiter carries certain risks. Negotiating early guarantees more control over the situation for both adversaries, especially for the one with the least chance to win in court. This approach is generally beneficial within company structures and relationships. It is better for shop managers and individual workers to resolve work performance and human resource issues in a cooperative, mutually benefiting manner than to bring in the union steward and set up an us-versus-them relationship that requires a winner and a loser. What is the managerial goal? Is it to find the most effective way to meet both short- and long-term goals of the organization, or to prove who is in charge? Is it to find ways to respect all employees because of their dignity based on their being made in God's image?

How does a manager maintain professional ethics and courtesy?

In the Decker and Associates scenario, Jay and Tonya also would be well advised to find a mutually beneficial solution without taking the matter before their managing broker or an even higher authority. Determining that solution may prove difficult when a commission is at stake.

Ask the Pro

Melvin Hornsby is the owner and operator of H&H Pro Audio, a company that sells and installs sound equipment for churches, schools, and businesses in a multi-state area. Melvin has owned this business for nine years.

Melvin and his wife attend a local church where he serves as Sunday school superintendent and song leader. The couple also has formed a singing quartet called Jesus' Own. This group ministers regularly in area churches.

In addition to H&H, Melvin has been involved in commission sales for ten years in a variety of settings. Today he manages the commission sales staff of H&H. It was that experience in commission work that first attracted the authors to him for advice on the Decker and Associates case. The result of the conversation appears below:

Q: From your experience in commission sales, how realistic is the Decker and Associates scenario?

Hornsby: This case is not uncommon at all.

Q: Do such matters usually work out well?

Hornsby: They can be uncomfortable. However, it is possible to sit down and discuss matters, such as how much time we each have spent with these clients, and work out a compromise.

Q: How might those negotiations work?

Hornsby: Jay made a cold call and has spent a little bit of time with these people already. In addition, he has a showing scheduled. Tonya has six months invested. Maybe a 60/40 or even a 70/30 split would be in order.

Q: Is that what the broker will impose if they can't work it out?

Hornsby: I think the broker will lean more toward giving Tonya the commission. She spent the bulk of the time and has been with him the longest. She would probably take the total commission if it comes to that.

Q: If she sees that developing, why would she bother to negotiate with Jay?

Hornsby: To keep peace, to keep a co-worker as a friend, and to show respect for another. Everyone needs to do all they can to maintain positive attitudes between salespeople.

Q: Does a commission arrangement automatically set up competition?

Hornsby: Yes, but that doesn't necessarily mean it's bad. Commissions allow you to see in your paycheck how you are doing. It serves as a motivator.

Q: In your experience, what are the chances that Jay and Tonya will voluntarily negotiate this matter in a mutually beneficial way?

Hornsby: It is possible to work it out, but usually you need a manager to intervene.

Q: In a more general way, what is the biggest challenge to you as a Christian in business?

Hornsby: As a Christian, I have certain standards. For example, I prefer not to solicit bars. It's a choice not to pursue that type of a business for a sound-system installation. Of course, there is some lost income, because bars usually need elaborate sound and lighting systems. Some employees have quit working for me when they realized the company was not going to seek that type of business, because they wanted to capitalize on the revenue that can come from a bar. As a business owner and salesman, I think that leaves 98 percent of the country open for buying products and services. I believe in having some standards and sticking to them. That's important!

You Be the Consultant

Examine Jay and Tonya's situation in light of these questions:

1. What course of action would you advise Jay to take in his negotiations with Tonya? Which parts of your personal ethics statement support this advice? How would you advise Tonya? Would your advice be supported by any of the Bible-based ethical principles? If so, how?

2. Is it possible for Jay and Tonya to find a win-win outcome in this situation? Defend your answer.

3. Let's say that Jay and Tonya cannot find an agreeable solution. The matter goes before the principal broker in the firm, Mr. Decker. He asks for your advice in dealing with the dilemma. What Bible-based ethical principles should he consider? Explain why they apply.

4. Is either the win-win or the win-lose strategy inherently more ethical than the other? Explain giving specific Bible-based ethical principles and/or principles from your personal ethical statement. How would your answer differ from a utilitarian perspective? How would your answer differ from the perspective of Kantian ethics?

5. Imagine that at Decker and Associates you are the broker charged with developing a policy manual to prevent conflicts such as that faced by Jay and Tonya. Using your personal statement of ethics as a basis, state three policies the manual should include showing how they are supported by your personal statement.

Endnotes

1. Christopher T. Timura, "International Negotiation Pedagogy," *International Negotiation* 15, no. 2 (2010): 155–61.
2. Peter J. Goodman and Roger Fisher, *Win-Win Career Negotiations: Proven Strategies for Getting What You Want from Your Employer* (New York: Penguin, 2002), 3–32.

Notes

20

The Christian Manager as Ethical Global Citizen

The earth is the LORD's and all that is in it, the world, and those who live in it.

— Psalm 24:1 (NRSV)

Chapter Challenges

A careful examination of Chapter 20 should enable the reader to:

- Recognize the ethical environmental issues facing managers.
- Understand three global ethical responsibilities facing today's managers.

Case Study

The Ken Eastland Farm

Ken Eastland looked carefully down the half-mile lane leading to his barnyard. Although few strangers came around this part of the farm, Ken had heard rumors in town that Environmental Protection Agency (EPA) representatives were working in the area again. There was a need to be especially careful in mixing herbicides.

The EPA had spent a great deal of time in Ken's county since the Rock Creek fish kill a few years ago. Unidentified chemicals in the creek had killed fish for nearly twenty-five miles downstream. That summer Ken and every other farmer in the area had been suspect in the investigation. Just to be safe, everyone seemed to be overreacting—diluting herbicides and right-of-way sprays to well below the label's recommended proportions. As a result, weeds threatened to take over the county! Now, with the heat off for the most part, Ken had quietly returned to his more normal practice of increasing the recommended strength.

Of course, Ken cared about the environment. In fact, he had several large fields near the river. For years, he had always sprayed according to label instructions. No regulator had to tell Ken the impact of runoff in those locations. The effects were obvious. However, Ken found certain other regulations for the use of chemicals ridiculous. "It's hard enough to make a living on a small farm," Ken complained to a friend recently, "without Uncle Sam protecting the weeds on the farms of good citizens."

"Good morning!"

Ken turned with a start to face a tall, well-dressed stranger. "What are you doing sneaking around?" Ken gruffly demanded.

"Sorry to startle you," the stranger apologized. "I am Jerry Kirkwood from Worldwide Employment Services."

"Sounds like some government agency," Ken responded suspiciously.

"Hardly," Jerry smiled. "We are a private employment agency that matches farmers such as you with the plentiful supply of inexpensive farm labor around the world."

An Interesting Proposition

Ken's anxiety turned to curiosity. He moved Jerry away from his mixing operation by offering his hand as he stepped outside the barn. "What's on your mind?" he asked Jerry.

"I thought you might be needing some help," Jerry answered.

"You're looking for a job?" Ken asked with surprise. "We don't get too many applicants here, and I don't recall ever seeing a farmhand applicant in a shirt and tie."

"No! It's not me," Jerry said, smiling warmly. "My firm represents men from Honduras who are new in this country and looking for a better life."

"Sorry," Ken said. "I've got enough on my mind without having to watch for border agents because I've hired illegal immigrants."

"I assure you, all of our people have appropriate entrance papers and work permits," Jerry continued. "In fact, many will be studying toward United States citizenship very soon."

"I don't get it," Ken confessed. "What's the catch?"

"No catch," Jerry responded. "Honduras is one of the poorest countries in this hemisphere. Many of its people do whatever is necessary to come to our land of opportunity. My company loans them transportation money and locates farm jobs where they can earn the minimum wage for their state. That's two days' pay every hour for most people in Honduras. And they're used to working from sunup until sundown."

"The hours sound right for this farm," Ken quipped.

"This and every family farm in America," Jerry continued. "The Honduran work ethic matches the need of America's family farms. That is the basis of our work at Worldwide Employment Services."

"A couple of questions come to my mind," Ken said.

"Good," Jerry responded. "Worldwide Employment Services has absolutely nothing to hide. We're happy to answer your questions."

"Well, first off, what's in it for you? Is this Worldwide-whatever a charity? How do you make a living?"

"Our income is derived from two sources," Jerry explained. "Like any other employment agency, we collect a small finder's fee from the employing farmer. In most cases the fee is only three hundred dollars, and we don't expect that for six weeks. That gives you plenty of time to make sure your help works out before you pay us. Then we also ask you to withhold 10 percent from the employee's weekly check. That's how the farmhand repays our travel and opportunity loans."

"Ten percent off the minimum wage . . ." Ken calculated. "That leaves very little left for him. There's no way he could make it."

"Of course he can," Jerry argued. "You or I couldn't, but that's more money than these folks have ever seen. They usually live ten or twelve to a house and eat beans and rice. It's just like home for them, except here they have money for the beans."

"Sounds almost like slave labor," Ken observed.

"Not at all," Jerry said. "No one has to sign up, and no one has to stay. Any time they want to repay their loans and move on, they are free to do as they please. They just recognize a great opportunity. I hope you will, too."

"Check with me in a few days," Ken said. "With twelve hundred acres of corn and beans and a few head of cattle, God knows I could use the help. But right now, I've got chemicals to mix."

On Background

Issues of Environment and People Worldwide

One author has rejected the terms *globalization* or *multiculturalism* to describe the twenty-first-century business environment. He opts instead for the term *cosmopolitanism,* noting that "there are two strands that intertwine in the notion of cosmopolitanism. One is the idea that we have obligations to others, obligations that stretch beyond those to whom we are related by ties of kith and kind, or even the more formal ties of a shared citizenship. The other is that we take seriously the value not just of human life but of particular human lives."[1]

The twenty-first century has seen rapid increases in transportation and communication technology. Business once focused on the repeat customers of a single small town. Today the marketplace has expanded to planetary dimensions. Along with the marvelous new opportunities are increasing ethical tensions. For example, as a relatively small scale farmer and businessman, Ken currently faces two ethical questions with worldwide dimensions.

The first involves environmental issues. On one hand, increasingly tight governmental regulations designed to preserve the environment have threatened business and industry. National attention was drawn to the northwest United States a few years ago. Preserving the habitat of the endangered spotted owl threatened logging concerns and the families that depended on the timber industry for their livelihood.

On the other hand, when business has been allowed to police itself, all too often the global environment has suffered. Oil spills, hazardous materials' dumping, and unscrubbed air emissions are examples of environmental abuse.

The Christian and the Environment

The Christian in business recognizes that human beings are the pinnacle of God's creation. In Genesis 1:28, God gave humans, represented by Adam and Eve, dominion and rule over all creation. Recognizing God's call to rule as good stewards, Christians especially recognize an ethical responsibility to conserve God's creation. This requires Christian businesses to adopt in-house procedures and purchasing practices that reduce the strain on nature's resources. This is being a good steward of God's resources, and in many cases, such practices will increase the company's bottom line by reducing waste.

Christians also acknowledge that dominion implies rule and lordship. This means that human beings do not have to be subject to the rest of the creation. Many would say that the spotted owl controversy in the northwest forests of the United States is an example of this concept being out of balance. Environmentalists were able to shut down much of the timber industry, causing economic hardship to the region and especially to the thousands of persons who lost their jobs and homes. The well-being of a bird was given precedence over that of humans. However, this concept does not relieve humans of the responsibility to examine both short- and long-term effects of our interactions with nature and natural resources and to make decisions that reflect responsible use of God-given power.

The Christian and People from around the World

The second global ethical issue facing Ken concerns the responsibility of American business managers to people from other countries. Such issues usually fall into one of three categories:

- ethical dealings with customers
- ethical dealings with employees or potential employees
- ethical issues revolving around nondomestic sources of natural resources

As with environmental concerns, ethical managers can arrive at vastly different conclusions about these issues. An examination of the expiration dates on foods processed in the United States, such as peanut butter and canned peaches, in supermarkets in developing countries might reveal recent shipments of goods that are six months or more beyond the expiration date. Wholesale dealers might argue that the United States Department of Agriculture (USDA) set unnecessarily stringent standards and that these food products are safe for human consumption for many months or even years to come. They might claim that there is no health risk and therefore their practices do not violate ethical principles. Members of the developing society might be grateful for the food. Or they might argue that because of the economic strength of United States companies, they are using the poor nation as a dumping ground for foods that the United States government declares unsafe for its own people's consumption; they might say, "You are violating our dignity as God's creation for selfish economic gain."

For some Americans, the practice of using immigrant employees at a time when so many jobs are being outsourced to other nations raises questions. On the one hand, is it ethical to further strain the fragile economic status of our unskilled labor force by encouraging unskilled laborers to enter our country? Is expanding the profit margins of already prosperous companies an ethical motive for finding a cheaper labor pool? Is it ethical to seek out a workforce that is willing to live in misery with the hope of helping their loved ones back home through the small amounts of money they can send from their low-paying jobs? On the other hand, is it ethical to deprive companies of a workforce that is willing to do jobs that many of its citizens are not willing to do? Is it ethical to deprive hardworking immigrants of the opportunity to better the standards of living of themselves or their families? Is it ethical for the United States to deprive itself of people who often spur the economy by their new creative energies? These are just a few of the thorny issues that surround the use of cheap immigrant labor in the United States. And we have only tangentially touched the issues raised by the use of cheap labor forces in other nations, not regulated by labor and wage laws.

One of the hottest issues in developing countries is potential exploitation of their natural resources by more economically stable and generally, more militarily powerful countries. What is the ethicality of the lion's share of the benefits going to the foreign companies or populace instead of to those of the country of resource origin?

Adding fuel to the fire, the economically powerful country often builds factories in the developing country to process the raw materials before exporting them. This is often done to reduce the cost of shipping. The ethical questions then concern potentially substandard wages and emissions standards. Many citizens in developing countries believe that US companies are really not interested in helping the local economy or people; they sense their land is being used as a pollutant dumping ground that would not be permitted in the United States. They question whether these companies are being godly stewards of nature and whether they are respecting their fellow human beings.

Again we can see that providing the proper balance between fiduciary responsibilities (e.g., to stockholders, local employees, and consumers) and responsibility to God's creation—including immigrants and citizens of other countries—is a difficult process that does not happen without earnest effort. In seeking ethical responses, Christian managers should consider Cain's question to God, recorded in Genesis 4:9, "Am I my brother's keeper?" The answer throughout Scripture is a resounding yes.

Finding a Way through the Maze

Christian managers honestly strive to find their way through the maze of conflicting expectations, barriers, and economic performance pressures that are part and parcel of the modern business environment. We offer a list of commonsense guidelines to help the reader begin to consider how to treat all people ethically, regardless of their country of origin or residence. The ethical concepts from classical philosophy in Chapter 3, Bible-based principles in Chapter 4, as well as the manager's own personal statement of ethics in Chapter 5 will provide the insights for solid, ethical decision making.

- At minimum, decisions should follow the laws of the host country. This does not exclude taking the higher road of Bible-based principles if the laws violate God's Word.
- Decisions should promote the general welfare of all people involved.
- Decisions should be designed to treat each human being as the businessperson would want to be treated.

Toward an Ethical
Christian Worldview

Psalm 24:1

The earth is the LORD's and all that is in it,
    the world, and those who live in it (NRSV).

The Bible declares in this verse and elsewhere that the planet and everything on it belongs to God. Human beings have been given the unique role among created beings to oversee God's creation.

In the Genesis account, humanity is the capstone of the creation event. All other beings are created first, as if in preparation for God's ultimate creative stroke. Further, human beings are the only products of creation made in the image of God (1:27). God instills the importance of this fact in the following verses:

And God blessed them. And God said to them, "Be fruitful and multiply and fill the earth and subdue it and have dominion over the fish of the sea and over the birds of the heavens and over every living thing that moves on the earth." And God said, "Behold, I have given you every plant yielding seed that is on the face of all the earth, and every tree with seed in its fruit; You shall have them for food. And to every beast of the earth and to every bird of the heavens and to everything that creeps on the earth, everything that has the breath of life, I have given every green plant for food." And it was so (Genesis 1:28–30).

In verse 28, the words *subdue* and *have dominion* represent a delegated authority by God for humans to tend to the care of the planet. Apparently this precludes the abuse of God's creation, because God describes the process as "very good" later in the narrative.

Ken Eastland does have an ethical responsibility and a moral right to oversee his farmland. He must determine whether the application of chemicals in violation of label directions constitutes an abuse of that authority.

How does a manager exhibit global citizenship?

Similarly, in Genesis 4, God holds Cain responsible for the well-being of his brother Abel. As previously noted, the implied answer to Cain's question, "Am I my brother's keeper?" is yes (Genesis 4:9). Ken Eastland also must decide whether sisters and brothers in Honduras are best served by participation in, or rejection of, the Worldwide Employment Services program.

Ask the Pro

Shane Davis farms approximately 2,200 acres, an operation he has farmed for forty-five years. His son now helps him run the farm. They grow corn and beans, along with an occasional specialty crop.

Along with his wife, Davis attends a small-town Baptist church where he has held a variety of positions over the past twenty-six years. He currently serves as chair of the administrative council of the church.

The authors asked Davis to evaluate the Ken Eastland case in light of his farming experience. Our conversation follows:

Q: How realistic is the dilemma in which Ken Eastland finds himself?

Davis: No farmers I know would adjust spray rates. Improperly used, chemicals can contaminate the soil. We have to live here a long time. We take better care of the land than that. Even if a farmer increased a rate, it would cost more money for little or no increase in effectiveness.

Q: So, there is a business reason as well as an ethical one not to do that?

Davis: Oh, yes!

Q: What about the question of hiring farm help?

Davis: I think something here isn't right. It isn't clear that it is illegal, but it doesn't sound right to me. A man working for a minimum wage won't last long. I would stay away from that situation.

Q: Isn't Ken likely to need the help?

Davis: Yes, but if it were me, I would hire someone close by who needs a job. I'd look for someone who knows the machinery and how to run it. Without speaking Spanish, I couldn't even instruct a Honduran employee properly.

Q: So the Ken Eastland situation seems pretty cut and dried to you?

Davis: Good farmers simply don't cut corners. It doesn't pay.

Q: What are some ethical problems with which farmers do struggle?

Davis: Spraying on a windy day is a big issue. Label directions warn that my bean spray could kill a neighbor's corn if it drifts. That becomes a real issue when you have a lot to get sprayed in a short time, and the wind is borderline, like say ten or twelve miles per hour. You need to get the work done, but need to be a good neighbor at the same time.

Q: So how do you solve the problem?

Davis: Even the best solutions don't always work. A few years ago, I sprayed most of a field on a borderline day, but I left the rows nearest my neighbor for a calmer day. I still don't know how, but I killed twelve to twenty-four rows of his corn on that calm day. Even when you try to do the right thing, accidents happen which require compensatory actions.

You Be the Consultant

Answer the following questions as you study Ken Eastland's situation:

1. Preservationists believe that the environment should be left as nearly as possible in an unaltered prehuman state. Conservationists believe that humans should manage the environment for the good of all species, using tactics such as controlled hunts and burning of certain vegetation. Which position most closely matches your ethic? Which position parallels Genesis 1:28? Explain why.

2. What advice would you give Ken Eastland about the use of herbicides on his farm? What Bible-based ethical principles support your advice? Which secular ethical principles? Which elements from your personal statement of ethics?

3. What answer do you believe Ken should give Jerry Kirkwood about hiring one or more Honduran immigrants? What are the ethical issues to consider in this decision? Which parts of your statement of ethics deal with those issues? How? How might one who holds to Kantian ethics respond? Why? If you held to utilitarian ethics, what might your response be? Why?

4. Describe an ethical process for filling the need in the United States for low-skilled labor. Defend your position with an eye to your personal statement of ethics. How would a Kantian ethicist view your response? Defend your answer. How would a utilitarian view your response? Why do you think so? Is your process supported by Bible-based ethical principles? Which ones and how?

Endnotes

1. Kwame Anthony Appiah, *Cosmopolitanism: Ethics in a World of Strangers* (New York: Norton, 2006), xv.

Notes

21

The Christian Manager as Ethical Human Resource Administrator

Let every person be subject to the governing authorities.
— Romans 13:1

Chapter Challenges

A careful examination of Chapter 21 should enable the reader to:

- Identify key elements of the Americans with Disabilities Act.

- Identify key elements of the Family and Medical Leave Act.

- Recognize three possible courses of action in response to laws regarding the ethical treatment of employees.

Case Study

Franks and Barnes Engineering Consultants

"Thank God, it's Friday," Ron Franks said as he headed for the parking lot of Franks and Barnes Engineering Consultants.

"With one less draftsman, there would be a lot more rough weeks," responded his partner, Jeff Barnes.

"That is definitely true, but we might save our company by letting him go," Ron said.

"It appears we have no real choice," Jeff agreed. "It is just too bad it has to happen. Maybe another idea will develop over the weekend. See you Monday, partner."

"See you Monday," Ron responded. "Have a great weekend."

Ron Franks and Jeff Barnes began their engineering consulting business more than thirty years ago in the basement of Ron's first home. The two had met at one of the finest engineering schools in the Midwest and had enjoyed college life together as fraternity brothers. The business had steadily grown over the years, gaining a reputation for reasonable fees and exceptional service. Franks and Barnes now employed two graduate engineers in addition to Ron and Jeff, three clerk-secretaries, and eight draftsmen.

Several years ago, during a time of unprecedented growth, the business moved into a large Victorian-style house just a block from downtown. The historic three-story brick structure provided ample room for the business and left a very positive impression on visitors and passersby.

Neither Ron nor Jeff had any training or interest in issues related to human resource management. In fact, they viewed the business aspects of their operation, in general, as just unavoidable—something they had to endure if they wanted to practice engineering. They saw themselves as engineers, primarily. Management and business matters were relegated to a distant second place.

"We're just engineering geeks," Ron had joked to Rhonda Sutton when he contracted with her firm to manage such matters as payroll, employee benefits, and accounting.

"And we love handling business details for you geeks," Rhonda assured him with a smile.

The Implications of Accommodation

There was no joking about the tension Ron felt when he looked out the window of his office on Thursday afternoon. He had been keeping an eye out for Jannette Lynn, with whom he had scheduled an interview. Franks and Barnes had just signed a lucrative contract to design a shopping center in Ohio. The additional business made it possible to hire another draftsman. Jannette had responded to the Franks and Barnes ad in a national trade journal. Her résumé demonstrated impeccable credentials. She had an impressive combination of experience and education and offered several excellent references. Ron had enjoyed a pleasant conversation with Jannette on the phone. She had not mentioned a wheelchair. But there she sat in a wheelchair on the sidewalk in front of the Franks and Barnes building, looking at the menacing fifteen steps leading to the front door.

Fortunately, Ron recovered quickly and bounded down the steps to greet Jannette. He suggested that they meet together over coffee at a restaurant less than a block away. He made it appear that he always conducted interviews in that handicap-accessible facility.

Throughout their conversation, Ron contemplated what Jannette's presence might mean to Franks and Barnes. In addition to the front steps to the main entrance, he visualized the computer-assisted drafting area located on the third floor. The cost of making the building accessible could reach nearly a quarter of a million dollars. In the process, the historic charm of the old structure could be lost. "Somehow," he thought, "I have to find a way to get rid of this potential employee."

A quick call to Rhonda Sutton after the interview confirmed his suspicions. "Of course you fall under the Americans with Disabilities Act (ADA)," she said. "The law clearly states that the act applies to employers with fifteen or more employees. Your firm currently is at fifteen, so you meet ADA requirements—which means you need to accommodate the needs of this woman if you hire her."

The next morning Ron and Jeff outlined a plan that would reduce their employee number to fewer than fifteen so that they would not fall under ADA requirements. It would mean working more hours personally than either of them desired. In addition, it could cost the company in overtime for employees. While they had never been much for long-term business plans, the current situation made it clear that the company would seek no new business in the near future. Although this troubled them, they were more worried about the cost of the alternative.

"How do we explain to Billy that since he was the last employee hired he will be laid off?" Jeff asked, referring to Billy Asbury, one of their draftsmen. Billy had been with Franks and Barnes for three years. He did fine work and had earned outstanding job reviews.

Ron responded, "I'll say something like this: 'Billy, I'm sorry, but you were the most recent draftsman hired and business is such that we have no choice but to let someone go.'"

On Background

Significant Federal Legislative Mandates

Americans with Disabilities Act

Ron and Jeff are apparently moving toward a decision with serious ethical as well as business ramifications. Rhonda and any others who may advise them will need to have some background on the *Americans with Disabilities Act* (ADA).

> *Americans with Disabilities Act*: 1990 federal law applying to businesses with fifteen or more employees and requiring accommodation for employees with physical or mental impairments.

As Rhonda suggested, the ADA applies to employers with fifteen or more employees. Passed in 1990, the ADA is administered and enforced by the Equal Employment Opportunities Commission (EEOC). According to the ADA, employment discrimination is prohibited against individuals with disabilities who are able to perform the duties that every other employee must do. That prohibition against discrimination holds even if the employer must change the work environment, redesign the job, or alter work schedules.[1]

The ADA covers "both physical and mental impairments affecting one or more life activities."[2] However, no accommodation is required for a person who does not meet minimal stated job qualifications. For example, had Jannette Lynn applied for an engineer's job, no accommodation would have been required of Franks and Barnes. Since she meets and exceeds stated qualifications for the draftsman position, accommodation would certainly be required.

A special provision does exist that allows an employer to plead undue hardship.[3] In reality, the EEOC has demonstrated reluctance to allow the successful use of that provision. Further, undue expense has specifically been eliminated as a reason for hardship.

Rather than search for exceptions, ethical managers recognize their responsibility to assist those with physical or mental impairments. Many find that the ADA does not severely limit their businesses. Even before the ADA was made law, they voluntarily behaved in accordance with its provisions, which merely describe what they had long held to be a part of their social and Christian responsibilities. Their view of the merits of treating people as they wished to be treated and belief in biblical and social norms for treating humans with dignity had been guiding principles.

It is true that accommodation may cost an enormous amount. Such costs can seriously erode the bottom line of any business. Some managers question this use of profits with potential for return to stockholders or other owners. They raise legitimate questions about whether it is ethical to hire a person who could cost the company a great deal in accommodation rather than an equally qualified nondisabled alternate, thus freeing funds for updating equipment or research and development activities that would benefit all present and future employees.

Family and Medical Leave Act

Employers who seek to perform ethically may also have differing views of the federally mandated *Family and Medical Leave Act* (FMLA) of 1993.[4] The FMLA provides up to twelve weeks of leave to eligible employees for the birth or adoption of a child, the care of a sick family member including a spouse, child, or parent, or the care required for one's own health concerns.

> *Family and Medical Leave Act:* federal law applying to most businesses with fifty or more employees and requiring those businesses to allow up to twelve weeks of unpaid leave for family emergencies.

Many employees and some managers see the *unpaid* provision of the FMLA as a serious limitation. They would prefer to see provisions for compensation during an employee's time off. Others applaud the fact that the FMLA guarantees employees the same or an equivalent position and conditions upon their return. Some businesses are put under severe strain when a highly skilled worker takes twelve weeks off, at a critical time in the company's operations or times of employee shortage, to care for an eligible relative. The FMLA applies to firms with fifty or more employees. While legally exempt, smaller companies may see an ethical responsibility and a benefit in voluntary compliance. This may be especially true in regions with a shortage of qualified workers or in close-knit organizations where employees and management have both personal and professional ties.

Three Scenarios

When laws such as the ADA and FMLA protect the rights of employees, companies can choose one of three general courses of action:

Minimum Compliance with the Letter of the Law

Often the rationale is stated: my decision is ethical because it complies with the related law. If that is always true, then the "separate but equal" clause as expressed in the Supreme Court decision *Plessy v. Ferguson* (1896), which established segregated seating on public buses and trains as well as separate restrooms in department stores, led to ethical treatment of African-American citizens. LaRue Hosmer's assertion that "The law is a guide to managerial decisions and actions, but it is not enough" certainly nullifies the use of the law as the sole definer of ethical behavior. Managers should also consider Hosmer's assertion that the absence of a law protecting the rights and dignity of employees is not an excuse for lack of ethical action on the part of management.[5]

Compliance Beyond What the Law Requires

Legal compliance represents a minimum ethical standard. Some managers choose to go beyond mere legal compliance and employ a values-based approach that reflects biblical and philosophical ethical principles.

Noncompliance with the Law

It is sad to say, some managers select the noncompliance course of action. Refusing to consider the ethical and legal implications of these acts, they choose instead to find ways to skirt the intent of mandates such as the ADA and FMLA even though they carry harsh penalties for noncompliance.

Toward an Ethical Christian Worldview

Romans 13:1–3

Let every person be subject to the governing authorities. For there is no authority except from God, and those authorities that exist have been instituted by God. Therefore whoever resists the authorities resists what God has appointed, and those who resist will incur judgment. For rulers are not a terror to good conduct, but to bad. Who would have no fear of the one who is in authority? Then do what is good, and you will receive his approval.

Believers have a responsibility to the government. Matthew 22:17 records an occasion when Jesus was asked by his enemies, "Is it lawful to pay taxes to Caesar, or not?"

He responded by borrowing a coin to use as an object lesson and asking them whose image appeared on the coin. "Caesar's," came the reply. "Then," Jesus continued, "render to Caesar the things that are Caesar's, and to God the things that are God's" (Matthew 22:21). In this exchange, Jesus left no room for doubt; his followers were to obey the government.

Paul goes beyond simple obedience in his exhortation to a young disciple named Timothy:

First of all, then, I urge that supplications, prayers, intercessions, and thanksgivings be made for all people, for kings and all who are in high positions, that we may lead a peaceable and quiet life, godly and dignified in every way. This is good, and it is pleasing in the sight of God our Savior (1 Timothy 2:1–3).

Ethical Dilemma

Can a manager succeed as an ethical human resource manager?

Of course, Ron Franks and Jeff Barnes maintain that they are following the strict interpretation of the law. They might further argue that excessive government interference threatens the success of their business. What must be determined is whether Ron and Jeff have held to the spirit of Romans 13 or merely obeyed the letter of the law. Have they treated Jannette Lynn in an ethical manner, as well as a legal one?

Ask the Pro

Karen Brown has spent five years as a loan officer in a credit union. Previously she worked for twenty-five years in consumer credit and finance positions for various financial institutions.

Karen sings in her church choir and teaches a preschool Sunday School class. She agreed to assist the authors with a discussion of business ethics in general, and the Franks and Barnes case in particular. The results of that conversation follow:

Q: Before we look at the Franks and Barnes case, tell us about your particular business. What are the ethical concerns associated with being a loan officer?

Brown: One of the biggest concerns involves people who are not ethical themselves and then don't seem to understand when I can't help them. For example, I recently had a potential client who was self-employed and had not reported all of his income over the past several years. He became very angry when we were forced to make a loan decision on what he reported to the federal government, rather than what he tells us now is his true income picture. He had behaved unethically and couldn't understand that there were consequences.

Q: That, of course, involves someone else's unethical behavior. Are there ever pressures on you to do the wrong thing?

Brown: On the one hand, loaning people money is helping them achieve a dream or solve a problem. On the other hand, sometimes making a loan could get people into trouble. I don't want to loan to people when it is not in their best interest to borrow.

Q: How do you deal with that situation? Doesn't your employer insist that you make as many loans as possible?

Brown: Thankfully, my employer doesn't pressure me to lend. In fact, we have very conservative lending policies. In addition, I am often in a position to do financial counseling with a prospective borrower with encouragement to develop a budget or wait a while for a new car or a bigger house.

Q: It sounds as if you have a very good relationship with your employer. I'm not so sure you would have the same attitude working at Franks and Barnes. How did you evaluate this case?

Brown: I think it is a sad situation when an employer is simply not willing to work with a disabled person and offer that person a position. What is even more sad is that they choose to eliminate a very good draftsman from the staff just so they don't have to accommodate the person and the law. Of course, there is a moral issue here, but more, they will lose business by being understaffed. Ironically, they are driven by money and are making decisions that in the long run will cost them profits.

Q: Are you saying that ethical decisions are good business?

Brown: I'm saying that if you make solid ethical decisions, especially on behalf of your staff, they will in turn be profitable for you as the employer.

Q: What alternatives do these managers have?

Brown: They could begin by viewing the expenditures necessary to accommodate Jannette as investment rather than expense.

Q: The modifications involve a lot of money. How far should they go? Do you see alternatives?

Brown: Of course, there are always alternatives. Jannette might work from home. They might lease another office that is accessible for part of the staff. I think they looked only at the expense of compliance with ADA and ignored the potential income from this qualified applicant's work and from the company's future growth. The ethical action is to find a way to accommodate her since she is qualified for the job.

You Be the Consultant

Answer the following questions as you analyze the situation at Franks and Barnes:

1. Is reducing their firm size to fourteen a good business decision for Franks and Barnes? Why or why not? Is it legal? On what do you base your answer? Is it ethical according to your personal statement of ethics? Explain how you drew that conclusion. How would one who has adopted Kantian ethics respond? Would a utilitarian react differently than a Kantian? How?

2. Propose an alternate plan that may work for Franks and Barnes. Defend it using your statement of ethics. Then respond to your plan on the basis of Kantian ethics, utilitarianism, and ethical egoism.

3. Suppose you were advising Jannette Lynn, Billy Asbury, and Rhonda Sutton in this matter. What might you suggest to each of them?

4. Admittedly, Franks and Barnes had "never been much for long-term business plans." In what way has that attitude led to the current crisis? Are there ethical implications of failing to plan? Defend your answer with principles from Chapters 3 and 4 (see also Chapter 7).

5. Should a company like Franks and Barnes conform to the standards of the Family and Medical Leave Act, even if the company falls far short of the minimum fifty employees? Which secular and Bible-based ethical principles support your conclusion? Why do you believe such minimums are placed in the federal law? Which secular and Bible-based ethical principles support your conclusion?

6. How would a manager following Kant's categorical imperatives view the Franks and Barnes plan? How would the answer change for one who adopted ethical egoism or utilitarianism?

Endnotes

1. Americans with Disabilities Act of 1990, 42 U.S.C.A. § 12101 *et seq.* (West 1993).
2. Jeff Hornsby, *Human Resource Development* (Muncie, IN: T.I.S., 2001), 109.
3. John M. Ivancevich, *Human Resource Management: Foundations of Personnel,* 5th ed. (Homewood, IL: Irwin, 1992), 101.
4. Family and Medical Leave Act, 29 U.S.C. § 2601.
5. LaRue Tone Hosmer, *The Ethics of Management,* 3rd ed. (Chicago: Irwin, 1996).

Special Assignment

Personal Statement of Ethics Update

Write a final draft of your personal statement of ethics. Be certain that the statement covers all of the situations presented in the case studies of this book.

Personal Statement of Ethics	
Name _____	Date _____

Conclusion

Becoming a more ethical manager is intertwined with becoming a more self-reflecting searcher for ethical and spiritual truth. To become an ethical manager, family member, or citizen, one must be a purpose-driven individual. There must be a desire to grow ethically, and that desire must have a proactive element that looks beyond the requirements of society. It involves more than compliance to society's laws and to God's laws. Compliance is action that is often motivated by fear. Personal ethical growth is not fear driven. It is the inculcation of the underlying principles regarding the value of people, the biblical absolutes, and the justice, love, righteousness, and other character traits of God into your being.

Knowledge of management theory and practice is not a guarantee of ethical management and decision making, though it can contribute to the level of ethicality found within a company. Insufficient knowledge and inadequate skill development in the managerial functions can set up situations where management of various levels may inadvertently make unethical decisions or set up systems and procedures that cause lower level employees to feel that they have no choice but to act against their ethical beliefs. A poor decision based on inadequate management knowledge may look harmless today, but it can place future managers in difficult situations where they are put under extreme pressure to ignore their ethical beliefs.

Ethical decision making requires a high level of personal discipline. The manager must be vigilant to exercise sound management principles and practices to minimize opportunities for ethical dilemmas. The manager must also be aware of how the company's actions and policies are affecting employees, vendors, customers, and other stakeholders. This requires always keeping one eye on the bottom line and the other on the humans involved in the business arena and the needs of society. These sound like simple things to do, but under the pressure of production schedules, investor expectations, and threats from global competitors, they require purposeful discipline on the part of conscientious managers.

Having a personal statement of ethics to serve as a framework to guide ethical decision making is very important. A manager, husband or father, wife or mother should not have to stop and analyze personal standards each time a decision needs to be made. However, since the sincere manager, father, or mother is a maturing individual, it is valuable to periodically review personal beliefs and values to see how they have matured and then adjust one's personal statement of ethics. Reflection is also very important to help see the degree of alignment between stated standards and actual practices in the crucibles of the business and personal worlds. Bible study, prayer, and reflection on beliefs, priorities, and practices are key tools in the maturation of an ethical decision maker.

Consider two important "Ps" in growth as an ethical manager. The first is *practice*. Knowledge of God's character and principles, skills in management and decision making, and ethical beliefs from the world of philosophy are of little value if they are not practiced. It is through practice that managers hone their proficiency in making ethical decisions and solving problems in ways that glorify God. It is important to understand that the old saying that "practice makes perfect" is not always true. *Reflective practice* is necessary for personal growth. Reflection calls a manager to test knowledge and skill levels and analyze what went right and what needs improvement. This habit of reflecting on one's performance minimizes the repeated performance of practices that are ineffective, unethical, and inappropriate in the workplace, home, and community.

The second "P" is *process*. It is very helpful to follow an established process for making major decisions. A formalized thought process such as the one below may be used when facing a decision involving the company's economic vitality and the company's responsibility to investors, employees, customers, vendors, the community, and the environment. See Chapter 6, "The Christian as Ethical Decision Maker" for an expanded explanation of a seven-step decision-making process. Consider also these six questions:

1. What people (stakeholders) will be affected by the decision? They should be identified as those who will benefit and those who will be hurt by the decision.

2. What economic needs or desires of the company and the affected stakeholders are being affected by the decision? (Who stands to gain and who stands to lose economically by my decision?)

3. Is the situation causing the need for a decision violating a company policy or the law? Will my proposed decision violate company policy or the law?

4. Will my proposed decision violate my statement of personal beliefs—including biblical and philosophical principles?

5. When I consider stakeholders, economic issues, the law, and my personal statement of beliefs, what appear to be the two or three best courses of action for me to take?

6. Of the courses of action listed above, which one will do the most good and the least harm to the company and the stakeholders while conforming to God's character and principles?

This or a similar process can help you become more consistently ethical in your managerial decisions. You may find that what starts as a managerial tool becomes a subconscious part of your decision making in your daily life—at work or at home.

It is the authors' goal and prayer that this book has helped the reader think through the potentially difficult issues faced by maturing managers who seek to glorify God as they interact with colleagues at all levels of the business world.

Notes

Glossary of Key Terms

Americans with Disabilities Act (ADA): 1990 federal law applying to businesses with fifteen or more employees and requiring accommodation for employees with physical or mental impairments.

Appeal-to-emotions strategy: uses emotionally charged language to influence stakeholders and distract the decision maker from relevant issues and data.

Biblical interrelational justice: type of justice that emerges when power is not abused by one party to gain an unjust domination over another.

Business ethics: the application of moral standards to the structures, policies, systems, and decision-making processes that facilitate the production and distribution of goods and services and affect the treatment of people within the organization and the greater society.

Business plan: detailed written statement of a business that comprises a strategic plan and an operational plan.

Categorical imperative: two standards that must be satisfied according to Kantian ethics. The first is act only on a maxim that you would be willing to become universal law. The second is to treat others as an end not a means.

Cognitive dissonance: discordant act of mentally holding two opposing views simultaneously.

Core values: principles around which a business is established and maintained.

Communication: interaction between two or more individuals.

Compensatory justice: type of long-term justice that emerges from compensation for injustices of the past.

Conflict stage: second stage of group or team development where team members often grow tired of one another.

Content: aspect of communication focusing strictly on the messages that are sent as opposed to the contextual relationship in which those messages are sent.

Contractual justice: justice that occurs when an exchange of promises creates a special relationship called a contract.

Control: managerial function that includes performance appraisal, production statistics, and budgetary systems.

Credibility of data standard: deals with the credibility of sources of information used in communications and decision making as well as the methods of acquiring this data.

Disciplinary action: process of dealing with employees who are ineffective, demonstrate personal problems, commit crimes, or violate company policy.

Distributive justice: type of justice that emerges from questions regarding the distribution of wealth.

Esteem needs: fourth level of needs according to Maslow's hierarchy involving the need for recognition.

Ethical egoism: ethical system where the ethical decision is determined by the self-interest of the decision maker.

Ethics: a system of moral values that is applied in a consistent way to one's personal, social, and business life.

Ethnocentrism: belief that one's culture is superior to all others.

Equality: along with justice and integrity a characteristic of the holiness of God.

Equivocation strategy: a presenter of data purposefully uses a key word or phrase that has two or more common meanings.

Family and Medical Leave Act (FMLA): federal law applying to most businesses with fifty or more employees and requiring those businesses to allow up to twelve weeks of unpaid leave for family emergencies.

Formation stage: first stage of group or team development where members develop rules for interaction and grow accustomed to one another.

Fundamentalist view: view of Scripture maintaining that biblical teaching is normative for today's culture except where the Scripture specifically suggests otherwise.

Holiness: attribute of God that issues in equality, integrity, and justice.

Integration stage: third stage of group or team development where members develop standards for effective operation.

Integrity: along with equality and justice a characteristic of the holiness of God.

Interpersonal communication: interaction between just two individuals.

Interpretive view: view of Scripture maintaining that the reader must determine the original intent of a passage and then apply that intent to today's moral choices.

Issue of fact: decisions that consider the truth or falsity of an assertion.

Issue of policy: decisions that consider what course of action should or should not be taken.

Issue of value: decisions that consider the relative worth or rightness of an issue.

Judeo-Christian worldview: those principles, attitudes, and values that influence every area of life and that grow out of an acceptance of God's standards as revealed in his creation and holy Scriptures.

Justice: along with equality and integrity a characteristic of the holiness of God.

Kantian ethics: ethical system developed by Immanuel Kant and based upon categorical imperatives.

Liberal view: view of Scripture maintaining that a biblical teaching is applicable to today's moral choices when it is clearly the word of God and not the writer's viewpoint.

Love needs: third-level needs according to Maslow's hierarchy including the need for interaction, acceptance, and membership in groups.

Manipulation: extreme form of motivation that is sometimes seen as coercion.

Mission statement: succinct statement of the fundamental purpose of the company which becomes the guiding light for every organizational decision.

Motivation: drive that compels a person to action.

Natural law: truths that transcend culture and thus are the same for all human beings.

Negative harm principle: specialized application of utilitarianism where stakeholders' health and safety are impacted.

Operational goals: specific goals which break an organization's plan into short-term action statements. The operational goals combine to form an operational plan.

Operational plan: composed of short-term and specific goals of an organization designed to meet the strategic plan over time.

Organizational chart: visual representation of an organization's structure.

Organizational communication: formal and informal rules within an organization that shapes the way interaction occurs.

Organizational level: those needs of the organization that drive decision making.

Performance appraisal: systematic review of an employee's job-related strengths and weaknesses.

Performance stage: fourth and final stage of group or team development where team members establish their own work goals and maximize productivity.

Personal level: lowest variable that drives the need for ethical decisions.

Physiological needs: lowest-level needs according to Maslow's hierarchy, including the need for air and water.

Positive discipline: process of employee discipline focusing on future behavior rather than past performance by offering positive reinforcements for appropriate behaviors.

Progressive discipline: process of administering employee discipline that increases in severity with each subsequent infraction.

Protected classes: groups protected by the Civil Rights Act of 1968 including race, color, national origin, religion, gender, familial status, and handicap.

Recruiting: process that is the first step in staffing wherein people are encouraged to apply for an open or potentially open position.

Red herring strategy: introduces unrelated information with the intent of diverting the decision maker's focus from relevant facts.

Relationship: aspect of communication focusing on the nature of the interaction instead of the content of the message.

Safety needs: second-level needs according to Maslow's hierarchy.

Selection: the process of screening potential employees who have been recruited. The second step in staffing.

Self-actualization: fifth and highest level of needs according to Maslow's hierarchy involving the need to maximize one's personal potential.

Servant leadership: assumes that the role of a leader is to facilitate the work of followers who are generally self-motivated. The servant leader generally engages in participatory management.

Societal level: needs that drive decision making stemming from the society at large.

Socratic model: process demonstrated by Socrates consisting of raising questions in such a manner as to elicit the most logical conclusion.

Staffing: basic managerial function usually broken down into recruiting, selecting, and training of employees.

Stakeholders: individuals or groups who have a stake in a particular decision.

Stalking-horse strategy: disguising or concealing of intentions (plans or objectives) by one or more stakeholders by proposing a fictitious solution that is not likely to be adopted.

Stereotyping: a positive or negative bias characterized by a preset notion about the qualities of members of a certain group.

Strategic plan: process of identifying major goals, policies, and strategies for an organization.

Straw person fallacy: distortion of the connection(s) of one or more stakeholders or of facts related to a managerial dilemma so as to confuse the decision maker, causing decisions to be made on false premises rather than the real issue.

Synergy: effect is greater than the sum of the parts. $1+1>2$

Theory X: view of employees in the McGregor model of management. In theory X employees are viewed as lazy and incapable. They must be closely supervised.

Theory Y: view of employees in the McGregor model of management. In theory Y employees are viewed as capable of self-management and self-motivation.

Thinking speed: rate at which a listener can process verbal words. Usually three times faster than the words are spoken.

Three-E equation: efficiency + Effectiveness + Ethics = Profits + Long-term stability training: The process of orienting employees to their job and its expectations. The third step in staffing.

Transparency of data standard: deals with the availability of important, accurate, and complete data to all involved stakeholders and the form in which the data is presented.

Truthful communications corollary: the principle of veracity—requires communications that are truthful in their content as well as in their intent.

Utilitarianism: ethical system built upon the belief that the decision where the end positives outweigh the end negatives is always the most ethical.

Vision statement: an expansion of the organization's mission which provides a statement of the perceived, achievable, and measurable future.

Win-lose strategy: conflict negotiation strategy based upon the assumption that when one person gains a benefit the other must lose in corresponding fashion.

Win-win strategy: conflict negotiation strategy based on the assumption that it is possible to maximize benefits for both parties simultaneously.

Work team: basic production unit that builds tasks and organizations around processes instead of functions.

Index

Scripture Index

About the Authors

Blake J. Neff

Blake J. Neff, an experienced university professor and academic program director, is a retired United Methodist pastor who currently serves as lecturer in communication at Indiana Wesleyan University. He holds a management degree from Kettering University, a ministerial degree from Asbury Theological Seminary, and the doctorate in communication from Bowling Green State University (Ohio). Neff's publications include *A Pastor's Guide to Interpersonal Communication* (Haworth Press), *The Complete Guide to Religious Education Volunteers* (coeditor, Religious Education Press), and *A Brief Guide to Extemporaneous Public Speaking* (coauthor, Triangle). He and Nancy, his wife of thirty-seven years, have three adult children and ten grandchildren.

Ted Batson

Ted Batson has extensive experience in international business in Central America, where he served fourteen years in managerial roles in not-for-profit organizations. He has a twenty-one-year academic administration career in a variety of state and private colleges and universities. Batson has designed and taught ethics courses at the bachelor- and master-degree levels for the past thirteen years at Indiana Wesleyan University. He holds a bachelor of science degree from The University of Southwest Alabama, a master's degree from the University of South Alabama, and a PhD from the University of Southern Mississippi. Batson completed additional studies in theology at Asbury Theological Seminary and serves as a lay pastor in the United Methodist Church. He and Anne, his wife of forty-seven years, have four adult children and fourteen grandchildren.

Acknowledgments

The authors gratefully acknowledge their mothers, Bertha Cummings Batson and Mary Brown Neff, who provided sound ethical teachings through biblical instruction and personal actions, and their wives, Anne Parks Batson and Nancy Meeks Neff, who encouraged the authors and proofread the early drafts. We also thank the successful businesspeople who were interviewed in the "Ask the Pro" sections.